David Foster Wallace's
Toxic Sexuality

New Horizons in Contemporary Writing

In the wake of unprecedented technological and social change, contemporary literature has evolved a dazzling array of new forms that traditional modes and terms of literary criticism have struggled to keep up with. *New Horizons in Contemporary Writing* presents cutting-edge research scholarship that provides new insights into this unique period of creative and critical transformation.

Series Editors
Martin Eve and Bryan Cheyette

Editorial Board: Siân Adiseshiah (University of Lincoln, UK), Sara Blair (University of Michigan, USA), Peter Boxall (University of Sussex, UK), Robert Eaglestone (Royal Holloway, University of London, UK), Rita Felski (University of Virginia, USA), Rachael Gilmour (Queen Mary, University of London, UK), Caroline Levine (University of Wisconsin–Madison, USA), Roger Luckhurst (Birkbeck, University of London, UK), Adam Kelly (York University, UK), Antony Rowland (Manchester Metropolitan University, UK), John Schad (Lancaster University, UK), Pamela Thurschwell (University of Sussex, UK), Ted Underwood (University of Illinois at Urbana-Champaign, USA).

Volumes in the series
David Mitchell's Post-Secular World, Rose Harris-Birtill
Life Lines: Writing Transcultural Adoption, John McLeod
New Media and the Transformation of Postmodern American Literature, Casey Michael Henry
The Politics of Jewishness in Contemporary World Literature, Isabelle Hesse
South African Literature's Russian Soul, Jeanne-Marie Jackson
Transatlantic Fictions of 9/11 and the War on Terror, Susana Araújo
Wanderwords: Language Migration in American Literature, Maria Lauret
Writing After Postcolonialism: Francophone North African Literature in Transition, Jane Hiddleston
Postcolonialism After World Literature, Lorna Burns
Jonathan Lethem and the Galaxy of Writing, Joseph Brooker

Forthcoming volumes
Northern Irish Writing After the Troubles, Caroline Magennis

David Foster Wallace's Toxic Sexuality

Hideousness, Neoliberalism, Spermatics

Edward Jackson

BLOOMSBURY ACADEMIC
LONDON · NEW YORK · OXFORD · NEW DELHI · SYDNEY

BLOOMSBURY ACADEMIC
Bloomsbury Publishing Plc
50 Bedford Square, London, WC1B 3DP, UK
1385 Broadway, New York, NY 10018, USA
29 Earlsfort Terrace, Dublin 2, Ireland

BLOOMSBURY, BLOOMSBURY ACADEMIC and the Diana logo are trademarks of Bloomsbury Publishing Plc

First published in Great Britain 2020
This paperback edition published in 2022

Copyright © Edward Jackson, 2020

Edward Jackson has asserted his right under the Copyright, Designs and Patents Act, 1988, to be identified as Author of this work.

For legal purposes the Acknowledgements on p. viii constitute an extension of this copyright page.

Cover design: Eleanor Rose
Cover illustration © Alice Marwick

All rights reserved. No part of this publication may be reproduced or transmitted in any form or by any means, electronic or mechanical, including photocopying, recording, or any information storage or retrieval system, without prior permission in writing from the publishers.

Bloomsbury Publishing Plc does not have any control over, or responsibility for, any third-party websites referred to or in this book. All internet addresses given in this book were correct at the time of going to press. The author and publisher regret any inconvenience caused if addresses have changed or sites have ceased to exist, but can accept no responsibility for any such changes.

A catalogue record for this book is available from the British Library.

A catalog record for this book is available from the Library of Congress.

ISBN: HB: 978-1-3501-1776-1
PB: 978-1-3502-4929-5
ePDF: 978-1-3501-1777-8
eBook: 978-1-3501-1778-5

Series: New Horizons in Contemporary Writing

Typeset by Deanta Global Publishing Services, Chennai, India

To find out more about our authors and books visit www.bloomsbury.com and sign up for our newsletters.

For Mom, Dad, Thomas, and Mary.

Contents

Acknowledgements	viii
Introduction	1
1 Responsibility: Investing against pornification	29
2 Risk: Securitizing male homosexuality	59
3 Contract: Gazing within masochism	89
4 Property: Privatizing feminist critique	119
5 Austerity: Sacrificing and scapegoating little men	149
Conclusion	177
Notes	183
Bibliography	195
Index	213

Acknowledgements

I would like to thank Martin Paul Eve, David Avital, Lucy Brown, Bryan Cheyette, Ben Doyle, and Joseph Gautham for their interest in publishing this book. My gratitude extends as well to the reviewers who provided very useful feedback on the book in its draft stages, and to the copyeditors who helped me to fine-tune it before publication.

This project exists because of financial support from the AHRC's Midlands4Cities Doctoral Training Partnership. Without this money, I could not have pursued the PhD from which this book arose. The expert guidance I received at the University of Birmingham was also instrumental to getting my research off the ground. Sara K. Wood, who first introduced me to David Foster Wallace's work, has been a fount of knowledge and advice for over a decade now, and I cannot thank her enough. Rex Ferguson and Michele Aaron were also excellent supervisors who helped to steer me in the right direction.

Alexander Moran provided me with invaluable intellectual, professional and friendly support as I wrote this book, and I am greatly in his debt. The following people also deserve special mention: Gerry Carlin, Nicola Allen, Tom Cobb, Ali Fletcher, Joel Nicholson-Roberts, Xavier Marco del Pont, Tony Venezia, Emma Southon, Clare Hayes-Brady, David Baldwin, Jonathan Prince, William Pryde, Simon Mole, Rachel Simmonds, David Evans, Ashley Connolly, Kauser Husain, John Taylor, Barry Worrallo, Anne Wilkinson, Ian Francis, and Gavin Pahal. Thank you all for your kindness and support.

Introduction

David Foster Wallace's short story, 'Forever Overhead', follows a thirteen-year-old boy's decision to jump off a diving board at a public swimming pool, and it ends with him about to leap. At its simplest, the story is an extended metaphor for initiation into manhood, in which the boy's new sexual feelings play a central role. His wet dream is 'a rush and a gush and a toe-curling scalp-snapping jolt' (1999b: 4) that produces 'a dense white jam that lisps between legs, trickles and sticks, cools on you' (4). Wallace would express reservations about such lyrical prose, describing the story in his contributor note to *The Best American Short Stories 1992* as 'heavy, meditative, image-laden, swinging for the fence on just about every pitch' (1992: 375). Such lyricism, though, imbues the boy's first sexual stirrings with emotional importance, to the extent that, for Zadie Smith, 'the unmediated sensory overload of puberty overlaps here with a dream of language: that words might become things' (2011: 262). One image in these paragraphs is evocative not only of such thingness, but of an economic realm that, for all intents and purposes, is alien to the experience at hand: the boy's 'sack is now full and vulnerable, a commodity to be protected' (Wallace 1999b: 4). As a commodity, the boy's scrotum takes on the meanings of the market. Consequently, his ejaculation – and also, perhaps, his semen itself – derives its value from the apparent fact of its scarcity. This strange image of a young boy's genitals is not incidental, but is actually indicative of how Wallace explores sexuality through reference to economic ideas throughout his career. As ejaculations go, in other words, this one is far more than just a wet dream that Wallace would later dismiss with embarrassment.

Critics have noted the link between sexuality and economics in Wallace's work before, but they have not subjected it to the sustained analysis it deserves. For instance, in *David Foster Wallace's Balancing Books: Fictions of Value* (2017a), Jeffrey Severs explores how economic ideas permeate Wallace's canon, and his analysis of *Brief Interviews with Hideous Men* – the collection in which 'Forever Overhead' appears as the third story – looks partly at how these ideas intersect with sexuality and gender. Those investigating Wallace's papers at the Harry Ransom Centre, meanwhile, have found evidence that confirms his comingling of the sexual and the economic. David Hering notes how 'one of the longest extant pieces of unpublished material' (2016: 134) from *The Pale King* relates to a 'magazine called *Money and Skin* that combines soft-core pornography and investigative business journalism' (134). Elsewhere, writing on Wallace's engagement with the work of Joseph Campbell, Lucas Thompson refers in passing to a draft note for *The Pale King* in which Wallace pinpoints the 'economics of sex' (2016: 219) in his characterization of Chahla Neti-Neti. This is a woman who, at least as this note outlines, handles the trauma of having lived through Iran's Islamic Revolution by giving sexual favours to her fellow workers at the Internal Revenue Service. It is she who takes the author-surrogate 'David Wallace' into a closet at one point in the novel and, in an instance of what Thompson acknowledges as crude Orientalist stereotyping (2016: 219), fellates him. On the basis of these details alone, it is fair to say that sexuality is never far from economics for Wallace, and that he connects them because of their disreputability; the perception, that is, that money is intimately related to 'skin'.

In fact, the tenderness of 'Forever Overhead' is an exception to this seediness, and Neti-Neti aside, it is the male characters in Wallace's work who embody it most thoroughly. This is partly a sign of Wallace's androcentrism, which David P. Rando (2013), Clare Hayes-Brady (2016), Mary K. Holland (2017), Daniela Franca Joffe (2018) and Peter Sloane (2019) have examined in detail.[1] While the sexuality here is gendered masculine – and usually, but not exclusively, heterosexually oriented – the economics in question relate to neoliberalism, which critics such as Marshall Boswell (2014), Ralph Clare (2014), Richard Godden and Michael Szalay (2014) and James Dorson (2014) have explored in relation to *The Pale King* especially. Definitions of neoliberalism abound, but David Harvey's widely cited explanation of the term, in his book *A Brief History of Neoliberalism* (2007), is a useful way to begin to understand what it means. For Harvey, neoliberalism is 'a theory of political economic practices that proposes that human well-being can best be advanced by liberating individual entrepreneurial freedoms and skills within an institutional framework characterized by strong private property rights, free markets, and free trade' (2007: 2). In the following chapters I consider five aspects of this political economic theory: responsibility, risk, contract, property and austerity. My goal is to show how these various aspects inform Wallace's depictions of male sexuality. I therefore unite two major areas of focus in Wallace Studies – his attitudes towards gender and sexuality, and his relationship to neoliberalism. By doing so, I argue that Wallace uses neoliberal logics to present male sexuality as being immutably toxic.

That Wallace presents male sexuality in this way will come as no surprise to some readers. Revelations of Wallace's abusive personal behaviour have coloured much of the popular and critical discourse on his work of late. Some of this falls into what Boswell calls (and perhaps too readily dismisses as) 'Wallace Snark', which in his words consists of 'blogs by women complaining about their boyfriends and, by extension, David Foster Wallace' (2019: 125). At the same time, though, there has been some genuine soul-searching on the topic of Wallace and sexism from leading Wallace scholars such as Hering (2018) and Hayes-Brady (2018). If one can boil this discourse down (outside of concerns with Wallace's personal life) to two central questions – are Wallace's texts misogynist and do they encourage misogyny in their readers? – then my answer to these questions is yes, but that it requires more exacting analysis. For a key pillar of my argument is that Wallace's sexual toxicity is not an example of unthinking prejudice, but rather of his determined attempt to present hideous sexual activities – such as addiction to masturbation, homosexual panic, objectifying gazes and sexual violence – as being integral to masculinity. As I will explain shortly, neoliberal logics, in addition to his peculiar attachment to antiquated notions of spermatic economy, lend Wallace the tools with which to naturalize this toxicity. Put simply, Wallace acknowledges and at times criticizes toxic male sexuality, but he refuses to entertain the possibility that men can behave otherwise – apparently, and tautologically, *because* they are men.

But why does Wallace feel the need to use neoliberal logics and seminal imagery to make this point? Why not just throw up his hands and declare that boys will be boys? Katie Roiphe offers the beginnings of an answer when she includes Wallace alongside Michael Chabon, Benjamin Kunkel, Dave Eggers and Jonathan Franzen in a group she dubs 'The Naked and the Conflicted'. For Roiphe, these writers 'have repudiated the aggressive virility' (2013: 63) of literary forefathers like Philip Roth, Norman Mailer and John Updike, and instead show 'an obsessive fascination with trepidation, and with a convoluted, postfeminist second-guessing' (2013: 70). In Wallace's case this registers as a tension between, on the one hand, writing about characters and situations that shore up patriarchal gender dynamics and, on the other hand, his awareness that to do so is objectionable. What results is an impasse between endorsing and critiquing toxic male sexuality – an acutely self-conscious instance of what Linda Hutcheon theorizes as postmodern literature's 'complicitous critique' (2002: 2).[2] One could read this as exemplifying what Hayes-Brady calls 'the Both/And dynamic central to Wallace's writing' (2016: 109), whereby he rejects binary either/or choices in order to occupy two or more positions at once. Or, following Thompson, who sees the same dynamic in Wallace's depictions of race, one could read his guilty self-awareness of expressing racist attitudes as the productive attempt to 'prompt similar self-examinations on the part of his readers' (2018: 208). These approaches have merit, but they do not consider the possibility that Wallace actually resolves this tension, and in ways that consolidate the sexist (or, as the case may be, racist) sentiments that trigger it in the first place.

Wallace does this by drawing on neoliberal logics and spermatic metaphors, which because of their seeming neutrality as economic processes and physical 'facts', allow him to present sexual toxicity as the immutable basis of masculinity. For example, in Chapter 4, I show how Wallace's attempt to privatize feminist critique in the 'Brief Interviews' stories casts toxic male sexuality as a matter of individual property rights, which though they might be transferred, debated or reclaimed, cannot be denied.[3] As a result, he preserves toxicity as the property of male sexuality and implies that the desire to change it is admirable but futile. The examples of sexuality in Wallace's texts that I focus on also follow spermatic metaphors of investing and releasing sexual energies as one would a form of capital. Thus in Chapter 1, which explores neoliberal logics of responsibility, I consider how Wallace's depictions of masturbation register an anxiety that semen has lost its value in a culture saturated with pornography. By appealing to ostensibly natural processes – the 'thingness' that Smith evokes – these metaphors cement the idea that toxic male sexuality cannot be reckoned with. As my opening example of the young boy's scrotum suggests, such recourse to the sexualized male body can at times be quite literal. Elsewhere, though, the spermatic metaphors I see in his work are far more implicit. Hence, in Chapter 3, I argue that an idea of male orgasm as the ejaculatory breaking of boundaries informs Wallace's suggestion that contracts, whether between writer and reader or employer and employee, need to be overcome.

To support these arguments, I will accentuate the many instances of negativity and violence that run throughout Wallace's texts. Boswell was the first to observe this current when, writing about *Oblivion*, he describes 'the dark but insistent tug of nihilism that is the dialectical obverse of his otherwise hopeful posthumanism' (2013: 162).[4] Mark McGurl, meanwhile, also stresses how Wallace is drawn to 'the seductive object – or nonobject – of a death drive, a destination of pure authenticity' (2014: 45–6). Male sexuality, in my reading, displays the nihilistic and death-driven qualities Boswell and McGurl detect in his texts – indeed, these are the very qualities which make it so valuably toxic for Wallace. In this light,

David Foster Wallace's Toxic Sexuality follows work done by McGurl (2014), Amy Hungerford (2016), myself and Joel Nicholson-Roberts (2017), Joffe (2018), and Jess Row (2019) in tackling Wallace's reactionary attitudes towards matters of gender and racial identity. At the same time, I hope to move beyond just tincturing Wallace's hopefulness with an obverse darkness. In my account, his sexual conservatism is more complicated (though no less objectionable) than is normally given credit for, while my suggestion that he endorses neoliberal logics encourages greater scepticism of his work's indictments of capitalism. Like the boy of 'Forever Overhead', though, there are several rungs that I need to climb before asking readers to take such leaps. Specifically, what do the terms that make up this book's title – toxicity, hideousness, neoliberalism and spermatics – actually mean?

Toxic how?

In a 2018 article for the *New York Times Magazine*, Lauren Oyler considers the profusion of the term 'toxic masculinity', and on the whole, she finds it wanting. Though it sounds 'vaguely academic', she notes that 'the concept is now invoked as the root cause for everything from sexual harassment to violence against women to mass shootings to the popularity of David Foster Wallace' (2018). As a lazy shorthand for harmful masculine gender norms, 'toxic masculinity' is perhaps a poor concept to use for the kind of close textual analysis that I wish to carry out in this book. Nevertheless, as Oyler's inclusion of Wallace in this list suggests, for many readers it does have some purchase, if only to describe the caricature of the Wallace fanboy. I want to retain this term, but also to specify it somewhat by focusing on toxic male *sexuality*. This is more fitting to my focus, and hones in on a particular strand of an otherwise baggy concept. Describing male sexuality in Wallace's work as toxic, rather than using his own less ethically charged term of 'hideous', also wrests some of the analytical ground on this issue away from his interpretive control, particularly as evidenced in his most explicit treatment of it in *Brief Interviews with Hideous Men*. I will at times use 'hideous' to unpack Wallace's artistic strategies, particularly in reference to that aforementioned short story collection, but even here I take it as a loose synonym for dynamics which I describe elsewhere as toxic. Finally, my preference for toxic over hideous better allows for the possibility that future critics can apply my theorization of the concept to images of male sexuality in other, non-Wallace contexts.

The male sexual toxicity I am investigating, which includes misogyny, abuse, 'perverse' desires, and a general emotional numbness, appears early on in Wallace's corpus. For most of his first novel, *The Broom of the System* (1987), Andrew 'Wang Dang' Lang functions as a prototype of Wallace's later hideous men. Critics have certainly noted how this toxicity exceeds the *Brief Interviews* alone. Mary K. Holland, for instance, reads Wallace's 1990 review of David Markson's novel *Wittgenstein's Mistress* as displaying 'anxieties about masculinity and its seemingly inherent tendency to coopt, disempower, or manipulate the female other' (2017: 5), a reading she then supplements with references to his fiction. Elsewhere David P. Rando, in his deconstruction of the irony/sentiment binary in Wallace's work, notes how Wallace is 'peculiarly invested in diagnosing male lovelessness as a form of hideousness' (2013: 579). I will expand on readings like these by interpreting sexual toxicity as a broader marker for negativity and violence. Both of these terms fit into Holland and Rando's analyses, but I understand them in reference to theoretical and literary contexts that neither of them consider. First, I approach negativity through Lee Edelman's theories of anti-futurity. Secondly, I follow Sally Bachner's analysis of violence as an unpresentable reality that, paradoxically, post-war American writers persist in trying to write about. A combination of these perspectives helps to illuminate how Wallace's texts promulgate the notion that male sexuality is, apparently, unchangeably toxic.

In his polemic *No Future: Queer Theory and the Death Drive*, Edelman argues that an ideology of 'reproductive futurism' (2004: 2) defines the limits of political discourse. This phrase refers to how 'the biological fact of heterosexual procreation bestows the imprimatur of meaning-production on heterogenital relations' (13), and in turn privileges the 'child ... [as] the perpetual horizon of every acknowledged politics' (3). For Edelman, to the extent that political thinking (of whatever stripe) is always aimed towards achieving a better tomorrow, then such thoughts cannot help but be expressed through heteronormative imaginaries (and regardless of sexual disposition – put crudely, gay parents are just as reproductively futurist as straight parents). Drawing on Lacanian psychoanalysis, Edelman argues that reproductive futurism only enjoys the hegemony that it does by virtue of abjecting the *jouissance* left over from our ascension into the Symbolic order. Associating this *jouissance* with the death drive, he argues that queers have had a historically privileged access to its negativity. By embracing negativity, then, rather than harnessing it into 'some determinate stance or "position" whose determination would thus negate it' (4), queers can rend the Symbolic from within, affronting reproductive futurism with its own 'self-constituting negation' (5). For Wallace, male sexual toxicity accords with this idea of queer negativity. Indeed, his suggestion that masturbation is a 'wasteful' sexual activity, and his depiction of anal intercourse between men as a source of disease and death, clearly bears upon ideas of anti-procreation.

However, although this negativity is important to how Wallace presents toxic male sexuality, his texts also tame it to confirm a 'determinate stance or "position"' (4) – namely, male gender identity. In doing so, they support the futurity that Edelman would rather abort. For instance, in Chapter 1, I show how Wallace focuses on masturbation's anti-procreative pleasures to responsibilize straight men, while Chapter 2 extends this analysis to argue that his texts securitize homosexuality for a similar purpose. Queer negativity describes the non-procreative sexualities that Wallace presents as toxic, then, but with the crucial distinction that he utilizes said negativity to reaffirm heterosexual masculinity. Notably, Edelman also describes reproductive futurism as 'a Ponzi scheme' (4), as corroborating how 'capitalism is able to sustain itself only by finding new markets' (2006: 822), and as matching 'the laissez-faire faith of neoliberalism' (2011: 112) in its demand that we all compete within established political frameworks. If there is an anti-neoliberal critique implicit in Edelman's work, though, it is one that Wallace's use of sexual negativity does not follow. It is by channelling such negativity through seemingly neutral economic logics of responsibility, risk, contract, property and austerity that he is able to suggest that male sexual toxicity cannot change. Neoliberal logics and sexual negativity work hand-in-glove in this regard, not in opposition to one another.

There is a danger here that, by drawing on these theories, I appropriate queer ideas for an analysis that is geared exclusively towards hetero-masculinity. Still, I am arguing that Wallace recuperates sexual negativity to reaffirm masculinity, *not* that his texts fulfil the disruptive function Edelman envisages. Moreover, as Marie Franco's 2017 and 2018 readings of S/M and narrative in Thomas Pynchon's *Gravity's Rainbow* show, critics can put queer negativity to illuminating use when analysing the largely white male canon of American postmodern fiction.[5] Notably, in *David Foster Wallace and the Body*, Peter Sloane lays some of the groundwork for this analysis, albeit without drawing on queer theory. He argues that for Wallace 'sex is never really about sex' (2019: 70), but 'about validation' (71); namely, it is 'the metaphysically and psychologically violent assertion of the male self' (72), which 'results in the reciprocal eradication both of personhood and even objecthood' (92). In Sloane's estimation, Wallace conceives of male sexuality as a violent, death-driven force that undermines the subject's attempt to find validation in it. I am sympathetic to this reading, which is in some ways close to my own, but I believe it only tells half of the story. Yes, Wallace presents sex as an arena for validation, but he *tames* the negativity that Sloane outlines, so that – far from short-circuiting the masculine 'self-through-power' (75) through orgasmic self-cancelling – he is able to ensure that toxic male sexuality survives to see another day.

In addition to taming queer negativity, this process works by intimating acts of violence. Maggie McKinley's *Masculinity and the Paradox of Violence in American Fiction, 1950–75* (2015), although concerned with a period that precedes Wallace's career by over a decade, is a good place to begin examining this. McKinley's analysis of texts by Ralph Ellison, Norman Mailer, Philip Roth, James Baldwin and others offers a helpful understanding of masculine violence as a form of liberation. Drawing upon the existentialist philosophies of Jean-Paul Sartre and Simone de Beauvoir, McKinley argues that the novels she looks at show how 'violence can be used as a tool to freely construct one's gendered identity with the aim of transcending a stagnant or oppressive situation' (2015: 12). This notion of violence as liberation is close to my reading of 'Brief Interviews' in Chapter 4, where I argue that Wallace partly uses the threat of violence as a means to affront feminist discourses that, ostensibly, attack men for such characteristics. The paradox of McKinley's title, meanwhile, refers to how violence 'in the name of liberation often reifies many of the cultural myths and power structures that these authors, or the protagonists who speak on their behalf, seek to overturn' (2). In other words, when the racialized men that she examines use violence to approximate or resist the power of a white heteronormative culture, they only end up reproducing the white, hetero-patriarchal systems that have consigned them to society's margins in the first place.

A broad concern with ameliorative cultural politics therefore motivates McKinley's study. By examining masculine violence in her chosen texts, she seeks to accentuate their potential opposition to essentialist ideas of masculinity that further aggression. Although I certainly share McKinley's sentiments, I do not read Wallace's texts in the same way. The toxicity that I detect in them works through and against such a well-meaning and progressive perspective, and indeed to affirm 'the cultural myths and power structures' (2) that McKinley describes. Furthermore, the violence that I focus on in Wallace's depictions of toxic male sexuality includes but exceeds McKinley's existential framework. In fact, these depictions often reach beyond the diegetic level of Wallace's represented worlds to figure as an extra-linguistic reality. In this regard I follow Sally Bachner's *The Prestige of Violence: American Fiction, 1962–2007* (2011), in which she argues that for many American writers of this period violence is 'the last redoubt of the real' (2011: 3). Although I share McKinley's emphasis on literary masculinities, and also take inspiration from her reading of violence as existential liberation, Bachner's argument that violence is a privileged conduit to reality in postmodern fiction will provide the main influence upon how I approach the term.

Bachner looks at novels by Pynchon, Margaret Atwood, Don DeLillo and others to argue that they 'locate in violence the ultimate source and site of authentically unmediated reality, even as they claim that such a reality cannot be accessed directly by the novel' (2–3). Working from the 'loosely Lacanian' (4) idea of the Real as an 'extralinguistic ontological order' (4), she posits that they are able to accrue prestige from trying to tackle this apparent unknowability; in other words, 'to know that it [i.e. violence] is unspeakable and to rephrase its unverifiability is to gain a new kind of authority in relationship to it' (11). As I will show in Chapters 3 and 4, Wallace's depiction of male sexual toxicity follows this prestige of violence. Bachner also argues that 'the foregrounding of a violence guaranteed by its material absence as the center of American life, enables a deeply therapeutic and illusory reckoning with that violence' (5). American writers, anxious about their complicity in violence that they do not have immediate access to (especially in the form of overseas wars), try to resolve this anxiety by crowning it as the authenticating aporia of their writing. Applying this dynamic to male sexual toxicity, it can be said that Wallace resolves the anxiety of furthering patriarchal violence by inscribing it as the unrepresentable 'real' of masculine identity.[6]

There is a strong critical precedent for reading Wallace as trying to puncture mediation and to access something 'real' by doing so. His work indeed fulfils Robert McLaughlin's account of post-postmodern fiction as 'aiming, perhaps quixotically, to reconnect with something beyond representation, something extralinguistic, something real' (2012: 213). Though Andrew Hoberek has shown how 'Wallace's interest in representing the unrepresentable' (2018: 39) connects him to the romance tradition in American literature, this pursuit of ineffability has for the most part given rise to the notion that Wallace is instigating broader aesthetic changes. As Casey Michael Henry notes, 'These divergences from "representation" have been touched on under a variety of titles – from "belief" to "sincerity" to philanthropic "gifting" – by various Wallace critics (McLaughlin, Scott, Konstantinou, Kelly, Smith)' (2019: 111). Henry's own take on this apparent rupture of representation is the most interesting for my purposes. For him, Wallace's use of the epiphany, which is 'tritely old in a realist sense, [but] transgressive in its potential for a dubiously shaded moment of revelatory violence' (113), creates ineffable connections between reader and text or author, and through 'dark ... subject matters' (112). This emphasis on revelatory violence accords with Bachner's reading of violence as figuring something 'real'. Like Bachner, though, and unlike Henry, I approach it more sceptically. Rather than offering a path beyond mediation, I see this violence as a strategic aporia, and one that authenticates the idea that toxic sexuality cannot be reckoned with.

Toxicity in my reading, then, has a twofold meaning. First, I use it to refer to the (tamed) anti-futurist negativity of non-procreative sexuality. Secondly, it designates a sexual violence that can supposedly broach an unrepresentable 'real'. There are no doubt overlaps and tensions between these meanings, but I allow for such criss-crossing in order to better accommodate for the different ways in which Wallace accepts the negativity and violence that make up such toxicity and presents them as the immutable underbelly of masculinity. He is not alone in this, of course, for these ideas demonstrate Wallace's imbrication in a culture of white male backlash. In 2012, the preeminent scholar of American masculinities, Michael Kimmel, noted that since the mid-1990s a 'vitriolic chorus of defensively unapologetic regression' (2012: ix) had arisen in men's attitudes towards gender issues. That he would publish *Angry White Men: American Masculinity at the End of an Era* in 2013 is evidence that the chorus still sings; that three years later Donald Trump would be president suggests that it shows no signs of shutting up. There may indeed be commonalities between Wallace's sexual politics and Trumpism, or the rise of the alt-right more generally.[7] However, I wish to ground Wallace's writing of sexuality in its historical and cultural contexts, and therefore build on what Joffe describes as 'the important work done by other scholars in recent years to decouple Wallace's writing from the largely ahistorical, universalist discourse that has surrounded the author since his death' (2018: 155). Indeed, doing so helps to militate against Wallace's contention that male sexuality cannot change.

That said, no piece of criticism is free from the social and disciplinary conditions from which it emerges, nor from the biases of the author who produced it. Accordingly, it behoves me to state how *David Foster Wallace's Toxic Sexuality* contributes to debates on toxic male sexuality and contemporary literature, and my motivations for writing it. A good way to do this is to turn to an important recent collection of essays on one of Wallace's major influences, Pynchon. In their introduction to *Thomas Pynchon, Sex, and Gender* (2018), editors Ali Chetwynd, Joanna Freer and Georgios Maragos suggest that, despite progress in social attitudes to gender since the time Pynchon started publishing, 'recent slippages back toward greater inequality make examinations of the role representational practices play in combatting or reinforcing such inequality particularly relevant and urgent' (2018: xiv). The same can be said for Wallace, perhaps even more so given the wider popular currency he enjoys compared to the ever elusive Pynchon. By unpacking the ways in which Wallace reinforces toxic masculinity, then, I hope to further this project of combatting inequality by scrutinizing representations that perpetuate it. At the same time, the variety and perspicacity of the essays that Chetwynd et al. collect – on topics ranging from the figure of the noir detective, pornography, and Pynchon's commonalities with *The Simpsons*[8] – all attest to the fact that one can analyse and critique a writer whose work is sexually problematic while still accounting for said writer's cultural importance and signature achievements.

This rather obvious point bears reiterating because, in Adam Kelly's words, 'it has recently become possible for prominent critics to argue that, on the basis of details found in his biography, Wallace's fiction can be dismissed as *a priori* misogynistic before it is even read' (2018: 96). He has in mind Amy Hungerford's call, in the concluding chapter of her 2016 book *Making Literature Now*, to stop reading Wallace.[9] The biographical details in question here are not to be dismissed, for she reminds us that Wallace's 'relationships with women featured stalking, yelling, throwing things, and trying to push his girlfriend from a moving car' (2016: 145). Naturally, Wallace scholars have responded negatively: Hayes-Brady suggests that Hungerford's ideas reproduce what she thinks she is resisting (2018), and Boswell 'is left scratching his head' (2019: 129). That you are reading this book is proof that I think Hungerford is wrong to reject Wallace *tout court*, but right nonetheless in stressing how prevalent sexual toxicity is in his work (or, more accurately, the small sections of it she has read). Going forward, I build on her insights by showing how he presents this toxicity as being immutable. To do that, though, I first need to show how this pessimistic idea of male sexuality has much in common with the neoliberal credo normally associated with British prime minister Margaret Thatcher: There is No Alternative.

Neoliberal Wallace

Neoliberalism is hard to define, and it has become a prerequisite for critics who wish to use the term to acknowledge this fact before they go ahead and use it anyway. Indeed, in their introduction to *Neoliberalism and Contemporary Literary Culture* (2017), an important collection of essays that I will refer to again, Mitchum Huehls and Rachel Greenwald Smith set out by acknowledging how other people have registered this difficulty, before offering a four part breakdown of the term's development nevertheless (2017: 5–12). My use of Harvey's definition earlier obscures the fact that his study, a Marxist investigation of how economic elites have restored their class power, is just one among many. As Huehls and Greenwald Smith explain, 'Neoliberalism only becomes more complicated as the decades pass, accumulating economic, political, social, and cultural valences, while insinuating itself materially, ideologically, normatively, and ontologically' (12). Accepting neoliberalism's hydra-like constitution is a productive way to examine how Wallace uses a *variety* of neoliberal logics. That said, and although I draw on thinkers whose approaches to the term differ, there is a thread to how I parse responsibility, risk, contract, property and austerity. I approach these logics from the materialist standpoint of having to do with the allocation of capital, but in ways that also shade into the ontological register of what (male) people 'are'. Specifically, I argue that Wallace uses neoliberal logics to position sexuality as a type of capital, while his recommendations for the management of this capital signals his disheartening sense that men can only ever be toxic.

This is where I most drastically part ways with the main current of Wallace Studies. For scholars who have considered Wallace's treatment of economics tend to argue that he resists neoliberalism. Attempts to elucidate what Severs believes is his 'antineoliberal vision' (2017a: 184) are notable across the field. For instance, in their complex Marxist readings of *The Pale King*, Godden and Szalay (2014), as well as Steven Shapiro (2014), explore how the novel engages with forms of capitalist abstraction during a period of neoliberal financialization. Hayes-Brady meanwhile uses neoliberalism as a marker for the 'cultural condition' (2016: 22) and 'radical individualism' (2016: 136) she believes Wallace writes against, while Boswell strikes similar chords in his analysis of *The Pale King* and civic responsibility (2014). As Thompson observes, 'Wallace's critique of late-capitalist US culture is so clearly visible throughout his work' (2016: 2). Indeed, this is evident in the most unlikely of places, such as in his 1990 book on rap music, *Signifying Rappers*, which he co-wrote with Mark Costello. Wallace is only being slightly tongue-in-cheek in this book when he refers to 'Supply Side democracy' (1990: 115), the 'Pursuit of Yuppiness' (137), and 'halcyon Demand Days' (135). Thus, though Ralph Clare is quite right to argue that *The Pale King* 'bring[s] together economic, political, cultural, and social explanations as to why the neoliberal revolution came to be' (2014: 199), Wallace was interested in this revolution long before the posthumous publication of his final, unfinished novel.

Nevertheless, some critics are starting to consider how Wallace may have had sympathy for, or even actively supported, neoliberal ideas. The revelation in D. T. Max's biography, *Every Love Story is a Ghost Story* (2012a), that Wallace voted for Reagan and supported Ross Perot (the latter because, as Max relates, Wallace told a friend that 'you need someone really insane to fix the economy' (259)) muddies the idea that a socialist or Marxist politics motivate Wallace's critique of capitalism; Severs, for one, rejects this possibility outright (2017a: 25). Elsewhere Greenwald Smith references Wallace's texts and their critical reception as exemplifying forms of neoliberal aesthetics (2014, 2015: 41). In a response to Greenwald Smith, meanwhile, Ryan M. Brooks teases out how Wallace's essay 'E Unibus Pluram: Television and U.S. Fiction' accepts 'the premise that capitalism's problems can be addressed at the level of personal values and relationships', expressing a neoliberal disavowal of 'impersonal economic and political conflicts' (2015). An essay that many take to be the cornerstone of Wallace's signature hostilities to postmodern culture is, in Brooks's estimation, steeped in a neoliberal attempt to substitute personal relationships for ideological antagonism. By showing how Wallace uses neoliberal logics in his depictions of male sexuality, I add to this strand of criticism that casts doubt on his anti-neoliberal credentials.

Brooks's reading in particular faults Wallace's poetics for displacing structural conflicts. My interest in how Wallace's texts suggest that male sexual toxicity is not subject to social change is generally in line with this contention, but with an important caveat. In my analysis it is not that Wallace presents structural antagonisms as interpersonal disagreements, but rather that his texts, at least in their depictions of sexuality, try to bypass political contestation altogether. His use of neoliberal logics, in other words, constructs male sexual toxicity as a non-political intransigency, confirming William Davies's pithy formulation of neoliberalism as '*the disenchantment of politics by economics*' (2016a: 6, italics in original). (Albeit, for my purposes, this would read better as the disenchantment of *sexual* politics by economics.) Wendy Brown also reads neoliberalism as a depoliticizing force, and her *Undoing the Demos: Neoliberalism's Stealth Revolution* (2015) will at times be essential to my analysis. However, her focus is on how neoliberal rationalities hollow out liberal democracy, and so her arguments, if less driven by Marxist thought than Brooks's, resemble his in their attention to political discourse. The dynamics I explore in Wallace's texts evoke the neoliberal context Brooks and Brown outline, but my investigation is geared to looking at how they seek to make debate over the nature of male sexuality redundant.

The terminology Brooks uses in his piece is also interesting for my purposes. He refers to 'the logic of neoliberalism' and 'neoliberal logic' to describe the refusal of structural politics that he sees in 'E Unibus Pluram', but leaves his understanding of 'logic' unspecified (2015). In this, he is similar to Davies, whose book *The Limits of Neoliberalism: Authority, Sovereignty and the Logic of Competition* (2016a) – despite offering what is perhaps the most theoretically vigorous account of what neoliberal competition means in practice – does not state what the phrase 'logic of' means. One can assume that Brooks and Davies use 'logic' in the descriptive sense of 'the science or art of reasoning as applied to some particular department of knowledge or investigation' (*OED Online*). I follow them in this light by approaching my five chapters' key areas – responsibility, risk, contract, property and austerity – as forms of neoliberal logic. This sense has the benefit of framing the areas that I wish to examine – for example, contract – not in regard to actual policy (such as the contours of a specific labour contract) nor as epistemological concerns (as in the question of how we come to actually know what a contract is). By drawing on the work of Walter Benn Michaels and considering a broadly neoliberal logic towards contract in Chapter 3, my focus will be on how Wallace resists contracts that, both for him and for neoliberal thinkers more broadly, place too many restrictions upon individual choice and agency.

This points to a more particular strand of what I take the term neoliberalism to mean in this book. As the example of contract implies, Wallace's writing positions male sexuality as a form of capital, free to invest in the pursuit of profit, but in need of being released from stricture. The logics I pick out thus inflect a common attempt to construct male sexuality as a form of individually possessed capital. The focus on construction here is key, for as Jeremy Gilbert observes, neoliberalism 'encourage[s] particular types of entrepreneurial, competitive and commercial behaviour' (2016b: 12) of the kind that 'the liberal tradition has historically assumed to be the natural condition of civilised humanity' (12). Although Wallace suggests that male sexual toxicity is an immutable reality, he also tries to inculcate this notion – both diegetically and at the level of the reading experience – rather than take it as pre-given. True to Judith Butler's theorization of gender performativity as being a series of acts that 'appears to produce that which it names, to enact its own referent' (1993: 70), Wallace's neoliberal logics produce the idea of male sexuality as a form of capital that they ostensibly only reflect. Indeed, as Butler observes in relation to the gendered body, such acts remove the 'political regulations and disciplinary practices' (1990: 186) that constitute performative constructions from view, thereby presenting as fixed something that is actually contingent.

My understanding of capital in this context is close to the Nobel Prize winning economist Gary S. Becker's theory of human capital, as articulated in works such as *The Economic Approach to Human Behavior* (1976). As Michel Foucault explains in his account of the importance of Becker's ideas to American neoliberalism, capital becomes 'the set of all those physical and psychological factors which make someone able to earn this or that wage' (2008: 224), a move that extends '*economic analysis to domains previously considered to be non-economic*' (ix, italics in original). Sexuality is not an explicit part of Becker's theories, but neoliberal thinkers who have been inspired by him – such as Richard Posner in his book *Sex and Reason* (1994) – have applied human capital theory to sexual behaviour. I will examine theories of human capital in greater detail in Chapter 1, particularly Wendy Brown's and Michel Feher's arguments that, in the former's words, human capital has in recent decades developed 'from an ensemble of enterprises to a portfolio of investments' (2015: 70). However, I will at times approach capital through reference to other capitalist processes. In Chapter 2, for example, I draw on the neo-Marxist thinkers Randy Martin (2002, 2007) and Max Haiven (2014) to suggest that Wallace securitizes homosexuality as a risky financial asset. This will require careful delineation of the frameworks I use to understand (human) capital, but maintaining a relative theoretical openness to this concept can better illuminate the ways in which Wallace presents male sexuality as a resource to liberate and invest.

Furthermore, by describing the areas of neoliberalism that I focus on as forms of logic, I also wish to evoke their being 'logical' in the sense of appropriate and sensible. For Wallace's neoliberal construction of male sexuality as capital is suggestive of how his work – in this aspect at least – implies that there is no outside to capitalism. In this regard his texts are indicative of the socio-economic context that they arise out of, a period that Davies calls '1989–2008: Normative Neoliberalism' (2016b: 127). These dates roughly map on to the publication of Wallace's first and last major works, 1987's *The Broom of the System*, and 2011's *The Pale King*. Davies argues that neoliberalism is normative during this period because the absence of alternatives allows for a 'constructivist ... neoliberal telos ... of rendering market-based metrics and instruments the measure of all human worth' (2016b: 127) to arise. Huehls and Greenwald Smith also offer a useful periodizing term (and include Wallace in its remit) when they dub the 1990s the sociocultural phase of Anglo-American neoliberalism. Here 'culture absorbs and diffuses neoliberalism's bottom-line values ... shifting neoliberalism from political ideology to normative common sense' (2017: 8). Wallace's dissatisfaction with this state of affairs is evident throughout his texts, but, in his suggestions that men should accommodate and calculate for their toxic sexuality as they would a form of capital, they are suggestive of its dominance. Indeed, common sense in this regard, whereby (to use Wallace's warning to African American students that they must use Standard Written English) 'This is just How it Is [*sic*]' (2005d: 109), is central to how Wallace furthers the idea that, though lamentable, male sexual toxicity is here to stay.

Hence, I am not arguing that Wallace writes against neoliberalism only to reproduce its logics, in a process that Jedediah Purdy describes as trying and failing to cut through the 'neoliberal knot' (2014). Similarly, I do not suggest – as Kelly does in his response to Brooks (2017: 55) – that in *The Pale King* Wallace offers the critique of neoliberalism that is otherwise implicit or absent in his preceding works. Wallace is not a card-carrying neoliberal, but he actively pursues logics that construct male sexuality as (human) capital. Rather than a betrayal of best intentions, or a mistake he makes up for later on, his use of these logics proceeds with a similar verve to his more manifest and critically well-canvassed interests in postmodernism, dialogic communication, civic responsibility and so on. That this aspect of his output has generally gone underexplored suggests its potential to force a rethinking of his politics. For to read Wallace's texts as endorsing the notion that male sexuality is a form of human capital dulls their oppositional edge in the various anti-neoliberal fights that critics regularly enlist them in – whether that be in favour of a 'democratic liberalism' (Kelly 2014b), against finance capitalism (Godden and Szalay 2014) or in resisting President Trump (Severs 2017b). My analysis runs contrary to these trends by emphasizing how Wallace follows key neoliberal logics in his treatment of male sexuality; other critics can perhaps consider how he follows these logics in different areas.

Yet why would they want to do so? Indeed, what are my own motivations for arguing that, when it comes to sexuality, Wallace is an ardent neoliberal? Although I distinguish myself from critics who read Wallace as being against neoliberalism, and who thus look for tools and insights in his work with which to combat it, I share the underlying premise of their investigations nonetheless; namely, that literary texts can be put to use in attempts to imagine worlds beyond the neoliberal. The central difference in my approach, then, is that I position Wallace as an example of the problem, not the solution. Further to this, I also wish to answer calls for readings that complicate what have become doctrinal ideas in Wallace Studies. As Ralph Clare suggests, 'The images of Wallace the Genius, Wallace the Tragic, Wallace the Depressed, or Wallace the Saint are essentially one-dimensional, reductive, and often supersede the work itself'

(2018: 6). I do not add 'Wallace the Neoliberal' to this list; indeed, focusing on a specific sexual-neoliberal strand of his canon does not mean invalidating the ways in which it takes aim at neoliberalism elsewhere. As Clare goes on to say, 'If in the process Wallace comes to contradict himself, then let it be of the Whitmanian variety, both generative and generous' (6). I am interested in these generative contradictions, even if one would be hard pressed to consider my readings generous; for I will continually show how Wallace's investment in male sexual toxicity works in lockstep with his investment in neoliberalism, thus generally puncturing hopes that he resists both.

Considerations of how male sexuality intersects with neoliberalism in literary and cultural texts are relatively scarce. The essay collection *Masculinities under Neoliberalism* (2016) suggests that there is scope for such work, but this book's sociological approach and its focus on gender at the expense of sexuality mean that it is of limited use for my analysis. However, there is an essay elsewhere that speaks directly to my concerns – C. Wesley Buerkle's 'Masters of Their Domain: *Seinfeld* and the Discipline of Mediated Men's Sexual Economy' (2011). Buerkle looks at the *Seinfeld* episode 'The Contest', in which characters place bets on how long they can refrain from masturbating. Drawing on the same ideas of spermatic economy that I will explain shortly, Buerkle argues that this episode shows 'the tensions and ambiguity experienced amid the social transformation from industrial modernism to consumerist neoliberalism as they manifest in discourses of masculine sexuality' (2011: 11). Buerkle's reading, particularly of masturbation as a form of sexual-economic 'waste', chimes with my analysis of Wallace's work, most notably in Chapter 1. Yet the contrast he draws between 'industrial modernism' and 'consumerist neoliberalism' leaves these terms inadequately theorized. His readiness to equate neoliberalism with consumerism means that the former becomes an empty synonym for the latter. By approaching neoliberalism as a set of specific logics – responsibility, risk, contract, property and austerity – I offer a more rigorous understanding of how they relate to sexuality in Wallace's handling. To do so, I now consider how the final key term in my trio, spermatics, sticks to the other two.

Theorizing semen

Reading economic discourses in relation to semen brings to mind a medium that regularly associates the monetary with the seminal – hardcore pornography, and in particular, the role of the 'money shot' within it. As Gail Dines explains, this phrase refers to when 'the man ejaculates on the face or body of the woman' (2011: xxvi), though, arguably, it need not be a woman who receives the ejaculate for it to be considered a money shot. Direct comparisons of semen and money, however, are rare in Wallace's texts. Perhaps the only instance occurs in section 24 of *The Pale King*, when 'David Wallace' receives fellatio from Neti-Neti. Having impacted his 'abdomen twelve times in rapid succession' (2012a: 311) with her head, she withdraws 'to a receptive distance' (311) for his semen. Godden and Szalay make much of this hinted at ejaculation in terms of the novel's concern with finance. Describing it as a money shot, they suggest that 'Foster Wallace's semen figures the contradictory structure of personhood called forth by a system of derivatives' (2014: 1311). My reading includes a focus on specific examples of semen, but it also moves beyond them to explore how Wallace's texts combine seminiferous and economic metaphors more generally. What Walt Whitman called the 'quivering jelly of love' (1996: 67) in 'I Sing the Body Electric' is therefore not my overriding concern, but rather how a discursive construction of semen in economic terms (such as spending, waste or scarcity) informs the neoliberal logics that I argue are at work in Wallace's texts.[10]

Whitman's poetry nevertheless offers a useful precedent, at least as expounded by Harold Aspiz in his essay 'Walt Whitman: The Spermatic Imagination'. As the only other piece of scholarship to use 'spermatic' as a tool for literary analysis, this essay is a good orienting point for how I approach Wallace. Aspiz identifies a 'spermatic trope' (1984: 395) in Whitman's poetry, whereby 'sexual arousal and visionary fervor lead him to an inspired vocalism which accompanies, or acts as a surrogate for, orgasms' (379). Aspiz uses spermatic to designate signifiers (love jelly) taken to be the natural expression of signifieds (semen) which have a one-to-one relationship with their referents (Whitman's semen). I want to retain the idea of semen as being more than just somatic excrescence, but also build from the understanding that signifiers often miss the signifieds and referents they refer to. This is despite Paul Giles's arguments that Wallace tries to revivify 'the idea of a romantic subject' (2012: 4) in posthuman environments, and Vincent Haddad's comparison of the homoerotics in Whitman's 'Crossing Brooklyn Ferry' with Wallace's depictions of male–male bonds (2017). While Aspiz uses spermatic to describe ejaculatory images and the metaphysical qualities they have in Whitman's poetry, I use it to refer to discourses of sexuality that, though carrying seminal meanings, at times lack grounding in (or direct reference to) actual love jelly.

Accordingly, I approach Wallace's writing of the body as a performative process, and thus one that helps to create the reality that it purportedly only reflects. However, this is not to suggest that Wallace follows Butler's attempts to problematize the categories of sex and gender altogether. In fact, the dynamics I focus on in his work support the idea that gender is the natural expression of an immutable sex. This is important to bear in mind given the various formulations of masculinity in relation to biological metaphors. Notable here is Arthur Flannigan Saint-Aubin's arguments concerning phallic and testicular masculinities. For Saint-Aubin phallic masculinity – defined by aggression, linearity and penetration – has traditionally foreclosed the possibility of testicular masculinity, which is passive, cyclic and receptive (1994: 239). The first major study of Wallace in relation to masculinity, Andrew Steven Delfino's *Becoming the New Man in Post-Postmodernist Fiction* (2008), builds upon Saint-Aubin's ideas to suggest that *Infinite Jest* blends phallic and testicular masculinities. Saint-Aubin and Delfino's readings tend to reconfirm the notion that the sexed body is a pre-discursive given. By contrast, I want to stress how the spermatic metaphors Wallace uses are contingent upon the discourses they inflect; in particular, male sexual toxicity and neoliberal logics. Doing so helps to push against Wallace's attempt to mobilize spermatic metaphors in his appeal to what Sloane describes as the 'brute fact of embodiment' (2019); more than this, it is essential in rejecting the idea that the 'fact' of masculinity is brutality.[11]

An important precedent for thinking about seminal imagery in relation to economics is the aforementioned idea of spermatic economy. G. J. Barker-Benfield first analysed this concept in his 1976 study *The Horrors of the Half-Known Life*. Focusing on Massachusetts minister John Todd, and his 1835 book of self-instruction *The Student's Manual*, Barker-Benfield describes spermatic economy as a form of Freudian sublimation *avant la lettre*. Conserving one's sperm, particularly from wasteful expenditure, entailed the 'need to divert energy away from the invariably tempting sexual expression [i.e. masturbation] and to concentrate it on higher goals' (1976: 183). Barker-Benfield reads Todd's masturbation phobia as being indicative of similar fears throughout eighteenth-century Europe, but which 'in America took hold during the early nineteenth century, possibly in the early 1830s, and was extraordinarily intense through the first third of the twentieth century' (1976: 167).[12] Though other framings of male sexual toxicity will be significant to my arguments in this book – such as AIDS-inspired notions of risk, and the emotional blockage and release prevalent in men's liberationist discourse – spermatic economy, and what Barker-Benfield describes as its 'connection between sperm and money' (1976: 186), is of particular importance. Though Wallace cannot be said to display a Whitmanian enthusiasm for ejaculatory vocalization, his texts are invested in nineteenth-century ideas of sexual frugality – of the kind, indeed, that *Leaves of Grass* repeatedly flouts.

Barker-Benfield's focus on masturbation phobia in the West partly mirrors the approach taken by another, much more famous study published the same year as *The Horrors of the Half-Known Life* – Michel Foucault's *The Will to Knowledge: The History of Sexuality Volume 1*. For Foucault 'the war against onanism' (1998a: 104) was a notable instance of the '*pedagogization of children's sex*' (104, italics in original). This formed one of the 'four great strategic unities' (103) by which nineteenth-century sexology's 'incitement to discourse' (105–6) rendered sexuality an object of power-knowledge. This book's theorization of biopower – 'power organized around the management of life rather than the menace of death' (147) – accords with Todd's emphasis on controlling semen. Indeed, ideas of spermatic economy follow the two poles that Foucault suggests are at work in biopower. On the one hand, biopower entails '*an anatomo-politics of the human body*' (139, italics in original), which disciplines the individual body to ensure its integration into forms of control. On the other hand, it entails a '*biopolitics of the population*' (139, italics in original), which focuses on 'the species body' (139); in other words, the broader population's 'propagation, births and mortality, the level of health' (139), and so forth. Concern with ideas of spermatic economy, particularly as expressed by Todd and other commentators, disciplines the individual body out of an interest in regulating the sexual expenditures of men as a group.

Biopower is therefore an apt framework through which to consider Wallace's images of male sexual toxicity. Indeed, I progress from an individualizing focus on responsibility in Chapter 1, to an emphasis on population with austerity in Chapter 5. However, biopower is also limited when it comes to unpacking capitalist logics, even though Foucault suggests that it was 'an indispensable element in the development of capitalism' (140–1). His idea that biopower allowed for 'the controlled insertion of bodies into the machinery of production and the adjustment of the phenomena of population to economic processes' (140) still leaves the nature of such production and processes unspecified. Focusing on Foucault's discussion of neoliberalism in his 1978–9 lectures at the Collège de France, Wendy Brown similarly points out that Foucault 'averted his glance from capital; in these lectures, when capital is mentioned, it is usually to heap scorn on the idea that it follows necessary logics or entails a system of domination' (2015: 75). For Brown this blind spot means Foucault cannot account for neoliberalism's 'undoing of democracy and a democratic imaginary' (2015: 78). At the same time, this aversion from capital allows its logics concerning value, investment or profit to escape scrutiny. To be clear, Foucault's work motivates my analysis – explicitly so in Chapter 4's treatment of feminist discourses of male sexuality, where I draw on his theories of authors and disciplines. Yet my focus is on unpacking the heterogeneity of economic logics through which Wallace writes about male sexual toxicity. Accordingly, I give more attention to capitalist processes that, on its own, biopower cannot capture.

A similar desire to work around Foucault's ideas of sexuality and power, and by paying attention to economic logics that fall outside of his purview, animates Michael Tratner's *Deficits and Desires: Economics and Sexuality in Twentieth-Century Literature* (2001). Tratner argues that economics and sexuality share a '"mutual representability": the terms in one discourse turn out to be useful to represent elements in another' (2001: 5). From this basis he suggests that 1920 to 1960 saw a congruence between a 'Keynesian orthodoxy in economics that oversaving is harmful, and the prevalent view of sexual theorists from Wilhelm Reich through Alfred Kinsey to Bernie Zilbergeld that repression is harmful' (6). Discussing writers such as Virginia Woolf and Zora Neal Hurston, Tratner explores how a Victorian morality of saving gave way in the early to middle decades of the twentieth century to a readiness to go into debt, both economically and sexually. However, there are problems with Tratner's reading; as Patrick Mullen observes, he 'readily adopts the broad contours of the repressive hypothesis that Foucault is at pains to complicate – the narrative that associates the nineteenth century with repression and the twentieth century with liberation' (2002: 781). I am indebted to Tratner, but I do not suggest that Wallace's work, or the neoliberal moment it comes out of, signals a new turn in a dialectic of sexual repression and liberation.

Furthermore, by presupposing a division between economics and sexuality – so that 'different realms of behaviour and discourse find that they "glow" in each other's reflected glory' (6) – Tratner's notion of mutual representability cannot capture how neoliberal logics collapse such distinctions. If neoliberalism in Simon Springer et al.'s words entails 'the extension of competitive markets into all areas of life' (2016: 2), then sexuality in this state of affairs is economic from the start. Thus, neoliberal logics are not separate to Wallace's sexual representations, but immanent to them. Understood in this way, his texts are suggestive of a situation Jean Baudrillard describes whereby 'the possibility of metaphor is disappearing in every sphere' (2009: 8). As a result 'all disciplines ... lose their specificity and partake of a process of confusion and contagion' (9); sex, for one, 'is no longer located in sex itself, but elsewhere – everywhere else, in fact' (9). Baudrillard names this transsexuality, which as Rita Felski explains, means 'a general social process of implosion and de-differentiation which renders all terms commutable and indeterminate' (1996: 339–40). As an indication of how neoliberalism naturalizes economic logics in the realm of sexuality, Baudrillard's arguments usefully stress how ideas of mutual representability rest on unstable distinctions.[13]

Baudrillard's dislocation of sexuality from any stable frame of reference can be read as a typically postmodern manoeuvre. In his 1996 book *Postmodern Sexualities*, William Simon goes so far as to state that 'human sexuality is really nothing, at least nothing specific' (145); in fact it 'is always inherently something else' (154). There are dangers in this attempt to make sexuality a discontinuous lens through which to view things elsewhere, not least of which is the loss of its phenomenal and embodied aspects. In a 2015 review essay entitled 'No Sex Please, We're American', Tim Dean assesses recent publications in queer theory to find it lacking on this front. More provocatively, he also argues that because 'regarded as insufficiently serious, sex [in these publications] must yield to weightier issues. To be properly queer in the academy today means ... to stop thinking about sex in favor of what are perceived as more urgent problems' (2015: 616). For Dean, legitimating sex as an area of academic enquiry has meant betraying the 'messiness of the erotic' (616) in order to focus on identitarian and progressive political goals instead. Put simply, one does not talk about sex, but rather about sex as a means to other conceptual ends. By labelling Wallace's spermatics as neoliberal, and by focusing on a gendered idea of sexuality, my project confirms Dean's critique – indeed, it subordinates the consideration of sex, simplistically understood as bodies in congress seeking pleasure, to sexuality as an indication of identity or 'truth'. Worse than this, my recourse to queer theorists like Edelman serves to elucidate how imbricated male sexual hideousness and neoliberal logics are in Wallace's texts.

However, if Dean's review helpfully points to lacunae in current theoretical writing on sex, his approach is unhelpful in its prescriptivism. As Lauren Berlant and Edelman note in their reply to Dean (for he attacks their co-authored *Sex, or the Unbearable* (2013) in particular), he 'underimagines' (2015: 627) sex as '"embodiment" or what he calls "bodily desire," without considering for a moment that desire may not spring from the body alone' (626). I follow Berlant and Edelman by focusing, in their words, 'on what sex induces in material and conceptual relations and not on sex as something immediately recognizable when we see it' (627). Hence, my analysis of sexuality in Wallace's work facilitates an investigation of what one might consider to be the weightier issue of neoliberalism. This is not out of a disregard for the erotic messiness that falls outside of this approach, but out of an interest in the conceptual entanglement between male sexual toxicity and neoliberal logics in his texts. Wallace's oeuvre is in fact lacking in the kind of sex Dean suggests contemporary queer theorists ignore. But to conclude from this absence that Wallace is uninterested in sexuality would be narrow minded; even though, as I will at times demonstrate, he often displays the same disdain for progressive sexual politics Dean does.[14]

That said, despite my sympathy for Berlant and Edelman's arguments over Dean's – and in spite of drawing on Edelman's work concerning queer negativity – my approach does not generally follow their concern with affect, non-sovereignty and forms of attachment in *Sex, or the Unbearable*. This is because my interest lies less in aesthetic, phenomenological understandings of political economy (as explored in Berlant's *Cruel Optimism* (2011b)), and, when I make recourse to psychoanalytic ideas (as Edelman does in *No Future*), it is mainly to illustrate how Wallace manipulates them for his own uses. As my focus on specific neoliberal logics suggests, political economy motivates my investigation to a greater degree than it does either Berlant or Edelman. Thus, neo-Marxist readings of neoliberal economics, alongside queer theories of negativity and recent work on violence in American fiction, provide my main methodological inroads. As such, this book can be seen as a small contribution to a recent line of studies that mesh queer theoretical insights with an emphasis on political economy. These include Kevin Floyd's complex blending of Marxism and queer thought in *The Reification of Desire* (2009), James Penney's suggestion in *After Queer Theory* that neoliberal capitalism has made queer identity politics redundant (2014), and recent studies on the relationship between queer theory and anti-capitalism by Holly Lewis (2016) and David Alderson (2016). My interest is first and foremost on Wallace, but in elucidating his use of neoliberal logics in particular, I hope to modestly further these lines of enquiry.

With my key terms now defined, it is worth reiterating my argument. This book argues that Wallace conceives of male sexuality through neoliberal logics of responsibility, risk, contract, property and austerity. Informing such conceptions are spermatic metaphors of investment, waste, blockage and release. These dynamics allow him to ground masculinity in an immutable sexual toxicity, characterized by negativity and violence. By figuring male sexuality as a neutral economic issue, and as lending itself to spermatic metaphors, Wallace presents such toxicity as a fact that must be accommodated for, rather than changed. He carries out this process, I argue, in order to resolve an abiding tension in his representations of gender – namely, that of focussing near exclusively on male characters and perspectives in the knowledge that this focus shores up patriarchal power relations. In this way, Wallace tries to turn an area of potential political contestation (the idea that men are sexually toxic) into a disinterested economic issue (toxicity can only be managed, not transformed). Overall, I offer a revisionist reading of his work as being indebted to neoliberal logics, which allow Wallace to reaffirm masculinity on the basis of its apparently immutable sexual toxicity. This is, no doubt, a suspicious argument. I pour cold water on Wallace's anti-neoliberalism by stressing his sexual and gender conservatism[15] – a move that, from a certain point of view, means using his work's most objectionable aspects as the most effective tools with which to criticize it. My hope, though, is that this approach answers the outstanding question of *why* Wallace is so sexually toxic, and, specifically, by demonstrating *how* he is so.

What's to come

Chapter 1, 'Responsibility: Investing against pornification', argues that Wallace tries to responsibilize men into conceiving of sexuality as a form of financialized human capital. He does so out of the conviction that the spread of pornography has devalued sex as an arena for emotional connection, chiefly by encouraging men to waste their spermatic resources on the non-reproductive pursuits of casual sex and masturbation. By investing in the value of their sexuality as a form of capital, and in turn the value of the emotional experiences they derive from such, Wallace suggests that men can resist pornification's degrading influence. I begin with close readings of 'Back in New Fire' and 'Big Red Son'. These essays depict male sexuality through metaphors of labour and exchange, only to replace them with a focus on financial self-appreciation. Yet, despite their suggestions that sex can facilitate emotional intimacy, both essays ultimately endorse displaced forms of sexual abstinence, in which men accept their sexual toxicity and choose not to act upon it. This chapter ends by examining how such displaced abstinence, which preserves toxicity as a fact not to be challenged, also rests on the sexist alignment of women with pornification. By looking at the stories 'Think', 'Adult World (I)', and 'Adult World (II)' in particular, I show how the responsibilization that Wallace presents as being desirable for men registers as being damaging for women. Indeed, in these stories Wallace attacks what he suggests is a feminist complicity with neoliberal logics in order to bolster the need to responsibilize heterosexual men.

While Chapter 1 closes with a consideration of gender difference, Chapter 2, 'Risk: Securitizing male homosexuality', focuses on differences of sexual orientation. Wallace presents male homosexuality as an abject risk to heterosexuals, who, in coming into contact with it, are revealed to harbour mysterious psychological interiorities. However, not only is he aware of this homophobia, he manipulates it as one would a financial asset. Specifically, his texts securitize male homosexuality: they treat it as a risky asset that, once combined with the safer asset of heterosexuality through the security of the closet, allows for positive emotional returns. To support this argument I trace Wallace's depictions of gay men and same-sex desire from *Broom* up until *Infinite Jest*, which marks his last sustained engagement with homosexuality as I am investigating it. Though the purpose of this securitization develops from text to text – from creating broad comedy, to meditating upon paternal relationships, and to a need to shore up psychological models of selfhood against biomedical models – the underlying logic remains the same. Within these dynamics male homosexuality figures as a sexual toxicity more abject than that which 'Back in New Fire' and 'Big Red Son' suggest inheres in heterosexual men. The risk of such non-reproductive abjection, though, makes it amenable to securitization, and in turn to how Wallace's texts suggest that male sexuality – whether heterosexually or homosexually oriented – is immutably toxic.

Chapters 1 and 2, then, are concerned with male sexual toxicity as a form of sexual non-reproduction. Underlying this concern are metaphors of investment and waste (and risk) that evoke spermatic economy. My next two chapters shift emphasis: from non-reproductivity to violence, and from investment and waste to spermatic metaphors of blockage and release. In Chapter 3, 'Contract: Gazing within masochism', I argue that Wallace mobilizes the male gaze as a means by which to reform what he envisages as the implicit contract between reader and text. Drawing on Walter Benn Michaels's work on this topic, I show how a neoliberal desire that contracts respect individual self-determination, rather than allow one party to dominate another, drives this need for reform. At fault here, for Wallace, are theories of masochism which suggest that being subservient within a contract is a form of agency. In *Infinite Jest* Wallace tries to remind readers of their capacity for sadistic male gazing, and in turn of how they are not subject to the text but its equal – especially when it comes to instances of violence that are seemingly beyond representation. To grasp how he does this, I look first at 'E Unibus Pluram: Television and U.S. Fiction' and 'David Lynch Keeps His Head', which are in part concerned with male gazing, contracts and masochism. In doing so, I argue that Wallace works within but against masochistic contracts in his pursuit of a greater equality between reader and text. This equality only makes sense, though, if one downplays how the text has more power than the reader does in gesturing at unrepresentable violence.

Chapter 4, 'Property: Privatizing feminist critique', also examines how Wallace tries to protect individual self-determination. Here, though, I consider how he does this against the perceived threat of feminist critique. Focusing on the stories that make up the 'Brief Interviews', I make explicit an aspect of male sexual toxicity in Wallace's texts that I have heretofore only touched upon. Namely, this is the fact that such toxicity, for Wallace, is in part a discourse promulgated by a feminism that he presents and caricatures as attacking men. Through reference to Foucault's theories of discourse and authorship, I argue that the 'Brief Interviews' stories reclaim this apparently feminist notion of male hideousness as heterosexual men's private property. In doing so, they imply that the critique this discourse sets out to make can be made more efficient – in effect, they privatize it. Encouraging men to speak about sexual hideousness as a type of private property, these stories imply, is a more efficient way to critique male chauvinism than Q's questioning. In fact, Wallace suggests that Q's interviewees embody forms of sexual violence that the vaguely defined 'feminism' she stands for cannot comprehend. Thus, engaging with these hideous men offers a potential release from the blockage that, ostensibly, Q's overly rigid feminist position creates. In keeping with how privatization's emphasis on efficiency over ideology sidesteps political debate, however, the 'better' feminist critique that these stories apparently provide ultimately reaffirms the idea that male sexuality cannot be changed.

My final chapter, 'Austerity: Sacrificing and Scapegoating Little Men', draws on various elements from the preceding chapters' parallel threads (namely, non-reproductivity, investment, and waste on the one hand, and violence, blockage, and release on the other) to account for how male sexuality in *Oblivion* and *The Pale King* accords with the logics of neoliberal austerity. These texts, I argue, envisage a shared spermatic budget that some men, through their sexual overspending, have run into a deficit. Though Wallace acknowledges how hideous men are responsible for such unbalancing, and indeed presents them as figures to critique, he follows the austerity logic of displacing responsibility for such onto pathetic schlemiels, or little men. After tracing the genealogy of this trope in Jewish culture, I argue that *Oblivion* and *The Pale King* respectively present little men as detestable figures to scapegoat and as admirable avatars of sacrifice. With the latter, they exemplify a responsible self-denial that helps to balance an inflated spermatic budget. With the former, Wallace scapegoats little men for failing to take such responsibility, in the process implying that capitalism and male sexuality share an inevitable toxicity. The austerity processes at work here not only compound how it is futile to try and change this toxicity, but in doing so they also indicate how Wallace – even when he is at his most anti-capitalist – mobilizes neoliberal logics to suggest that male sexuality is irredeemably, immutably awful.

1

Responsibility

Investing against pornification

In his essay 'The Braindead Megaphone', George Saunders argues that media sensationalism during the 1990s helped to debase the quality of public discourse. To illustrate this, he references President Bill Clinton's affair with White House intern Monica Lewinsky. Saunders mimics the media frenzy concerning Lewinsky's infamous blue dress, which bore the traces of Clinton's semen: 'more at five about The Stain! Have you ever caused a Stain? Which color do you think would most effectively hide a Stain? See what our experts predicted you would say!' (2008: 6) The satire here partly takes aim at a culture that allows for sexual images and meanings to proliferate in public. As such, Saunders articulates a fear that Tom Wolfe also shares, particularly in his essay 'Hooking Up'. Here Wolfe asserts that 'every magazine stand was a riot of bare flesh' (2012: 5), instances of 'web-sex addiction were rising in number' (5), and 'sexual stimuli bombarded the young. … At puberty the dams, if any were left, were burst' (5–6). This 'lurid carnival' (5) that Wolfe outlines implies the greater cultural presence of pornography in particular – in fact, he suggests that pornography has become so normalized that the term itself is now redundant (5). Whether or not this is true, the twenty-first-century boom in easily accessible, hardcore pornography has arguably borne out Saunders's and Wolfe's concerns. In fact, given president Donald Trump's boast that fame and money allow him to grab women 'by the pussy',[1] the scandal of Lewinsky's dress now feels quaint, a lewd historical curio from a time before standards *really* began to fall.

Wallace shares Saunders's and Wolfe's worries.[2] In the essays 'Back in New Fire' and 'Big Red Son', and in the stories of *Brief Interviews*, he laments how a glut of pornography disenchants sex as an arena for emotional connection. Anxieties over pornography's saturation of the cultural mainstream are not unique to the 1990s, of course, but I am not interested in whether or not this decade differs from others in this regard.[3] Rather, I wish to explore how the idea that this was the case informs Wallace's depictions of male sexuality. Wolfe's image of dried-up dams in fact resonates with the spermatic metaphors that underpin Wallace's concern with pornography. Wallace presents men who, when faced with an abundance of pornographic media, waste their sexual resources in casual sex or masturbation. Consequently, he suggests that men need to invest these resources more responsibly, if they want to emotionally connect with others. As Matthew Eagleton-Pierce observes, appeals to individual responsibility have 'become common in the context of neoliberalism' (2016: 156), especially as politicians promote logics of 'self-governance and self-care' (160) while they dismantle forms of state support. In Wendy Brown's more precise definition, responsibilization tasks subjects with 'undertaking the correct strategies of self-investment and entrepreneurship for thriving and surviving; it is in this regard a manifestation of human capitalization' (2015: 133). Wallace tasks male characters and readers in a similar way. Indicting pornography for inspiring non-reproductive sexual activities, he encourages them to manage their sexuality as a form of human capital, to be wisely invested in the pursuit of greater interpersonal intimacy.

Furthermore, responsibilization in this context constructs what Brown describes as 'financialized human capital' (33) in particular. Past theories of human capital, such as those put forth by Gary S. Becker, focused on how investments in one's education or lifestyle can determine future income, whether monetary, psychic or otherwise. However, recent decades, for Brown, have witnessed a shift towards 'a new model of economic conduct' (34), whereby the goal 'is to self-invest in ways that enhance its [human capital's] value' (33). Though an interest in securing returns on investments persists, it now jostles with an understanding of human capital where the objective is to increase one's value. The ways in which Wallace sexually responsibilizes men accords with this idea of value appreciation. Pornography is indeed such a marker for non-reproductivity in his texts because it devalues male sexuality as a means by which men can emotionally connect with others. Severs has explored at length how Wallace is interested in 'economic, monetary, mathematical, semantic, aesthetic, and moral meanings of value' (2017a: 10). In the essays and stories that I examine in this chapter, Wallace envisages male sexuality in relation to the first two terms in this list. He suggests that if men increase the value of their sexuality as a form of financialized human capital, they will be able to form more meaningful connections with their partners.

These dynamics are indicative of what various commentators have described as financialization. Natascha van der Zwan provides a useful breakdown of this term. If, at its simplest, finance refers to the management of money, and financial capitalism denotes a system in which financial processes dominate, then financialization designates 'the web of interrelated processes – economic, political, social, technological, cultural etc. – through which finance has extended its influence beyond the marketplace and into other realms of social life' (2014: 101). One such realm, in Wallace's texts, is male sexuality. Indeed, in her overview of scholarship that focuses on 'the financialization of the everyday' (111), Van der Zwan explains how, for political scientists like Rob Aitken, 'financialization has created a new subjectivity: the "investing subject" ... [an] autonomous individual who insures himself against the risks of the life cycle through financial literacy and self-discipline' (113). Wallace's suggestions that men need to invest their sexual resources more responsibly accords with this idea. True to Randy Martin's assertion that 'economic fundamentals ... become flustered under the financial gaze' (2002: 11), his texts also inculcate this subjectivity at the expense of ideas of male sexuality that, as I outline them, centre on labour and exchange. This inculcation is necessary, Wallace suggests, if men are to counter the emotionally deadening effect that pornography has on sex.

Commentators have coined a variety of terms to describe the greater presence of pornography in contemporary societies. These include pornocopia (O'Toole 1998), pornified (Paul 2006), pornification (Nikunen, Paasonen and Saarenmaa 2007), and porning (Sarracino and Scott 2010). As Gerry Carlin and Mark Jones note, 'Authors and publishers compete to effectively signify the pervasiveness of pornography by forming neologisms combin[in]g porn with various suffixes' (2010: 188). My preference in this chapter is to use Nikunen et al.'s term, which they employ in order to capture how 'texts citing pornographic styles, gestures and aesthetics – and to a degree pornography itself – have become staple features of popular media culture in Western societies as commodities purchased and consumed' (2007: 1). However, I will at times stretch this focus on 'styles, gestures and aesthetics' to include sex aids as well. Hence when Jeni Roberts purchases a vibrator in 'Adult World (II)', I read this as being part of the pornification that Wallace explores and deplores. That said, there are limitations to reading pornification as 'commodities purchased and consumed' alone. Wallace often depicts pornography in conjunction with consumerism, and in order to suggest that they are mutually objectionable. However, his presentation of male sexuality as financialized human capital also departs from this realm. Accordingly, ideas of investment and valorization are far more significant to my analysis in this chapter than commodification.

Furthermore, although complaints about commodification are useful in explicating anxieties about pornification, they presuppose that sexuality can or should exist outside of economics. As such, these complaints are indicative of what Brown describes as one of the 'four deleterious effects' (2015: 28) of neoliberalism that its critics tend to identify – the *'unethical commercialization of things and activities considered inappropriate for marketization'* (29, italics in original). Jeremy Gilbert provides a good example of this worry about – in Brown's words – 'crass commodification' (30). In his Introduction to the essay collection *Neoliberal Culture*, Gilbert notes in passing that the 'commodification of sex [at the hands of the pornography industry] ... is one of the most striking characteristics of neoliberal culture today' (2016a: 19). To some extent, Wallace's depiction of sex confirms this line of argument. Kiki Benzon is right to say that Wallace explores how, in 'a culture governed by neoliberal principles' (2015: 33), consumer 'pleasure itself may preclude a conscious, critical engagement with the world' (33). Yet similar to how, as I noted in my Introduction, C. Wesley Buerkle's equation of neoliberalism with consumerism does not account for the former's particularity, reading Wallace's engagement with pornification in terms of commodification alone elides how he envisages male sexuality as an economic resource from the get-go. Essays such as 'Back in New Fire' certainly critique pornification as a form of commodification, but they also urge men to increase the value of their sexuality as financialized human capital.

Additionally, reading Wallace's objection to pornification as an objection to how it fans individualism – so that sex, in Gilbert's words, becomes a 'consumptive rather than a relational act' (2016a: 19) – is only helpful to some extent. Wallace undoubtedly suggests that pornification undermines sex as an arena in which men can emotionally connect with others. In this light, his treatment of pornification is part of what some critics argue is Wallace's key concern – as Clare Hayes-Brady puts it, this is his 'insistence on striving for connection' in pursuit of a 'dream of complete intimacy' (2016: viii, 7). For Vincent Haddad this focus on intimacy is 'a physical, potentially erotic, transfer as well' (2017: 3), a reading that Casey Michael Henry has furthered with his argument that, in *Brief Interviews with Hideous Men* especially, Wallace's 'relational model ... is most accurately described as sexual' (2019: 139). Nevertheless, it would be short-sighted to argue that Wallace re-energizes sex as a relational space, if for no other reason than what Jonathan Franzen describes as a 'near-perfect absence, in his fiction, of ordinary love' (2012: 39). Though a failure of relationality provides the animus for his problem with pornification, the solutions he posits actually reaffirm an individualistic ethos. By encouraging men to increase the value of their sexual resources by investing them in more responsible behaviours, Wallace highlights the importance of self- rather than other-directed action. Instead of creating emotional bonds with others, then, these processes have the paradoxical effect of transforming non-reproductive pleasures into what Wallace suggests is a worthwhile sexual abstinence.

This goes some way to explaining why the essays and short stories that I examine in this chapter, despite their professed concern for how pornification undermines sex as a form of emotional connection, reaffirm the sexual non-reproductivity that they lament. Thus 'Back in New Fire' and 'Big Red Son' respectively instruct and imply that men should refrain from sex, rather than take part in the relational bonds that both essays suggest it can facilitate. The fact that these others with whom Wallace implies men need to connect are women, moreover, also explains why his texts bolster such non-reproductivity. For despite his attention to how men engage with, and, in 'Big Red Son', perpetuate a pornified culture, Wallace often aligns the dangers of pornification with women. It is fair to read this as sexism, an example of the longstanding association of mass culture and femininity that Andreas Huyssen outlines in his book *After the Great Divide* (1986). In the texts I examine, such sexism revolves around the suspicion that female sexual agency furthers consumerism – hence Jeni's purchasing of a vibrator in 'Adult World (II)'. My concern lies less in accounting for the reasons for this suspicion, and more in exploring how it informs Wallace's construction of male sexuality as financialized human capital. To some extent, it is central: for by aligning pornification with women, Wallace makes the need for men to resist the former – by valorizing their own sexual resources – an important part of his call for men to resist the latter.

The readings that I pursue here will at times appear counter-intuitive. The 'Adult World' stories, for instance, critique the sexual self-investments that I focus on, albeit in relation to women. Nevertheless, by showing how these texts are still indebted to logics of responsibilization, my readings are indicative of the revisionist approach that I adopt more generally. Hence, this chapter argues that Wallace urges men to invest their sexual resources in conducts that increase their value as a means to create emotional bonds with others. To the extent that these conducts either proscribe or preclude orgasm, however, then this process ends up implying that non-reproductivity is central to masculinity. This occurs by virtue of how Wallace's proposed conducts endorse displaced forms of abstinence, and also in how his suspicion of female sexual agency means he prioritizes scenarios that foreclose intercourse with women. My argument unfolds in two stages. First, I show how Wallace's hostility to casual sex and masturbation supplants ideas of labour and exchange with an emphasis on financialized human capital.

Secondly, I explore how his attempt to critique these processes when carried out by women ultimately works to stress their desirability for men. By preserving the negativity that Wallace suggests pornification inspires, his texts imply that men must control, rather than challenge, their sexual toxicity.

The labour of 'Back in New Fire'

'Back in New Fire' is Wallace's most direct engagement with sexual mores. It is also, perhaps, his most controversial text, arguing as he does that AIDS is 'a blessing, a gift' (2012c: 171) that could 'be the salvation of sexuality in the 1990s' (168). Wallace makes this argument based on the threat of 'heterosexual AIDS' (168), and does not mention homosexuals beyond an oblique reference to 'brave people' (172) suffering from the illness. In his review of *Both Flesh and Not*, a collection of Wallace's non-fiction that includes 'Back in New Fire', Charles Nixon calls Wallace's logic here 'indefensibly graceless and uncaring, and, in fact, [it] has virtually nothing to recommend it' (2013b). It is hard to disagree with this, though one can perhaps caveat Wallace's position by pointing to the essay's original place of publication – Dave Eggers's less literary precursor to *McSweeney's*, *Might* magazine. This magazine included issues with titles such as 'For the Love of Cheese' and 'Are Black People Cooler than White People?' To some extent, *Might*'s satirical tone can help explain Wallace's provocative stance in 'Back in New Fire'. That said, *Might*'s approach was tongue-in-cheek rather than broadly parodic, and there is a substantial difference between the racist cliché that blacks are cooler than whites and the deeply uncaring suggestion that AIDS is a blessing. Moreover, there is no doubting Wallace's earnestness in this essay when he proposes that AIDS can deliver Americans from pornification's 'erotic despair' (2012c: 171), namely, by compelling them to consider sex as a way to emotionally connect with others.

For Wallace the ''60s "Revolution" in sexuality' (2012c: 170) led to the sexual hangover of the 1970s, when sex reached a cultural 'saturation-point' (170), the legacy of which his 'bland generation' (171) inherit. Such excess includes 'swinging couples and meat-market bars, hot tubs and EST, *Hustler*'s gynaecological spreads, *Charlie's Angels*, herpes, kiddie-porn, mood rings, teenage pregnancy, Plato's Retreat, disco' (170). This list contains only two expressly pornographic phenomena – '*Hustler*'s gynaecological spreads' and 'kiddie-porn'. It therefore deploys what Rosalind Gill, in her criticism of arguments that document the 'sexualisation of culture' (2009: 139), calls 'a violent generalizing logic that renders differences invisible' (139). For Wallace the 'rampant casual fucking' this pornification inspires has indeed degraded 'human sexuality's power and meaning' (2012c: 171). This idea resembles a similar complaint that Edelman perceives in P. D. James's dystopian novel *The Children of Men*, which depicts a crisis of human fertility where sex has become 'meaninglessly acrobatic' (James 1992, cited in Edelman 2004, 13). As Edelman notes, James's hostility towards such acrobatics points to how 'the specifically heterosexual alibi of reproductive necessity' (2004: 13) renders all pleasures outside of pronatalism 'inherently destructive of meaning' (13). Though 'Back in New Fire' is not concerned with what Edelman calls 'the Child as the image of the future' (3) per se, its suggestion that sex is only meaningful when it is generative – in this instance, of forms of emotional connection between partners – follows the logic of reproductive futurism.

Wallace assesses pornification's detrimental effects on sexuality from the viewpoint of heterosexual men in particular. Though he personalizes his reflections (as in the comment 'I realize that I came of sexual age' (2012c: 170)), he also positions himself as talking directly to and for straight men. For example, he opens the essay with a Rapunzel-like scenario in which 'a gallant knight' (167) must 'slay the dragon' (167) to win a 'fair maiden. "Fair maiden" means "good-looking virgin," by the way' (167). This demonstration of insider knowledge appeals to patriarchal notions of unspoiled womanhood. Wallace reiterates these notions when he attests that 'any knight, from any era, can tell you what "win" means here' (168). Any knight, or any heterosexual male, will thus feel 'a slight anticlimactic droop to his lance' (169) when he discovers that 'here's the fair maiden, wearing a Victoria's Secret Teddy, and crooking her finger' (168–9). Though there is a camp comedy to this image that suggests Wallace's critical distance, it is still congruent with the essay's overall argument. That is, a pornified culture – which, as the 'Victoria's Secret Teddy' implies, Wallace associates with female sexual agency – supplants the impediments that heterosexual men require to keep their lances stiff with an emasculating sexual abundance. More than this, such a culture obviates the need for men to labour towards their objects of desire.

For the 'disappointment in Sir Knight's face' (169) when he finds his beloved too easy to access points to how, for Wallace, 'sexual passion … [is] a vital psychic force in human life – not *despite* impediments but *because* of them' (169, italics in original). In other words, men need to work for their 'sexual passion' if it is to have meaning. Severs describes the importance of work in Wallace's texts as a 'fundamental means of creating value and resisting consumerist forces of infantilization' (2017a: 22). Mary K. Holland, meanwhile, reads this importance in relation to Wallace's depiction of masculinity generally. Writing on his review of David Markson's *Wittgenstein's Mistress* (1988), and honing in on terms that resonate with the image of Sir Knight, Holland argues that in Wallace's texts the male 'subject's experience of being comes only as pursuit ("Quest") of the desired feminine Other who is herself constituted of lack ("Absent Object")' (2017: 4). To some extent 'Back in New Fire' follows this Lacanian framework, whereby, in Holland's words, a 'masculine-centered notion of desiring subjecthood' (2) means men are constantly working towards an absent object. This reading is compelling, but it cannot account for how 'Back in New Fire' ultimately redirects this work – or to deploy a more explicitly economic term, labour – away from a feminine other, and towards the male subject.[4] As I show shortly, Wallace supplants the other-directed labour that he attacks pornification for undermining with a focus on how men can appreciate the value of their sexuality.

To grasp how this occurs, it is useful to turn to the work of Michel Feher. Brown's suggestion that 'when everything is capital, labor disappears as a category' (2015: 38) is indeed indebted to Feher's essay 'Self-Appreciation; or, The Aspirations of Human Capital'. Here Feher theorizes 'the decline of the type of free labourer and its gradual replacement by a new form of subjectivity: human capital' (2009: 24), which he describes as 'a defining feature of neoliberalism' (24). However, Feher's understanding of human capital differs from that put forth by Becker, who for Feher 'largely remains a neoliberal theorist trapped in a utilitarian imagination' (27). This is because, for Becker, 'investments in human capital should essentially be analysed in terms of the returns they produce, that is, in terms of income' (27). In the neoliberal context that Feher outlines, though, 'our main purpose is not so much to profit from our accumulated potential as to constantly value or appreciate ourselves – or at least prevent our own depreciation' (27). 'Back in New Fire' presents male sexuality in this context, whereby, in Feher's words, the concern is with 'appreciation rather than income, stock value rather than commercial profit' (27). If the free labourer of liberalism rests upon a distinction between 'a subjectivity that is inalienable and a labor power that is to be rented out' (29), financialized human capital of the kind that Brown and Feher postulate collapses this divide. Significantly, it also turns a productive idea of labour – whether in the liberal sense of producing saleable commodities, or in Becker's sense of self-investing to produce forms of future return – into a concern with increasing one's value.

The economistic imagery that Wallace deploys in 'Back in New Fire' is suggestive of this concern. For instance, Wallace states that 'erotically charged human existence requires impediments to passion, prices for choices' (2012c: 171); that it is 'impediments that give the choice of passion its price and value' (169); and that 'the higher the price of choice, the higher the erotic voltage surrounding what people chose' (170). One can of course read 'price', 'value', 'choice' and 'charged' outside of an economic register, especially the latter term, which with 'voltage' suggests the figurative electrification Wallace believes sex has lost. However, that Wallace locates the roots of pornification in 'the erotic malaise of the '70s' (170) adds support to reading this term in relation to economics. As the IRS worker Chris Fogle observes in *The Pale King*, American culture during the 1970s was, for him, characterized by 'waste and drifting, which Jimmy Carter was ridiculed for calling "malaise"' (2012a: 225). One can read this term as being suggestive of the economic crises that dogged Carter's time as president – most notably, the rise in inflation. Melinda Cooper explains how 'by the late 1970s, commentators from across the political spectrum agreed that inflation represented a threat to the moral fabric of American society' (2017: 29). For, 'by creating uncertainty about the future value of money … inflation had the effect of shortening time horizons and inducing a desire for speculative indulgence among the consumer public' (30). In 'Back in New Fire' Wallace aligns the emergence of pornification with these crises in the value of money. Inflation and pornification respectively devalue money and sexuality, chiefly by encouraging gratifications that waste what should be treated as a precious resource.

For Feher, one of the consequences of this emphasis on value appreciation is that it becomes 'possible to govern subjects seeking to increase the value of their human capital … by inciting them to adopt conducts deemed valorizing and to follow models of self-valuation that modify their priorities and inflect their strategic choices' (2009: 28). This aptly describes how 'Back in New Fire' responsibilizes men to invest in behaviours that will conserve rather than waste their sexual resources. For instance, Wallace hopes that the threat AIDS poses to heterosexuals will encourage men to enjoy sex 'through non-genital touching, or over the phone, or via the mail; in a conversational nuance; in an expression; in a body's posture, a certain pressure in a held hand' (2012c: 172). Notably, except for 'non-genital touching', which steers sex away from an emphasis on orgasm, Wallace imagines types of 'sex' that either keep partners out of physical contact or touching in the most chaste way possible – holding hands. This signals a telling contradiction in 'Back in New Fire'. The essay posits that AIDS offers the required hazard to make sex valuable again. But, when it comes to imagining just what this valuable because dangerous sex will be, Wallace idealizes scenarios that withdraw from danger, rather than, in accordance with the essay's own logic, arguing that men continue to have sex but in manners pleasurably circumscribed by an awareness of the risk it carries. The fire that will re-enchant sexuality in a pornified culture, then, is one in which no one gets burnt.[5]

This contradiction suggests ambivalence about the body as a source of pleasure – indeed 'sexuality is, finally, about *imagination*' (172, italics in original). Most pertinently, though, the scenarios that Wallace proposes here mobilize fantasies of relationality that, ultimately, encourage men to increase the value of their sexuality by not expending it.[6] Moreover, this non-expenditure takes on a distinctly individualist character by the essay's closing remarks. Wallace ends 'Back in New Fire' by stating that 'fire is lethal, but we need it. The key is how we come to fire. It's not just other people you have to respect' (172). The change from 'we' to 'you' in these lines not only signals an attempt to enlist the reader into respecting AIDS's fire, or the other people Wallace assumes (but struggles to imagine) men want to have sex with. What Wallace leaves unsaid, but which the reader can conceptually finish, is that men need to respect themselves. In this sense, 'Back in New Fire' exemplifies what Iain Williams describes as a 'prominent contradiction' (2015: 311) in Wallace's texts: their 'appeal to vague, universal abstracts, coupled with a desire to protect the singularities of the individual' (311). This contradiction does not create an impasse, though, but rather is key to the essay's effect. 'Back in New Fire' appeals to the idea that sex can 'erect bridges across the chasms that separate selves' (2012c: 172) in order to imbue the individual self-valuation that it ultimately condones with a sense of emotional importance.

Interestingly, this dynamic appropriates discourses that surrounded gay men during the AIDS crisis, and applies them to heterosexual men. Michelle Marzullo explains how 'the terror over the emergence of AIDS encouraged a rhetoric of responsibility that incited gay and bisexual men to behave as good citizens through creation of a safe sex ethic' (2011: 767). I will return to how Wallace's texts appropriate elements of gay male experience and culture in the following chapter, where I argue that he securitizes the threat of AIDS and homosexuality for the emotional benefit of heterosexual men. For now, it is important to note that although 'Back in New Fire' gestures towards such a safe sex ethic in its mention of the 'conscientious use of protection' (2012c: 172), it prioritizes behaviours that, by avoiding intercourse, ultimately end up foreclosing the need for such protection in the first place. Significantly, this puts the essay at odds with Feher's call for subjects to defy 'neoliberalism from within – that is, by embracing the very condition that its discourses and practices delineate' (2009:

21), but in order 'to express aspirations and demands that ... neoliberal promoters had neither intended nor foreseen' (25).[7] If Wallace presented male sexuality in 'Back in New Fire' as financialized human capital as a way to re-energize sex as a relational activity between two (or more) partners, then this would indeed be the case. However, the essay does so to urge individual men to increase the value of such capital, despite its pronounced interest in sex as a site of relationality. Consequently, this logic supplants an emphasis on other-directed labour with a focus on how men should appreciate the value of their sexual resources.

It is similarly important to stress how this emphasis on self-appreciation mobilizes responsibility as a distinctly neoliberal concept. For as Susanna Trnka and Catherine Trundle observe, 'advanced liberal responsibilization projects [i.e. neoliberalism] have a particular political agenda attached to ideas of self-care and should not be misrecognized as subsuming the entire category of self-responsibility and self-cultivation' (2017: 9). With this in mind, Trnka and Trundle propose the concept of 'competing responsibilities' (3) so as not to lose sight of how multiple ideas of responsibility are in circulation, 'sometimes reinforcing neoliberal responsibilization, and at other times existing alongside or undercutting it' (22). Of the three alternative ideas they posit – 'other forms of personal responsibility; care for the Other; and social contract ideologies' (3) – the second, care for the Other, would appear most applicable to 'Back in New Fire'. For the essay conveys a desire for what Trnka and Trundle describe as 'intimate, face-to-face relationships that predicate a fundamental, if often understated, mode of social obligation' (3). Wallace's depiction of male sexuality here as a kind of financialized human capital in need of valorization, however, works against the possibility that the essay escapes a focus on individual self-care. Indeed, as capital to be appreciated, male sexuality in this essay (and as my following analyses show, in 'Big Red Son' and the stories in *Brief Interviews* too) is the target of an economizing logic in which responsibilization plays the key role.

That this self-appreciation endorses a displaced form of sexual abstinence, moreover, suggests how 'Back in New Fire' ultimately reaffirms the non-reproductivity that it sets out to criticize, albeit, in the guise of responsible self-denial, rather than hedonistic excess. The essay acknowledges the negativity Edelman posits in non-procreative sex – in his words, 'sex as the site of drives not predetermined by any fixed goal or end' (2011: 111) – but does not ventilate its death-driven implications. Edelman's critique of fellow queer theorist Judith Halberstam is applicable here – Wallace 'strikes the *pose* of negativity while evacuating its force' (Edelman 2006: 822, italics in original), with 'pose' referring to how Wallace's recommended sexual behaviours amount to abstinence in all but name.[8] As such, the essay manipulates this negativity to affirm what Wallace suggests is a positive 'fixed goal or end' – men's capacity for hoarding, in order to valorize, their sexual resources. However, this is not the hoarding of external objects or of labour power, both of which place the subject in a possessive relationship to that which they hoard. As Feher suggests, 'Neoliberal subjects do not exactly own their human capital; they invest in it' (2009: 34). Consequently, 'while they can considerably alter their human capital – by means of either diversifying or modifying their behaviors and social interactions – they can never sell it' (34). Human capital is indivisible from the individual, who by modifying his behaviours – in this context, replacing casual sex with behaviours that prevent orgasm – can increase its value.

This indivisibility has important implications for how the responsibilization 'Back in New Fire' endorses ultimately implies that male sexual toxicity is immutable. Though this essay takes issue with 'guys [who] now applaud their own casual sport-fucking' (2012c: 168), the fact that it reaffirms such non-reproductivity in oblique forms of abstinence suggests a reluctance to question what Wallace variously calls 'erotic will' (168), 'sexual passion' (169), and 'human will' (169). Put differently, the essay implies that men can modify what they do with their hideous desire for non-reproductive sex (i.e. by supplanting orgasm with emotional connection), but not their tendency to desire such non-reproductivity in the first place. Furthermore, the behaviours that Wallace promotes – holding hands, communicating by the mail and so on – position this controlled yet unchanged negativity as a basis for masculine gender identity. For to the extent that 'the dragon can help us relearn what it means to be truly sexual' (172), then Sir Knight's quest is still necessary. Yet rather than an external obstacle that 'knightly friends' (168) must slay for their sexual pleasure, the dragon necessitates that men direct such labour towards increasing the value of their sexual resources. The tamed negativity that the essay holds up as worthwhile may change Sir Knight's purpose from sexual conquest to self-appreciation, but this change reaffirms ideas of masculinity based in self-assertion and implicit aggression – indeed, as knightly.

Pornification in 'Back in New Fire', and the danger of AIDS for heterosexuals that Wallace aligns with such, provides the occasion to reaffirm male gender identity on the basis of a tamed negativity. This dynamic, whereby Wallace appropriates the same negativity that he laments in order to stress its intransigency, will recur throughout my analysis of how he writes about male sexual toxicity. In 'Back in New Fire', the neoliberal logic in question – that of responsibilizing men into investing in their sexuality as a form of financial human capital – replaces labour with a focus on self-appreciation. In fact, the essay appeals to a liberal idea of inalienable subjectivity and rentable labour power, wherein incommensurable notions of 'erotic will' (168), though deriving their meaning from the labour that Sir Knight deploys in the face of cultural impediments, will always persist outside and in excess of such. It does so, though, to propose a neoliberal remedy to the problems that Wallace sees arising from pornification's 'casual carnalcopia' (168). As I will now argue, a similar process is at work in how he depicts masturbation as a failure to exchange. Indeed, the following section adds more substance to what I have hitherto described only as 'sexual resources'. Wallace's depictions of masturbation are illustrative of the spermatic metaphors that, as I unpack them in this and subsequent chapters, underpin his writing of male sexuality.

Masturbation and exchange

Commenting in his essay 'The Nature of the Fun' on the challenges of writing fiction, Wallace suggests that writers need to move beyond the stage where they are 'writing just to get yourself off … – since any kind of masturbation is lonely and hollow' (2012e: 197). The offhand tone here, 'since' working with the clause's hyphenated isolation from the larger sentence to convey what is seemingly a common fact, compounds the essay's casual assurance that masturbation is harmful. These remarks are indicative of Wallace's hostility towards masturbation throughout his work.[9] However, the suggestion that 'any kind' of masturbation is bad elides how his texts overwhelmingly consider male masturbation. In fact, only two instances of female masturbation appear in his output: Jeni Roberts's auto-eroticism in 'Adult World (II)', and the suspicion in *Infinite Jest* that Enfield Tennis Academy student Carol Spodek has retained 'the same single large-grip Donnay stick for going on five straight years' (1996: 636) because she uses it to masturbate. Lucas Thompson notes how 'autoeroticism, in Wallace's work … functions as a recurring trope, consistently linked to such negative states as loneliness, ennui, artistic self-indulgence, self-serving metafiction, political avarice and – perhaps most importantly – solipsism' (2016: 80). Though I agree with Thompson's observations, he does not account for the importance of gender in these dynamics. He also deflects attention away from masturbation's negativity *qua* masturbation – namely, as a type of failed sexuality that, as I will now show, Wallace associates with men in particular.

The most obvious example of this pessimistic estimation of male masturbation is *Infinite Jest*'s Organization of North American Nations, or ONAN – the North American superstate made up of the United States, Canada and Mexico. This acronym points to the Genesis story of Onan, who, as Thomas W. Laqueur relates, 'spilled his seed upon the ground rather than into the wife of his dead brother' (2004: 15) and was struck down by God as a result. Associations between this tale and masturbation arise in particular from the anonymous 1712 pamphlet *Onania*. In Laqueur's description, as 'masturbation's primal text' (25) *Onania* outlined the 'dangers of the "abominable practice" of "self-pollution"' (25). He explains how this pamphlet helped to perpetuate the idea that 'just as in the world of trade and commerce one must discipline one's use of scarce resources, so in the spermatic economy men need to save and to husband their precious bodily fluid' (195). As Mia, the protagonist of Siri Hustvedt's novel *The Summer Without Men* describes it, Onan's crime and the lessons that anti-masturbatory tracts continue to draw from it amount to a 'waste-not-want-not-for-children argument' (2011: 123). Nevertheless, Wallace takes this need to control men's sexuality as a precious resource seriously. In ways that confirm Thompson's suggestion that his texts 'most importantly' (2016: 80) use masturbation to convey solipsism, he depicts wasting one's sexual resources as a sign of men's failure to emotionally connect with others.

Greg Tuck's research on representations of masturbation and the money shot offers a useful inroad to understanding how this works. In his analysis of various media texts from around the millennium, Tuck argues that male masturbation inspires revulsion because it is not 'socially or emotionally productive. It is not just "not partnered sex", it is "anti partnered sex"' (2009: 91). Though it can be said to support consumer capitalism's focus on individual gratification, the fact that masturbation signals 'a failure to exchange' (86) means that it has also, for Tuck, 'profoundly threatened the workings of the market. This is the paradox at the heart of masturbation that continues today' (86). Such failure to exchange only makes sense in a reproductively futurist imaginary, where *successful* exchange occurs when a woman receives the semen. This may be within reproductive acts or, as Tuck's analysis of films like *There's Something About Mary* (1998) and *Happiness* (1998) suggests, in the abject form of the money shot (Tuck 2003). Within this imaginary, what a man 'buys' from his female partner when his ejaculate lands either in or on her is the meaning of a masculinity that fulfils its 'natural' progenitive function. The masturbator's deviation from this framework affronts the exchange upon which such meaning rests. Consequently, in ways that recall

Wallace's complaints about casual sex in 'Back in New Fire', heteronormative culture tends to represent male masturbation as being hideously meaningless.

Tuck refers to a number of thinkers to illustrate this conception of male masturbatory hideousness, including Kant, Freud and Lacan, but his most useful example for my purposes is the 2000 horror film *The Cell*, starring the American pop singer and actor, Jennifer Lopez. Highly indebted to 1991's *The Silence of the Lambs*, *The Cell* concerns a serial killer who masturbates to films he has made of his victims drowning. For Tuck, what makes this serial killer 'truly obscene ... is that he consumes his own production and therefore does violence to the concept of market exchange as well as to his victim' (2009: 88). Orin's addiction to casual sex in *Infinite Jest* corresponds with this description, albeit, unlike Tuck, Wallace seems to suggest that even partnered sex can harbour such masturbatory negativity. In one scene the narrator describes Orin's sex with a mysterious hand model, and notes that he 'need[s] to be assured that for a moment he *has* her ... that there is now inside her a vividness vacuumed of all but his name: O., O. That he is the One' (1996: 566, italics in original). The pleasure Orin takes from sex entails denying his partner any agency, so that he can instead make love to himself as 'the One' – thus confirming Catherine Nichols's description of his addiction as an 'unregenerative form of masturbation' (2001: 10). Orin here resembles the serial killer in *The Cell*, reducing the other in Tuck's words to a 'masturbatory prop' (2009: 88). Though he may ejaculate on or in his various female partners, the implication is that he might as well be masturbating, for the meaning of these encounters ultimately amounts to '*O*' (Wallace 1996: 566).

In fact, reading this italicized '*O*' as – to borrow a description from Wallace's story 'B.I. #20', in part about a serial killer – 'the Ur-void, the zero' (1999n: 268), and thus signifying the absence of value, highlights a limitation to Tuck's approach. Besides eliding the possibility that, as Orin's trysts suggest, partnered sex can also facilitate masturbatory negativity, Tuck's analysis rests on an understanding of exchange that neoliberalism supersedes. In particular, human capital in Foucault's famous formulation transforms *homo economicus* from being a 'partner of exchange' (2008: 225) into being an 'entrepreneur of himself' (226). As Brown notes, though, one of the many permutations of neoliberalism that Foucault could not foresee was 'the way that financialization has altered the figure of human capital' (2015: 70). Hence, Feher's reading of this dynamic again proves to be more useful for my purposes. His argument that neoliberalism now encourages subjects to valorize their human capital through responsible self-investments is illustrative of how, as I argue shortly, Wallace implies that men must increase their sexual value from that masturbatory *O*. Orin's satyriasis does fail to validate a progenitive idea of masculinity – chiefly because it purchases a reproduction of himself as 'the One' that denies his female partners the agency required to act as recipients in a (heteronormatively conceived) sexual exchange. However, as with labour in 'Back in New Fire', Wallace's depictions of masturbation appeal to an ideal of exchange even as they responsibilize men into conducts that prioritize self-appreciation.

Pornification provides an important backdrop for these dynamics. To some extent Wallace links Orin's masturbatory use of sexual partners with pornography when his father, James, gets wind of the fact that he plans to watch an 'old hardcore X-film' (1996: 955). The terms in which James warns Orin about porn's deleterious effects – such as that it will create 'an impoverished, lonely idea of sexuality' (956) – echo Wallace's description of masturbation in 'The Nature of the Fun'. James asks Orin to wait until he has 'experienced for himself what a profound and really quite moving thing sex could be' (956) before he watches pornography. Though one should avoid interpreting James as merely a surrogate for Wallace, the former's wish echoes Wallace's yearning for meaningful sex in 'Back in New Fire'. Notably, James's hope that Orin will avoid pornography so that he can experience such meaningful sex 'for himself' (956) frames his intervention as a concern for the value of his son's individual feelings – *not* those of his potential partners. Thus James, like Wallace, evokes the danger of a 'lonely idea of sexuality' (956) to – paradoxically – lament how porn devalues an individual experience of sex. Masturbation here remains implicit, despite Orin's admission that 'I did myself raw for years on end on that hill' (136). In his essay 'Big Red Son', though, Wallace makes these connections direct, along with his suggestions for conducts men can undertake to appreciate the value of their spermatic resources.

Hal's description of his brother Orin's attempt to watch '"adult" films, which from what I've seen are too downright sad to be truly nasty, or even really entertainment, though the adjective "adult" is kind of a misnomer' (955), in fact echoes the title *Premier* magazine published 'Big Red Son' under: 'Neither Adult Nor Entertainment'. In its account of Wallace's attendance of the 1998 Las Vegas Adult Video News awards and adult consumer expo, 'Big Red Son' expounds upon the industry's venality in particular. Wallace advances this complaint alongside his description of Las Vegas as 'an enormous machine of exchange – of spectacle for money, of sensation for money, of money for more money, of pleasure for whatever be tomorrow's abstract cost' (2005a: 9). If Las Vegas is a 'machine of exchange' it is one in which such exchange is of and for groundless ephemera ('spectacle' and 'sensation') that are hermetically recursive ('money for more money') and which exalt immediate pleasures, despite 'tomorrow's abstract cost' and in the service of hedonistic individualism – 'an empire of Self' (10). The implication is that a porn awards show and expo have their natural home in a city brimming with corrupted exchange. Indeed, if 'for centuries you basically had to marry a person to get to see' (16) their faces in orgasm, then porn cancels this exchange (whereby one 'buys' sexual insight with marriage). To use Wallace's phrase in 'Back in New Fire', porn has so reduced the 'price of choice' (2012c: 170) for men that they no longer need to fear that, in choosing to have sex, they have to exchange something of value.

As in 'Back in New Fire', in 'Big Red Son' Wallace prioritizes pornification's effects on men. Observing that 'feminists of all different stripes' (2005a: 18) have advanced 'well-known and in some respects persuasive' (18) critiques of pornography, Wallace suggests that 'antiporn arguments in the 1990s are now centered on adult entertainment's alleged effects on the men who consume it' (18). As an example Wallace gives an excerpt from David Mura's *A Male Grief: Notes on Pornography and Addiction* (1987), which, despite being 'a bit New Agey' (19), he implicitly endorses. Mura argues that men who are in 'thrall of pornography try to eliminate from their consciousness the world outside pornography' (Mura 1987, cited in Wallace 2005a: 19), affirming the masturbatory failure to exchange evident in Orin's sex addiction. Wallace's recourse to a text that bears the hallmarks of self-help literature, moreover, points to how he responds to such failed exchange by promoting self-appreciation. In the face of how difficult it is to measure the self-appreciation that Feher theorizes (though Brown offers the intriguing example of 'social media "followers"' (2015: 34)), he suggests that 'it is arguably the psychological discourse of "self-esteem" … [that] is the most accurate correlate of practices and policies that aim at maximizing the (self-) appreciation of human capital' (2009: 28–9). Wallace's relationship to what Feher describes as this 'major cultural phenomenon' (29) which 'peaked in the 1980s and 1990s' (29) is complex.[10] For my purposes, it is enough to say that the brief glimpse we receive in 'Big Red Son' of a remedy to masturbation's failure to exchange focuses on increasing the value of one's emotional well-being.

Specifically, in a footnote to his suggestion that one used to have to marry a person in order to see them during orgasm, Wallace relates the story of a Los Angeles police detective – '60, happily married, a grandpa, shy, polite, clearly a decent guy' (2005a: 16) – who watches porn for 'those rare moments in orgasm or accidental tenderness when the starlets dropped their stylized "fuck-me-I'm-a-nasty-girl" sneer and became, suddenly, real people' (16). From this story Wallace considers the possibility that 'occasionally, in a hard-core scene, the hidden self appears' (17), thus affording the kind of emotional connection with others that he postulates in 'Back in New Fire'. Indeed, 'it turned out that the LAPD detective found adult films *moving*' (16, italics in original). This episode stands in stark contrast to the grotesquery that Wallace documents elsewhere in 'Big Red Son', most notably in the figure of porn producer Max Hardcore (real name Paul Little) – a man who would be jailed in 2007 on ten counts of obscenity charges. Unlike these men, the detective uses porn to access forms of emotional reality unavailable in other mediums, particularly Hollywood film, where even 'gifted actors … go about feigning genuine humanity' (16). Porn therefore enriches the detective's emotional life. In place of a masturbatory response and its failure to exchange, he increases the value of his experience (or at least, his perception) of sex. Furthermore, that he does not expel any semen – Wallace makes no reference to the man masturbating to these films – suggests that this boost in personal well-being is akin to appreciating his spermatic resources.

One can suggest, then, that Wallace presents the detective as displaying a more responsible approach to porn than those who masturbate to it. This activity's affront to progenitive exchange gives way to the kind of emotional enrichment Wallace suggests that sex can provide, and without expending the detective's semen to boot. The irony of course is that such responsibilization merely sublimates a masturbatory compulsion into a less explicit form of self-attention. As Nixon observes, 'Not only does the purported detective control the interpretation of this moment of "humanness", he is not required to communicate with it in any way. … Wallace's argument is therefore self-cancelling' (2013a: 219). In other words, whatever 'human' communion this approach to porn may facilitate, it remains one sided. Rather than conclude that this self-cancellation signals how Wallace is caught in a contradiction, however, it is more useful to ask what it achieves. For to the extent that the detective's (and his profession here is telling) search for 'erotic joy' (2005a: 17) in porn forecloses orgasm, then it is comparable to Wallace's proposed sexual conducts at the end of 'Back in New Fire'. The dynamics here are reversed – the detective engages with porn, he does not withdraw from it – but the effect is the same. Specifically, Wallace responds to the problem of men wasting their spermatic resources by highlighting the desirability of a displaced form of sexual abstinence.

This displaced abstinence similarly transmutes a direct form of sexual negativity, namely masturbation, into the indirect non-productivity of swapping one's own orgasm for the sight of other people's. A more dramatic instance of such transmutation, and one that suggests how Wallace preserves such negativity to reaffirm male gender identity, is apparent in his choice of dedicatees for 'Big Red Son'. These are 'testosteronically afflicted males' (3) who are castrating themselves because 'their sexual urges had become a source of intolerable conflict' (3) in a pornified culture that promises 'perfect, whenever-you-want-it release' (3). To these 'tormented souls' (3) Wallace proposes an alternative: undergoing the '1.4 years of nonstop continuous porn-viewing' (5) the AVN Awards judges have, at least purportedly, put in to assess the year's entries. As a result, they 'will never thereafter want to see, hear, engage in, or even think about human sexuality ever again' (5). Wallace's tone here is comic, but this suggested course of action nonetheless accords with the self-cancelling logic Nixon observes in the detective. For to fry one's 'glandular circuitboard' (5) through sustained porn viewing is not an alternative to castration but a means to achieve it through other means. Watching so much porn will not allow these men to escape their sexual negativity, but it will allow them to responsibly control it in ways that, as in 'Back in New Fire' (but lacking that essay's sense of optimism), affirms male sexuality's seemingly intransigent negativity.

The fact that 'Back in New Fire' and 'Big Red Son' supplant labour and exchange with an emphasis on value appreciation, but only to in turn reaffirm a negativity that should by definition lack value, is not a contradiction. In fact, the former can be said to run alongside the latter. For the negativity in question here provides an affirmation that Edelman's theories deny; in his words, negativity 'can have no justification if justification requires it to reinforce some positive social value' (2004: 6) (with 'positive' here understood as any cognizable or determinate end, rather than an ethical good). Both essays mobilize and indeed tame such negativity in order to affirm heterosexual masculinity as an identity defined by its propensity for non-reproductive desires. That such negativity is tamed, moreover, makes it amenable to the self-management that responsibilization calls forth. In this regard, though 'Back in New Fire' and 'Big Red Son' display a manifest desire for men to responsibly invest in valorizing their sexual resources, both essays also exhibit a latent desire for men to responsibly control their sexual negativity as, itself, what makes them men. Pornification is the motivating cause for these dynamics in both 'Back in New Fire' and 'Big Red Son', but these essays are not the only places in Wallace's oeuvre where pornification, responsibilization and financialized human capital intermingle. The next section considers selected stories from *Brief Interviews* to show how the presence of these same elements there – though consistent with my earlier analysis – are also inflected by a suspicion of female sexual agency.

The difference gender makes

Wallace's predominate focus on men in 'Big Red Son' means that considerations of female sexuality in relation to pornography fall by the wayside. As Nixon argues, the various degradations that Wallace outlines here 'are perpetrated against women, and yet the essay's condemnation never appears to consider a woman's perspective at all. It devalues a female perspective almost as much as do the pornographers Wallace describes' (2013a: 219). This seeming disregard for women's experiences of pornography is more explicit in 'Back in New Fire'. In addition to the Victoria Secret clad temptress who frustrates Sir Knight's ability to labour towards his desire, Wallace ignores how the impediments that once made sex a 'deadly serious business' (2012c: 170) – such as 'illegitimate birth; chaperonage; madonna/whore complexes … back-alley abortions' (169) – were disproportionately deadly to women. In a generous reading, this blindness to female experience confirms Wallace's generally (self-aware) androcentric focus. In a less generous reading, it confirms what many readers and commentators have come to acknowledge with either anger or regret – his misogyny. The rest of this chapter explores how Wallace's penalization of female sexuality critiques the neoliberal logics I have examined thus far. He formulates this critique to imply that although financial self-appreciation is objectionable when carried out by women, it is appropriate for men.

These dynamics are evident in the short story 'Think', which dramatizes 'Back in New Fire' by transposing that essay's Sir Knight and Fair Maiden into a suburban setting. Just under two pages in length, 'Think' recounts the crisis moment when a father and family man faces seduction by 'the younger sister of his wife's college roommate' (1999f: 61) who has allowed her breasts to 'come free' (61). If the Fair Maiden of 'Back in New Fire' wears a Victoria's Secret Teddy, this woman's 'expression is from page 18 of the Victoria Secret's catalogue' (61). Her 'knowing, smoky smile, Page 18' (61) is 'media-taught' (61), and 'he realizes she's replaying a scene from some movie she loves' (61). This woman embodies the pornified culture that 'Back in New Fire' suggests has devalued male sexuality. Notably, the story's free indirect discourse implies that this man is already compromised by the pornification his seductress represents. The sentence 'even if she's never kept her heels on before she'd give him a knowing, smoky smile, Page 18' (61), in its suggestion of that man's own observation on events, signals his familiarity – right down to the page number – with the same Victoria Secret's expression she has adopted. The challenge facing the male protagonist is therefore not only to stop and 'think' about the dangers of an affair, and so to resist the woman's advances, but also to resist the pornified fantasies – such as asking her to keep her heels on – that are already at play in his mind.

Despite the suggestion that both characters are complicit in pornification, it is the woman who personifies its injunction to meaningless pleasures. Again blurring distinctions between third person narrator and the man's own perspective, the story relates that 'she could try, just for a moment, to imagine what is happening in his head. … Even for an instant, to try putting herself in his place' (62). Wallace frames her failure to empathize with the man through images that highlight temporal foreclosure; not for a moment can she consider how she is endangering his loyalty to his wife and son. The recriminatory tone here emphasizes the man's contrasting acts of imaginative empathy. For instance, 'he knows what she might think'; 'he imagines'; 'she is, he thinks'; 'he realizes she's replaying a scene' (61). Whereas she acts impulsively, the man is actively empathizing with her to try and resist the temptation to have an affair. That Wallace genders this scenario upon such conventionally patriarchal terms speaks to the sexist traditionalism evident in this story. In fact, to the extent that this woman embodies an Eve-like impulsive sensuality, and the man displays cognitive labour, then with 'Think' Wallace offers a rewrite of the fall of man; only this late twentieth-century Adam manages to resist temptation.[11] In addition to this, though, the father's attempt to empathize with this woman belies how his response to the situation – falling to his knees and beginning to pray – encourages an individual responsibilization in which he can conserve, and therefore appreciate, the value of his spermatic resources.

The story's last sentence, 'and what if she joined him on the floor, just like this, clasped in supplication: just this way' (62) resembles the end of 'Back in New Fire' in what Greg Carlisle describes as Wallace's 'undefined-climax technique' (2013: 17). This puts 'the work of completing or making decisions about the narrative on each individual reader' (17). One would be hard pressed to find a better description of responsibilization or, coincidentally, a better metaphorical designation for a frustrated orgasm. The man's praying shields against the chance of non-reproductive sexual expenditure but, in accordance with my previous examples, it also works to sublimate this negativity into a situation where nobody comes, which Wallace's undefined climax asks the reader to condone. Most relevant to my present analysis, though, is how this situation positions the woman. As the dupe of pornified texts, she embodies how such texts urge people to treat sex (confirming Gilbert's complaint) as a consumptive instead of a relational activity. Furthermore, when Wallace spotlights her breasts as having been '*freed*' (1999f: 61, italics in original), entailed in the suggestion of her lust is a *free*-market ethos of gratification through consumption. Obliquely, her sexual agency follows patterns that neoliberal logics set out for her. When one considers 'Think' in relation to the 'Adult World' stories, Wallace's association of female sexual agency and neoliberal logic is even more apparent. In these stories he explicitly links female (and indeed feminist) sexual agency with human capitalization, financialized and otherwise.

This diptych recounts the efforts of a woman, Jeni Roberts, to discover what is wrong 'with her technique in making love' (1999j: 137) that leaves her husband so distant. By story II, she discovers that he is a 'Secret Compulsive Masturbator' (1999k: 156), addicted to porn films he buys from the eponymous Adult World store. Wallace's depiction of Jeni in stories I and II differs in terms of the human capital she exemplifies. In the former Jeni, unaware that her husband is addicted to masturbation, tries to improve 'their sexlife [sic] together' (1999j: 138) by working on 'her ability' (138) as a lover. Accordingly, she gathers 'her nerve together' (139) to buy 'a Dildo … to practice her oral sex technique on' (139). Jeni engages in sexual consumption, then, to optimize her sexual skillset, with the aim of securing validation from her husband. Indeed, her insecurities arise from her failure to solicit such psychic 'income', to the extent that, in a nightmare, her husband lights her cigarette but 'refused to give it to her, holding it away from her while it burned itself all the way down' (145). Becker's idea of human capital, where one self-invests to maximize future returns, applies here. It is worth reiterating that, for Becker, such returns do not necessarily involve money. For instance, he asserts that schooling is an investment in human capital not only because it may 'raise earnings' (1976: 15), but because it can 'add to a person's appreciation of literature over much of his or her lifetime' (15–16). By approaching her sexuality as human capital, Jeni invests in her utility as a lover in order to maximize the psychic income she can receive from her husband.

Jeni fails in this endeavour, and by 'Adult World (II)' realizes that he 'has "interior deficits" that … ha[ve] nothing to do with her as a wife[/woman]' (1999k: 159). As a result of this new awareness, she relinquishes Becker's idea of human capital in favour of the financialized model that Feher theorizes. In addition to quitting smoking, considering psychotherapy, and embracing 'masturbation as a wellspring of personal pleasure' (1999k: 160), 'Jeni Ann Orzoleck of Marketing 204' (155) even 'establishes [a] separate investment portfolio w/substantial positions in gold futures & large-cap mining stock' (159). These combined financial activities and self-esteem boosting exercises demonstrate how Jeni embodies the financialized human capital that Wallace urges men to adopt in 'Back in New Fire' and 'Big Red Son', whereby self-appreciation becomes more important than securing future returns. However, unlike in those essays, 'Adult World (II)' presents these responsibilized behaviours – which lead Jeni to the conviction that 'true wellsprings of love, security, gratification must originate within self' (159) – as objectionable. The story prompts us to see Jeni's 'authentic responsibility for self' (160) as working in lockstep with pornification. Central here, Wallace suggests, is how feminist ideas of sexual empowerment function as a smokescreen for perpetuating pornified consumerism, so that by the diptych's end Jeni, in contrast to her past unease, has 'revisited Adult World svrl [*sic*] times; becomes almost a rglr [*sic*]' (160).

In addition to her worry in 'Adult World (I)' that her husband prefers 'the familiar Missionary Position of male dominance' (1999j: 148), in 'Adult World (II)' we learn that, weeping for him, Jeni 'notes this & speculates on significance of "weeping for" [= 'on behalf of'?] men' (1999k: 158). Wallace thus aligns Jeni's developing awareness of patriarchal expectations with her attempt to valorize her sexuality (and her life generally) as financialized human capital – the word 'speculates', in this light, is telling. That the story ends with Jeni 'mastrbating [*sic*] almost daily' (160), and with appliances that she has bought from Adult World, furthers this comingling of financialization and feminist discourse. Tuck relates how, particularly in the wake of texts such as Nancy Friday's *My Secret Garden: Women's Sexual Fantasies* (1973) and Betty Dodson's *Liberating Masturbation: A Meditation on Self Love* (1974), second-wave feminist thought has often championed masturbation 'as a political act, evidence of women's sexual liberation' (2009: 84). Jeni's final vibrator of choice – the 'Scarlet Garden' (1999k: 160) – indeed contains an echo of the title of Friday's book. The irony then that Jeni's 'new hi-tech mastrbtory [*sic*] appliances are … manufactured in Asia' (160) is that a big part of her newfound sexual autonomy derives, circuitously, from the influence of her husband – a man whose job involves checking 'on the status of the yen' (1999j: 139), as well the 'riyal, the dirham, the Burmese kyat' (141), and so forth.

Wallace thus implicitly indicts sex-positive feminist ideas in these stories for pushing Jeni further into the grasp of financialized logics. One could read this indictment as serving its own feminist ends, by showing how an arguably superficial focus on self-empowerment via sexual pleasure reaffirms a consumerist ethos. In fact, Wallace hints at such a reading in how these stories play upon 'Yen' and 'Jeni' as near homonyms. That Jeni buys her husband a license plate which reads 'YEN4U' (149) signals this link, which becomes clearer when we learn that her full married name is 'Jeni Roberts' (151). Breaking this name down into Jen i Rob, one can suggest that, insofar as Wallace is equating 'Yen' with 'Jen', her name suggests 'Yen I Rob' (or even 'Yen I Robbers', or 'Y/Jen I Rob Hers'). This signals how the husband figuratively 'robs' other currencies, in what Richard Godden and Michael Szalay explain as the requisitioning by the United States 'of monies from the world's credit nations, in support of its deficit' (2014: 1293) after President Richard Nixon's 1971 decision to end the gold standard. Yet it also points to how he robs Jeni's own 'I': explicitly in 'Adult World (I)', where his 'inner deficits' (1999k: 157) become her life's concern, and implicitly in 'Adult World (II)', where his financial activities facilitate her use of vibrators manufactured in Asia. To some extent, Wallace's penalization of Jeni's sexual empowerment implies that what appear to be feminist acts of self-actualization actually imbricate her further into being controlled by men.

One could conclude that Wallace joins scholars such as Johanna Oksala (2013), Nancy Fraser (2013), and Catherine Rottenberg (2018) here in exploring the challenges that neoliberalism poses to feminist thought. Indeed, Jeni exemplifies the situation Rottenberg describes in *The Rise of Neoliberal Feminism* whereby women are now urged to 'build their own portfolios and to self-invest … as human capital' (2018: 16). However, to stop there, though it might salvage Wallace's credentials as offering a form of feminist critique, would be to miss the double standard that is still in operation in these stories. While Jeni's responsibilization is something to object to, Wallace implies that the husband would benefit from such 'adult' self-control. Jeni's change from 'utter child' (1999j: 144) to self-managing adult is ironic because her 'authentic responsibility for herself' (1999k: 160) renders her complicit in a falsely empowering consumerism. By contrast, her husband's failure to demonstrate the 'adult' resolve to break his addiction implies that responsibilization for him is desirable. After all, it is his 'trips to Adult World to purchase/view/masturbate self raw to XXX films' (1999k: 156) that create the problems that Jeni is compelled to remedy in the first place. References to the husband's infantilism, as in how he 'looked … like a child on his side sleeping' (1999j: 143), compounds how his addiction to masturbation shows a lack of self-management. Indeed, Jeni's suspicion that he is masturbating 'into the toilet' (145) and 'trash basket' (146) rather than climaxing with her suggests that he is quite literally wasting his spermatic resources.

Severs argues that 'in a traditional version of "Adult World," the story might resolve itself by forcing the husband's yens back from masturbation and market contingencies to more stable husbanding' (2017a: 155). For him the fact that this diptych resists such resolution is suggestive of Wallace's desire to explore the 'Asian Flu' currency crisis of 1997. This reading is interesting, and certainly deepens our sense of how closely imbricated sexuality and economics are for

Wallace. However, a simpler answer for why the husband does not responsibilize himself is that Wallace is attached to the negativity his masturbation represents. The Secret Compulsive Masturbator remains outside both the narrator's and the reader's purview; in this regard his addiction remains, at least notionally, a secret. As Simon Cook puts it, 'Wallace has isolated this man, making his feelings as inaccessible to the reader as they are to his wife, and any conclusions about psychological damage remain conjecture' (2017: 123). We only learn the facts of his auto-eroticism through Jeni, whose perspective Wallace mediates through multiple layers of third person narration. Furthermore, her sexual experiences move from demure euphemism (as in remarks such as 'the head of his thingie' (1999j: 137)), to the bathetically pornified (as when she purchases the 'Scarlet Garden MX-1000® Vibrator with Clitoral Suction and Fully Electrified 12 Inch Cervical Stimulator' (1999k: 160)). The consumerism Jeni comes to embody is another facet of a culture that, as Adam Kelly notes, Wallace depicts as being 'radically over-exposed, with many secrets appearing in open view' (2010: 138). In contrast, then, the husband's inaccessibility – at least in how both stories refuse to broach his subjectivity – is an exception to such pornified overexposure.

However, consistent with how Wallace evokes such non-reproductive negativity only to tame it, 'Adult World (II)' ends with a gesture to reproductive futurism as a corrupted but worthwhile ideal. Wallace closes the story on the ironic note that Jeni and her husband 'were now truly married, cleaved,** one flesh ... [and] were ready thus to begin ... to discuss having children [together]' (1999k: 161, asterisks and second brackets in original). The sardonic humour of bracketing 'together' as an afterthought to having children here works on the notion that heteronormative marriage defines the natural parameters in which child-rearing takes place, a seemingly obvious supposition that Jeni and her husband's masturbation devalues. In David Coughlan's reading, the end of 'Adult World (II)' shows how for Wallace 'masturbation and pornography ... have become the dangerous supplements to sexual intercourse, which both displaces and yet also enables what might be termed the natural meaning of sex: procreation' (2015: 168). The idea that the natural meaning of sex is procreation says more about how the 'Adult World' stories elicit this traditionalist view than it does about Coughlan's narrow mindedness. As he puts it, if in these stories 'no person is fully present to the other, in sex or in love' (168), then Wallace's parting joke at Jeni and her husband having a child presents this disconnection as being indicative of the failure of reproductively futurist ideals. Rather than mobilizing the husband's – and Jeni's – masturbatory negativity as a means to question such ideals, Wallace uses it to backlight the couple's lack of communion.

Moreover, although both Jeni and her husband embody a masturbatory negativity by the story's end, they do not do so on equal terms. For by the '7th, 8th yr [sic]' (1999k: 161) of their marriage the 'Hsbnd mastrbtes [sic] secretly, J.O.R. openly' (161). Jeni's openness aligns with a pornified culture's sexual overexposure – that her 'new dresser/vanity ensemble contains no sachet drawer' (160), which was where she once hid her sex aids (1999j: 140), compounds her lack of shame. While Wallace uses Jeni's transformation from neurotic lover to brazen masturbator to signal how she has let go of her desire for the 'revelational pleasure of coming together as close as two married bodies could come' (138), the husband begins and ends these stories as a Secret Compulsive Masturbator. Hence, whereas Jeni's masturbatory negativity evokes deterioration in the kind of sexual-emotional connection Wallace pines for, the husband's non-reproductivity figures as an unchanging constant. As in 'Back in New Fire' and 'Big Red Son', the implication is that though he is in need of investing his spermatic resources more responsibly, the husband's propensity for such non-reproductivity is beyond reform. Furthermore, the monikers of the dildos and vibrators that Jeni uses before she settles on the Scarlet Garden – 'Penetrator!!' (1999k: 160) and 'Pink Pistollero' (160) – evoke a militarism that in turn suggests her masturbatory empowerment involves masculinization. Hence, if Jeni's actions speak to the toxic non-reproductivity that, as I have been arguing, Wallace links with male sexuality in particular, Jeni can only buy substitutes for such rather than, like her husband, exemplify it by virtue of her gender alone.

'Adult World (I)' and 'Adult World (II)', and to a lesser extent 'Think', convey how Wallace's suggestion that men need to invest in the value of their spermatic resources works at the expense of women who carry out similar processes. In the 'Adult World' stories in particular, Wallace implies that the husband should manage himself like a better 'adult' while implying that Jeni's self-management is something to be concerned by. This is despite how, in the husband's job monitoring currency markets, Wallace aligns finance with non-reproductive sexuality, and as a central plank of what Severs notes is the story's interest in exploring how 'global capital … is the warping force flowing through these characters' (2017a: 154). More than any of the texts I have looked at so far, the 'Adult World' stories show how male sexuality is a conceptual snag in what is, at times, Wallace's evident desire to write against neoliberalism. It is a snag because his texts' response to pornification subscribes to the neoliberal logic of responsibilization, whether that be to encourage men to appreciate their sexuality as financialized human capital or, more obliquely, to cultivate their propensity for non-reproductive desires as being central to masculinity. Jeni's sexuality – and, as will become more apparent in subsequent chapters, female sexuality throughout Wallace's texts – acts as a foil for the male sexual toxicity I am exploring.

Conclusion

Wallace casts a critical eye on financialization at various points throughout his fiction. This criticism at times takes the form of incidental metaphors; for example, in *Infinite Jest* the sociopathic Randy Lenz, reflecting on his dislike for those who only pretend to listen to him talk, 'has a keen antenna for people like this and their stock is low on his personal exchange' (1996: 547). Elsewhere in the novel, Wallace refers to the anxiety among students at Enfield Tennis Academy of 'how the coaches are seeing you, gauging your progress – is your stock going up or down' (686). In both of these instances Wallace uses financial images to signify decidedly negative emotional states. His criticism of finance can also take more sustained narrative form, as in the 'Adult World' stories, but also in the uncollected story 'Crash of '69' (1989e). This story focuses on a man who, as Severs explains, 'is "always wrong" in predicting successful stocks – and thus supremely valuable to financial firms, who do the exact opposite' (2017a: 66). Indeed, for Severs '"Crash" initiates Wallace's contention that financial value and the irrational – if not the psychotic – are aligned' (66). In their analysis of corporeality and financial abstraction in *The Pale King*, Godden and Szalay further this alignment, going so far as to see Wallace's hanging corpse as the author's last comment on how 'physical forms ... melt into air, or float upon it, within a financial bubble (about to burst)' (2014: 1312). Given these details, it would seem undeniable that Wallace envisages finance as a malign force, and one that he sets out to both interrogate and critique.

My goal has not been to invalidate this reading. More work can be done to explore how, as Severs, Godden and Szalay argue, Wallace follows in the footsteps of his postmodern compatriots William Gaddis and Don DeLillo in critiquing finance. Similarly, it would be brash to subsume Wallace's interest in responsibility completely into the neoliberal fold; there are ways, as Boswell explores, in which civic responsibility in *The Pale King* in fact works against neoliberalism (2014). Nevertheless, I have argued in this chapter that a financial logic of value appreciation not only drives Wallace's depiction of male sexuality in relation to pornification, but ties these depictions to a broader neoliberal focus on individual responsibility. Moreover, I have suggested that this is not an oversight on Wallace's part – in other words, these are not logics that he either exhibits or recapitulates despite his otherwise best intentions. Rather, it is a sign of how he enthusiastically endorses the neoliberal concern with responsibilized human capital. Starting with close readings of the essays 'Back in New Fire' and 'Big Red Son', I have argued that Wallace responds to the perceived threat posed by pornification by supplanting ideas of male sexuality based upon labour and exchange with an emphasis on financial self-appreciation. Spermatic metaphors of conservation and investment were important here, particularly with regards to masturbation as a form of waste. Ending with an extended reading of the short stories 'Think' and 'Adult World (I)' and 'Adult World (II)', I argued that these stories show the difference that gender makes to such dynamics. If women's responsibilized sexual self-appreciation is objectionable to Wallace, he suggests that the same process is sorely needed for men.

Notably, if men follow Wallace's call to responsibly manage their toxicity, and in doing so, increase the value of their spermatic resources as a form of financialized human capital, the toxicity in question remains unchallenged. In fact, it becomes the basis on which Wallace can evoke the seemingly inevitable fact that, when it comes to non-reproductive activities like casual sex, masturbation and porn consumption, men will not change. Of course, this process implies that there is something objectionable about those three activities. As such, it points to Wallace's assumption that non-reproductivity is a problem. I have been less interested in the content of this assumption – that is, Wallace's sexual traditionalism – than in how it motivates the process whereby he turns a culturally contingent understanding of male sexuality ('men engage in wasteful sexual behaviours') into the expression of natural gender characteristics ('men engage in wasteful sexual behaviours *because they are men*'). The responsibilization I have analysed here indeed retroactively constructs the idea that men can only channel their sexual negativity more productively, rather than try to change it. This idea sidesteps the possibility that we can eliminate misogyny of the kind Wallace documents in 'Big Red Son', or perpetuates in 'Back in New Fire' and 'Think'. That the 'Adult World' stories articulate elements of feminist critique nonetheless – namely of how neoliberal logics have hijacked the sexual autonomy Jeni evinces – suggests the limits of Wallace's sympathy for progressive gender politics. He can endorse a feminism that can point to its own failings, in other words, but not one that challenges men's toxic behaviours.

I will return to what this suggests about Wallace's attitudes to feminism in Chapter 4, where I argue that in the 'Brief Interviews' stories he tries to 'improve' feminist critiques of male sexual toxicity. For now, the fact that it is *men's* sexual negativity in consideration here points to how, as I have stated throughout,

Wallace invokes such negativity only in order to tame it. In other words, while for Edelman, 'the death drive dissolves those congealments of identity that permit us to know and survive as ourselves' (2004: 17), the texts that I have examined in Chapter 1 invert this process, manipulating negativity to affirm masculinity. This taming, as I will show in my next chapter, has an economic correlate in Wallace's texts in the financial process of securitization. As I explain in detail shortly, this process refers to making a risky asset saleable by combining it with a more secure one. Explicating securitization in this manner, I argue that his texts not only envisage sexual negativity differently when it comes to gender (as I argued in relation to 'Think' and the 'Adult World' stories), but also in relation to sexual orientation. So far in this book I have presumed that the masculinities under analysis are heterosexually geared. I will now complicate this presumption, if only because Wallace shows a fascinating preoccupation with homosexuality. As usefully negative as male heterosexuality is for Wallace, male homosexuality – and particularly as he articulates it in relation to anal intercourse – offers a more abject ore to mine.

2

Risk

Securitizing male homosexuality

Early on in his account of accompanying Wallace on the 1996 book tour for *Infinite Jest*, David Lipsky observes how 'everywhere we've gone, restaurants, 7-Elevens, if someone asks, "You two together?" David has said, "Yes, but not on a date"' (2010: 44). When Lipsky asks whether this response is indicative of the Midwest being '*more homophobic*' (44, italics in original), Wallace answers that 'it comes off as a joke, but it also communicates that, like – I don't know, I've got a fair number of gay friends here. Who've had some terrible stuff happen to them, and have just …' (45). Wallace manipulates a mild homophobia here to signal his distance from prejudice while, at the same time, facilitating his and Lipsky's progress through public space as heterosexuals. This self-aware deployment of anti-gay sentiment, and in order to serve a bond between heterosexual men, is also evident in his fiction. Though homosexuality is an intermittent focus of attention throughout his work – figuring prominently in the short story 'Lyndon', for example, but reduced to the briefest of mentions in *The Pale King* (2012a: 446) – it is often important to Wallace's abiding concern with emotional intimacy. Indeed, Vincent Haddad (2017) argues that male homoeroticism is the incipient and unintentional by-product of Wallace's focus on author–reader connection. Building on this insight, I wish to focus on Wallace's more explicit images of homosexuality, and particularly in relation to HIV/AIDS. I argue that he presents homosexuality as a risk which, if heterosexual men appropriately manage and invest in it, can allow for desexualized, emotional intimacies of the kind that Wallace and Lipsky enjoy on their road trip – never actually dating, but strangely besotted nonetheless.

Despite his self-conscious manipulation of homosexuality, though, Wallace writes about it in ways that play upon men's ignorance of such, whether in relation to themselves or to other men. In this respect, he works with what Eve Kosofsky Sedgwick describes as 'the relations of the closet – the relations of the known and the unknown, the explicit and the inexplicit around homo/heterosexual definition' (2008: 3). For Sedgwick male homosexuality since the end of the nineteenth century has had an 'indicative relation … to wider mappings of secrecy and disclosure, and of the private and the public' (70). The historical context of Sedgwick's theorizations of the closet, and in turn of Wallace's own presentation of it, are significant here. In a 2007 preface to her 1990 book *Epistemology of the Closet*, in which she explored many of her key ideas concerning knowledge, secrecy and sexuality, Sedgwick relates how the 1980s was a decade when 'something called "sodomy" was illegal in half the United States' (2008: xiii), and when the emergence of AIDS allowed for a 'fusion of homophobic stigma with deadly medical mystery' (xv). Sedgwick reflects upon how these conditions 'imprinted a characteristic stamp on much of the theory and activism of that time' (xv), her own included. Wallace displays this imprint in his depictions of homosexuality, anal sex and AIDS. 'Back in New Fire', for one, is a provocative document of its time, showing an oblique homophobia in the face of the medical crisis Sedgwick evokes in her preface. In the texts I examine in this chapter Wallace is more overt in his homophobia, which functions as an essential ingredient in helping straight men feel close to one another.

Wallace's interest in writing about homosexuality should therefore not be taken as a sign that he was in some sense a queer writer, or that he pursues a queer project. Haddad stops short in this regard, noting that despite Wallace's 'intimate relational mode, I do not intend to read Wallace as an affirmative "queer" figure, nor his fiction as constructing queer relational modes' (2017: 25). Wallace shies away from the anti-identitarian edge one would normally associate with queer theory. As James Penney puts it, 'The most paradigmatic gesture of queer theory since its inception has been to insist that gender and/or sexuality subverts claims to identity' (2014: 9). This gesture runs counter to Wallace's belief, as I explore throughout this book, that sexual toxicity is the immutable fact of heterosexual male identity. Furthermore, the importance of homosexuality for Wallace lies in how it offers a glimpse into the emotional and psychological lives of straight men. This can sometimes take the shape of specifically Freudian models of the psyche, as it does in *Broom* and *Infinite Jest*, or of a more general sense of macho emotional repression, as it does in *Girl with Curious Hair*. The point, though, is that Wallace appropriates the risk of male homosexuality to facilitate intimacies between straight men who, in the process of coming into contact with same-sex desire, are shown to contain hidden and often mysterious interiorities. In short, male homosexuality in Wallace's work allows for insights into what goes on inside male heterosexuals.

For this process to work without compromising the heterosexuality of those involved, a notional distinction between such men and the same-sex desires they appropriate must remain in place. The closet's importance to Wallace's depictions of homosexuality, in this regard, lies in how it controls the risk of openly acknowledging same-sex desire while simultaneously teasing such. The apparent danger of homosexuality, though bracketed in the process of being appropriated, imbues the straight male intimacies Wallace explores with their sense of urgency. Given this, his representations of male homosexuality can be usefully thought of as attempts to securitize a risky asset. As Matthew Eagleton-Pierce explains, 'Securitization is a form of financial engineering whereby credit-risky assets are packaged with higher-quality assets in order to enable the sale of the former to a wider market' (2016: 73). Wallace combines the perceived risk of homosexuality with the higher-quality asset of heterosexuality to form a psychologized understanding of the closet. As a security, this closet enables same-sex desire to enter the empathic exchanges that his texts evoke between men in ways that, though they may query and even destabilize heterosexuality, do not undermine it. Indeed, if in Max Haiven's words 'securitization relies upon an underlying logic of risk management' (2014: 75), then intimations of homosexuality provide a valuable amount of risk for Wallace to manage in his depictions of male–male intimacies.

Securitization has entered public consciousness in recent years as a result of the 2007–09 subprime mortgage crisis. In the events leading up to this crisis, and the global recession that it helped spark, investment banks like Goldman Sachs and Lehman Brothers securitized disparate home mortgage loans – large proportions of which were high risk, but fraudulently rated (closeted, even) as low risk – into Collateralized Debt Obligations (CDOs). When the underlying assets in these CDOs turned bad, a general loss of confidence in their value soon followed.[1] Given that Wallace died on the eve of the crisis, his texts do not reflect its specific dynamics. However, as Randy Martin (2007) notes, these processes of financial securitization have been at work in the United States since the 1980s, and are important to the rise of particular neoliberal logics during this period and since. Notably, securitization has been instrumental to shifts in attitudes towards risk in US culture. In Martin's words,

> What began as the financial service industry's embrace of risk-management tools ... has been refigured as a subjectivity of consumer finance that infuses domesticity with risk. The space of security is now that of securitization. Risk is not unilateral but operates a kind of moral binary, sorting out the good from the bad on the basis of capacities to contribute. ... Those who cannot manage

themselves, those unable to live by risk, are considered 'at risk'. The epidemic that began with the 1980s, AIDS, is defined by moralizers as caused by 'high-risk' behavior. (2007: 37)[2]

For Martin securitization has been central to the dissemination of risk-management activities in everyday life. His example of the AIDS epidemic is especially relevant for my purposes. As I argued in Chapter 1, 'Back in New Fire' presents the threat of heterosexual AIDS as a motivation for men to manage themselves more responsibly. The essay thus positions AIDS as a risk that, when appropriately securitized, can serve the interests of heterosexual men. While 'Back in New Fire' does not explicitly address male homosexuality, in this chapter I show how Wallace's more direct references to it follow a securitizing logic.[3]

The effect of this logic is to legitimize risk, so that, in van der Zwan's words, 'the possibility that something might happen is not to be feared, but to be embraced: financial theory dictates that it is only through risk-taking that the individual can achieve the type of investment return necessary to sustain himself' (2014: 112).[4] My present investigation shares the last chapter's concern with financial processes. However, whereas my focus there was on value appreciation, here it is on forms of return. In other words, Wallace securitizes male homosexual risk so that heterosexual men can secure better emotional income. I thus share Brown's trepidation in following Feher's arguments to the letter. For, as she puts it, he 'appears to argue that the shift [from productive capital to finance capital] is thoroughgoing and complete. I am suggesting that both modalities are present today, that human capital on the entrepreneurial model is not dead and may cohabit in the same person with human capital on the investment model' (2015: 231). Further, this emphasis on returns – and so, on futurity – reiterates how Wallace engages with sexual negativity in order to tame it towards the ends Edelman tries to challenge. As I have previously noted, for Edelman homosexuality has a privileged association with the death drive, and is a 'future negating' (2004: 26) force whose 'risk informs the cultural fantasy that conjures homosexuality ... in intimate relation to a fatal, and even murderous, *jouissance*' (39, italics in original). This is true of Wallace's depictions of male homosexuality, but by securitizing such negativity to create emotional intimacies between men, he actually furthers a reproductively futurist ethos.

Moreover, one of the key spermatic metaphors in my last chapter – that of the waste that arises from casual sex and masturbation – undergoes a slight modulation here. For in the contexts I am working in, risk has seminal as well as financial connotations. Lisa Jean Moore observes that, in a culture where 'warnings about HIV/AIDS and STDS are plastered on bus stops, [and] broadcast through public service announcements on radio and television ... semen is directly associated with risk' (2008: 83). Though this association is largely implicit in the texts I examine, it is nevertheless pertinent. Indeed, if the self-appreciating dynamics I considered in Chapter 1 led to the paradoxical situation whereby responsible self-investment preserved forms of wasteful negativity, a similar process is at work here, albeit in ways that are less apparently contradictory. In other words, by suggesting that securitizing homosexual risk allows men to reap greater emotional returns, Wallace leaves the apparent link between male homosexuality and abjection unquestioned. The success of the securitizing processes I examine, in fact, reaffirms the idea that gay men are best understood as sources of disease and danger. In what follows I explore these dynamics in *Broom*, *Girl* and *Infinite Jest*. There are differences in how each text securitizes male homosexuality, but in all three Wallace presents it as useful to the extent that it is risky. Contrary to suggestions that his depictions of homosexuality are, for him, surprisingly considerate,[5] the images I unpack here show that Wallace *requires* gay men to be toxic so that he can securitize their sexuality as 'risky' – and, ultimately, in ways that work for the benefit of heterosexuals.

Entering The Flange in *Broom*

The plot of Wallace's first novel concerns Lenore Beadsman, a woman who is having an existential crisis over the possibility that she may not exist outside of discourse. She fears 'that there's nothing going on with me that isn't either told or tellable' (Wallace 1987: 119). Not least of her problems are the novel's two central male characters, her boyfriend Rick Vigorous, and the man who eventually woos her, Andrew 'Wang Dang' Lang. Both men attempt to control Lenore, leading Boswell to conclude that *Broom* displays a 'large-scale feminist critique of literary misogyny writ large' (2009: 41). Though I agree that male chauvinism is the target for much of the novel's satire,[6] *Broom* still affords Rick and Lang considerable moments of psychological depth. In addition to being a counterpoint to Lenore's sense of ontological instability, the depth that Wallace gives to these two men is also of a distinctly psychoanalytical kind. For instance, towards the novel's end, as Lang and Lenore lie next to each other semi-naked, the former confides his belief that '"without a thing there, believe me, you're nothing," Lang said. His finger was in the hot part of her legs again' (1987: 410). Lang is referring to the 'good old boy' (410) persona that he has now dropped for

Lenore, a persona he developed in high school because there 'you more or less got to have a thing' (410). The fact that he is pointing at Lenore's vagina, though, also implies that 'thing' means penis. Lang here unconsciously registers his subjection to the law of castration, suggesting that his chauvinistic 'Wang Dang' persona is a means by which he can disavow castration anxiety. He therefore points (rather literally) to how a Freudian schema of sexual development has informed his gender identity. As the dramatic irony between his speech and his action indicates, this is a schema he does not understand, positioning him as the bearer of a psychic interiority that Wallace only hints at.

These factors are central to Wallace's depictions of homosexuality in *Broom*. Rick, at one point, muses on how his son 'is, I happen to know for a fact, a homosexual' (78), and so confirms the sense of masculine inadequacy Wallace otherwise comically conveys through Rick's micro-penis. In fact, Rick suggests that his inability to display paternal discipline has led to Vance's homosexuality: 'I never once laid an angry hand to Vance Vigorous's bottom. Maybe that is part of the trouble' (300). The idea that not spanking Vance has contributed to his homosexuality bears a subtle irony, for Wallace implies that Rick's wish to be spanked is indicative of the character's own repressed homosexual desires. To understand how this is the case, one has to turn to Freud's essay 'A Child is Being Beaten'. Here Freud suggests that fantasies in which men are beaten by women correspond to a repressed desire to be loved by their father. In his words, 'The being beaten also stands for being loved (in a genital sense), though this has been debased to a lower level owing to regression. ... The boy evades his homosexuality by repressing and remodelling his unconscious phantasy' (2001: 198), so that 'his later conscious phantasy ... has for its content a feminine attitude without a homosexual object-choice' (198–9). Although Rick's efforts to have Lenore spank him come to naught, the aptly named Mindy Metalman is more accommodating (407–8). One can therefore read Rick's desire to be beaten as the expression of his unconscious desire to be loved by another man. The irony of his idea that spanking Vance would instil a stronger straight masculinity, however, is that Rick harbours closeted homosexual wishes himself.

The important point here is that Rick, like Lang, is subject to psychoanalytical frameworks of sexual development that, despite his neurotic self-awareness, he only has the vaguest sense of. Furthermore, for Rick at least, this intimation of psychological interiority centres upon repressed homosexual desire. Part of the novel's comedy in fact stems from Rick's inability to conceptualize his attraction to Lang. When talking to Lenore, for example, Rick notes that 'I'm really not sure why. There are affinities. ... But something ... I simply felt ... I don't know how to describe it' (1987: 289). Boswell convincingly argues that Rick and Lang are Wallace's parodic take on the writings of John Updike and Vladimir Nabokov, and notes how 'these two narrative lines – the Nabokovian and the Updikean, respectively – join together, not coincidentally, in a gay bar in Amherst called the Flange' (2009: 45). Wallace unites Rick and Lang in a gay bar as part of his parody of literary forebears, who he suggests are emblematic of straight male lechery and narcissism. This is a compelling insight into how Wallace reworks his literary predecessors, and Boswell substantiates it further with reference to Wallace's criticisms of Updike elsewhere.[7] However, this reading only partially accounts for how homosexuality functions in this scene. The precondition for comedy here lies in how Wallace securitizes male homosexuality as the dramatically ironic backdrop that facilitates Rick and Lang's encounter, and the intimacy they share with one another.

The bar's name is telling in this regard. A flange is a disk-shaped bolt with a hole in its middle, normally used to connect two separate pipes. By naming this bar 'The Flange', Wallace not only evokes an object that resembles an anus, but one that also serves to mediate and secure two interlocking things. Entering The Flange therefore amounts to figuratively entering a man's anus, and in order to create a strong homosocial bond between two straight men. Wallace reaffirms this association when Rick and Lang enter one of the bar's toilet stalls to locate their initials, which they carved there as students when The Flange was a fraternity bar. While these events take place, Wallace exploits the dissonance between Rick and Lang's growing intimacy (in chatting, they discover that they share several close, and predominantly female, acquaintances) and its potential libidinal implications for comedic effect. Rick, who is narrating the scene, recalls that 'it was something of a thrill, given the context. I tingle a bit even now, in the motel' (1987: 230). Similarly, Lang's sense that 'I need to get out. Just ... out, for a while' (233) resonates with being 'in' the closet, while his tipsy catachresis 'fine and Daddy – excuse me – fine and dandy' (233) implies repressed father issues of the kind Rick has. For these disjunctions to work, the scene must rest on the risk of both men acknowledging desires in their relationship that may be congruent with sexual attraction. Wallace not only evokes Sedgwick's theory of 'the potential unbrokenness of a continuum between homosocial and homosexual – a continuum whose visibility, for men, in our society, is radically disrupted' (1985: 1–2) – he plays it for laughs.

Rick and Lang's meeting is a scene of delicate risk management, whereby Wallace secures a dangerous asset – homosexual desire – in the form of an intense but desexualized intimacy between straight men. The risk that this security will turn bad – that their intimacy will reveal itself to be more than just homosocial camaraderie – makes their incomprehension of such potential desire for each other comic. Such unknowingness provides the tenuous security that their intimacy will not trouble their heterosexuality. In this light, when Rick refers to Lang as 'another inside outsider' (1987: 227), the immediate sense may be of 'another lonely alumnus' (237), but the phrase takes on further resonances. In one way, it points to how Rick and Lang are both inside and outside the closet, at the threshold of intimacies that could trouble their understanding of themselves as being heterosexual. In another way, it implies how their psychic 'insides', that is, their repressed homosexual wishes, are teasingly on the 'outside', whether through their behaviour towards one another or as represented through the gay bar. Psychological interiors, and the sexual metaphoric of being 'in' the closet, dovetail here as an asset pool Wallace can securitize to make fun of their encounter. That said, if the comedy instils a distance towards this intimacy, it is an intimacy nonetheless, and one that has great importance plot-wise; it leads, for instance, to Lang's reintroduction to Lenore, and so to the end of her relationship with Rick.

Given the absence of economic imagery in this scene, the objection can be made that reading a psychologized homosexual closet here as an asset-backed security is unwarranted. In comparison to the monetary terms in 'Back in New Fire', or Wallace's overt engagement with financial processes in the 'Adult World' stories, Rick and Lang's clumsy homoeroticism does not immediately lend itself to economic analysis. Nevertheless, my reading of this scene suggests how, as Brown (drawing upon the work of Koray Caliskan and Michel Callon) observes, neoliberalism as a 'governing rationality' (2015: 30) entails the '"economization" of heretofore noneconomic spheres, a process … [that] may not always involve monetization' (31). Reading the male homosexual closet in Wallace's texts as a financial security allows one to see how they are imbricated in neoliberal logics in ways that do not necessarily relate to explicit images of money. This emphasis on economized but non-monetized logics will remain important as I consider similar images of securitized male homosexuality in Wallace's later texts. The processes I have outlined in relation to Rick and Lang's encounter are in fact quite marginal within the scope of *Broom*'s more general concerns with post-structuralist language games, the philosophy of Ludwig Wittgenstein, and disappearing great-grandmothers. In *Girl*, however, securitized homosexual risk is at times central to how Wallace explores male–male intimacy, and particularly between fathers and sons.

Securing the future in *Girl*

Wallace's securitization of homosexuality in *Girl* is an important thread in the collection's preoccupation with paternal relationships. As critics have noted of the closing novella 'Westward the Course of Empire Takes Its Way' in particular, he uses these relationships to explore the transmission of cultural value from fathers to sons.[8] This focus on futurity resonates with how securitization works as a speculative process. Haiven observes that by combining dependable assets with those that are less secure (but possibly higher yielding), 'securitization effectively packages future probabilities as present-day commodities through the highly sophisticated manipulation of risk' (2014: 77). To the extent that risk, broadly defined, is an epistemological orientation towards the future (simply put, risk is the knowledge that something *may* happen), then securitization manipulates future probabilities so that, in the form of securities, they can be exchanged in present-day markets. As Martin emphasizes, securitization 'crash[es] the time machine by bringing the future into the present' (2007: 43). Wallace securitizes the risk of homosexuality in relationships between fathers and sons in *Girl* – again, through the motif of the closet – so that it can be utilized in the present. These bonds all the while exploit securitization's focus on *future* probabilities in their deference to the idea that fathers should transmit values to their sons; if only so said sons, in accordance with Harold Bloom's (1973) theories of poetic influence, can resist their forebears. Wallace's interest in paternal relationships as a site from which future cultural value (chiefly envisaged as fiction that facilitates intimacy) can be created limns with how securitization (here, of homosexual risk) is a way of speculating, in the present, on possible returns.

'Luckily the Account Representative Knew CPR' is a good example of these processes at work. The story relates how a young Account Representative, 'almost literally a junior executive' (1989b: 46), tries to resuscitate a Vice-President, 'old enough to be literally senior' (47), after he has a heart attack in an otherwise deserted parking garage. Woods Nash notes how as the Account Representative gives CPR, his interaction with the Vice-President is 'replete with sexual imagery' (2015: 106). For instance, he is 'straddling' (1989b: 50) the older man, '*having at*' (51, italics in original) the 'queer recession' (51) at his chest. This suggestion of libidinal desire, though, works alongside the story's confirmation of each man's heterosexuality. The Vice-President is 'married for almost thirty years, grandfather of one' (45), and the Account Representative has learned CPR from his ex-wife, 'whom, he remembered, all the students had volunteered to be straddled [by]' (51). Similar to Rick and Lang's meeting in *Broom*, Wallace securitizes the risk of homosexuality here so that, though both men are ignorant of it, it imbues their encounter with an otherwise inaccessible intimacy. For Kasia Boddy 'The literary implications of [this scene] become clear' (2013: 26) if one considers Wallace's desire for fiction that 'locates and applies CPR to those elements of what's human' (26) in the wake of meta-fiction's apparent neglect of such.[9] To the extent that Wallace dramatizes these ideas in 'Luckily', he does so by securitizing male homosexuality, manipulating its perceived risk to evoke a future type of art that will revive these sentiments. That the story ends with the Account Representative still administering CPR, and therefore with the question of whether or not he has saved the older man left open, adds to this sense of speculating on what might possibly arise from their encounter.

The specific risk that 'Luckily' securitizes also points to how *Girl*, and Wallace's texts more generally, equate anal intercourse between men with death. The story is thus suggestive of how, as I noted earlier in relation to Edelman's work, homosexuality figures as a privileged signifier of the death drive. Most obviously, the Vice-President's heart attack, and the homoerotic encounter that it instigates, positions homosexual desire firmly in the context of a risk to health. There are, however, more oblique suggestions that the garage in which the events of 'Luckily' occur is a figurative rectum. The 'Executive Garage [lies] below the Staff Garage below the Building's basement maintenance level' (46), accessible by 'the curving orifice of the Exit Ramp [which] spiralled darkly around and out of sight' (47). Given how Wallace anthropomorphizes 'the Building' (45) throughout the story, his focus on this locale as its deepest section, and the description of the ramp as an 'orifice', suggests that the garage – similar to how The Flange in *Broom* implies an anus – is a figural rectum. Amplifying the sense of burial, the 'ceiling [is] a claustrophobic eight-and-a-quarter feet' (46), it is made up of tombstone-like 'grey stone planes' (46) with 'thick concrete walls … [and] a cemented monoxide floor' (50–1). In these ways Wallace answers the title question of Leo Bersani's classic 1987 essay 'Is the Rectum a Grave?' in the affirmative.[10]

In 'Luckily', then, Wallace securitizes homosexuality's affront to futurity so that, though its association with death remains, it can be utilized as a source of managed volatility, and to stress the importance of patriarchal lines of inheritance. The closet as a device with which Wallace intimates and obfuscates psychological interiority is again significant here. However, in contrast to Rick and Lang, such interiority in 'Luckily' is not psychoanalytical. In fact, the intimacy that the Account Representative and Vice-President share suggests that masculinity generally harbours unknown interior depths. After the younger man has spotted the Vice-President approach, the narrator relates how he was 'preparing to feel that male and special feeling associated with the conversational imperative faced by any two men with some professional connection … the obligation of conversation without the conversational prerequisites of intimacy or interests or concerns to share. They shared pain, though of course neither knew' (48). Wallace presents the social conventions of white-collar masculinity as hampering these men's ability to express shared emotional pain. Importantly, though, if the Vice-President's heart attack provides an occasion for querying this restraint, it is at the level of narrative, not character. Wallace's erotic descriptions of their encounter, in other words, are distinct from the men's own experience of events. The closet is at work here in how Wallace depicts these office workers in the midst of an intimacy whose sexual implications are clear to readers but unacknowledged by the characters. Meanwhile, the interiority that Wallace gestures towards is not of repressed homosexual wishes, but of a broader sense of emotional life stifled by what is, seemingly, an exclusively heterosexual male reticence.

At first blush, however, Wallace does not seem to position heterosexuality in this story as the corresponding 'high quality' asset to homosexual risk. Before he begins the eroticized descriptions of CPR, he notes how in 'the silent but well-lit business-district street above … two lovers walked, stately, pale as dolls, arms woven, silent' (50). Assuming that these lovers are male and female,[11] their unfeeling procession contrasts with the eroticized panic of the two men's encounter. Unlike 'the happily married and blankly kind grandfather' (51) he tries to resuscitate, moreover, the Account Representative is 'newly divorced' (45) and 'again-single' (46). Although the description of the Vice-President as 'blankly' kind should give one pause before arguing he symbolizes heterosexual security (as should his heart attack), the fact remains that the Account Representative does not experience similar emotional guarantees – indeed, he is divorced from the 'Red Cross volunteer instructor' (51) who taught him how to carry out CPR. It is a procedure he was 'certified by her to do, one never knowing when it could save a life, he seduced utterly by his fiancee's [*sic*] dictum that you erred, in doubt, always on the side of prepared care and readiness' (51). As a source of risk management, his fiancée gives the Account Representative the skills with which he can try to save the older man. In this light, his heterosexual attachment *does* allow him to control a risky, potentially homosexual encounter with the Vice-President. As Nash notes, 'The narrator's language also echoes that used in many marriage ceremonies: The VP's "life" is "now literally" the AR's "to have and to hold, for a lifetime"' (2015: 106). Heterosexual bonds may have failed to ensure emotional connection, but Wallace still mobilizes traditionally heteronormative imagery as harbouring a much needed stability. This stability facilitates and securitizes the suggestion of homosexual desire as one man attempts to resuscitate the other.

In a generous reading this contradictory promotion yet denial of heterosexuality, along with the story's appropriation of homosexual desire as a valuable yet deadly risk, suggests how Wallace mobilizes libidinal desire to exhaust it, pursuing intimacies that are irreducible to sex or gender. This would certainly accord with Thompson's observation that 'Wallace tried either to erase or else look past various identity markers, including those of language, class, culture, gender, and race' (2018: 215) in his pursuit of more universalist, essentialist grounds on which people can feel in communion with one another. To stop here, however, would be to miss how Wallace still depicts heterosexuality in 'Luckily' as the more secure, productive asset. The description of the Account Representative 'clear[ing] the stricken executive's cervically pink throat of tongue and foreign matter' (1989b: 50) implies that their encounter, for all its evocation of homosexual desire, is actually an attempt to inseminate the older man with the life necessary for him to function as a patriarch. Wallace therefore imbues the story's same-sex encounter with a reproductively futurist ethos. As a risky asset, male homosexuality is contrary to such futurity, and so must be securitized in the story's otherwise heterosexual imaginary in ways that deny its specificity while exploiting its risk. If Wallace gestures towards intimacies in which the gender and sexuality of participants does not matter, he does so out of a concern with the need to strengthen hetero-patriarchal bonds.

This concern resembles an influential cultural critique of the late 1980s. Specifically, Wallace's treatment of the closet in *Girl* is similar to Allan Bloom's evocation of the same in his 1987 book, *The Closing of the American Mind*. As Sedgwick explains in her analysis of this book, for Bloom 'the history of Western thought is importantly constituted and motivated by a priceless history of male-male pedagogic or pederastic relations' (2008: 55). Bloom is frightened that the homoerotic passions underpinning patriarchal traditions with petrify, but, in Sedgwick's words:

> [the] other danger that, in Bloom's view threatens cultural vitality ... is not that these desires might be killed but that they might be expressed ... . [T]he stimulation and glamorization of the energies of male-male desire ... is an incessant project that must, for the preservation of that self-contradictory tradition, coexist with an equally incessant project of denying, deferring, or silencing their satisfaction ... So Bloom is unapologetically protective of the sanctity of the closet. (2008: 56)

The closet for Bloom functions like a financial security as I have been describing it. It must contain the energies of homosexual desire and exploit them for their vitality in the creation of future cultural value. At the same time, the closet must also prevent the risk of this desire's exposure. As well as positioning *Girl* as the articulation of concerns with cultural tradition, this comparison with Bloom helps one to see how elsewhere in the collection – and especially in 'Lyndon' – Wallace's manipulation of the closet talks to patriarchal lineages outside of a strictly literary context. For if Bloom's worry is that, in Sedgwick's phrase, the 'canonical culture of the closet' (2008: 57) is in danger, it is also the worry that, as in 'Lyndon', a more general national decline is imminent if men do not securitize homosexual desire.

'Lyndon' follows David Boyd, a closeted, fictional adviser to Lyndon Johnson. In a scene in which Johnson views anti-war demonstrators from the oval office, he reconsiders the aims of the Great Society to Boyd: 'These youths that are yippies and that are protestors and that use violence and public display. We gave it to them too easy, boy. I mean their Daddies' (1989c: 106). This suggestion of lax paternal authority, reminiscent of Rick's failure to spank Vance, equates a general failure of fathers with the disrespect 'the Youth of America' (106) displays for the country's patriarchs. Alongside this generational commentary, though, 'Lyndon' is also a highly character-focused story, centred upon Boyd's relationship to Johnson and the possible homoerotic desires it may harbour. As Boyd's surname implies, it is also concerned with how boys carry on paternal legacies. Wallace presents Boyd's homosexuality as an inability to generate the future along hetero-reproductive norms. Indeed, Boyd's admission that 'it was the Fifties and I was young, burned-out cool, empty' (77) informs the irony with which he views such expectations. After a former lover outs him before committing suicide, Boyd remembers 'invoking a sort of god of glands as a shaman might blame vegetable spirits for a lost harvest' (86) to explain his sexuality to his real father. This comparison subtly establishes Boyd's ironic self-awareness of biological explanations for homosexuality while retaining the image of male sexuality as naturally geared towards a reproductive, economic futurism. Put differently, attributing homosexuality to glands might be as silly as blaming spirits for a lost harvest, but it is still the case that a harvest has been lost. Hence Boyd's position as Johnson's amanuensis and figurative son, and so the person in whom the latter's paternal legacy must be carried forth, seems questionable because of his future-negating homosexuality.

Nonetheless, because Boyd's homosexuality is an unspoken secret in Washington, and the nature of his bond to Johnson a source of intrigue for other staffers, the closet as Sedgwick perceives it in Allan Bloom's work remains active. In other words, despite Boyd's firm self-understanding – 'I was a homosexual' (85), as he matter-of-factly puts it – his relationship to Johnson displays the same 'denying, deferring, silencing' (2008: 56) that Sedgwick suggests is so important to Bloom's concern for a homoerotically imbued cultural tradition. Hence, by the end of the story, Boyd and Johnson's potential desires for one another remain closeted. Before he visits Johnson's deathbed, Boyd tries to deny to Lady Bird the 'several stories about me and about how I'm supposedly in love with Mr. Johnson' (113). Lady Bird, a figure of enigmatic menace throughout, explains that Boyd offers Johnson a form of love she no longer can. Boyd, ailing and confused over his relationship to Johnson, then finds his lover Duverger next to the president in bed, the former near death from what is implied to be AIDS, and the latter ill from an unconfirmed heart attack. Who desires whom and in what ways in this closing scene is left unresolved, with Wallace exploiting the closet's power to mobilize and deny knowledge of homosexuality to its fullest.

Similar to how 'Luckily' tries to exhaust sexual and gender identity, and in pursuit of intimacies that ostensibly transcend both, there are signs in these final pages of 'Lyndon' that Boyd and Johnson's bond is also inexplicable by such frameworks. As Boyd knocks on Johnson's bedroom door, 'The gently feminine clink of Lady Bird Johnson's willow-necked spoon was the masculine sound of my heavy old undergraduate ring' (116). By collapsing feminine and masculine into equivalency, this image implies the redundancy of both. It is also significant that, as Boyd and Johnson have their final exchange, the dying Duverger is mediating between them; 'Duverger's narrow fingers' (118) even lie across the president's face as the two men acknowledge each other. Boyd's lover shares his surname with Maurice Duverger, the sociologist responsible for Duverger's Law. As Kenneth Benoit explains, this is 'the "law" that simple plurality electoral systems resulted in the two-party system' (2006: 70). Duverger's position in this scene – 'a frozen skeleton X ray, impossibly thin, fuzzily bearded' (1989c: 117) – is a rejection of this law envisaged in sexual terms. Having Duverger on the brink of death implies the similar frailty of a Duverger's Law of sexuality and gender; a law that, to follow this analogy, reduces the plurality of desiring positions to a binary system of masculine and feminine, heterosexual and homosexual, and so on.

As with 'Luckily', however, this possibly queer appeal to move beyond sexual and gender identity works by securitizing specifically male homosexual risk. In 1987, the year in which 'Lyndon' was first published, Duverger is risky in a very particular way. Catherine Waldby explains how 'the term "risk group" was first used in relation to AIDS in 1983 by the Centre for Disease Control (CDC)' (1996: 85), and that it specified 'initially the "three Hs" – homosexuals, haemophiliacs and Haitians – and intravenous (IV) drug users' (85). Fulfilling two of the CDC's categories, Duverger is very high risk. Lying next to Johnson, a man whom Wallace depicts as bombastically hetero-masculine throughout the story, Duverger represents the homosexual risk that must be managed in Boyd's intimacy with the president. Managing such risk, however, does not mean eliminating it. Though Duverger is sidelined here as a necessary mediator but skeletal AIDS victim, Boyd is sick too, and from a weak immune system. Duverger is the abject expression of a risk that, though shared by Boyd, manifests in the latter in a less volatile way. If Boyd is 'weak beyond description' (1989c: 109) and contracts 'violent flu' (109), he is not, like Duverger, near death. As such, his homosexual risk is manageable, and indeed exploitable, as a securitized asset that enables his intimacy with the heterosexual Johnson to trigger the closet's speculative energies.

Boyd and Johnson's closeted relationship – they might be lovers, close friends or intimate in ways that transcend sex and gender – therefore suggests that a certain amount of securitized homosexual risk is essential if the male–male pedagogies Bloom describes are to continue. 'Lyndon' ends with a passage extrapolating this sense of necessary risk into a rich metaphor for American global power. At Johnson's bedroom door, Boyd's narration shifts from its previous blank understatement to a tone of invocatory conviction:

> Forget the curved circle, for whom distance means the sheer size of what it holds inside. Build a road. Make a line. Go as far west as the limit of the country lets you … and the giant curve that informs straight lines will bring you around, in time, to the distant eastern point of the country behind you … the circle you have made is quiet and huge, and everything the world holds is inside: the bedroom: a toppled trophy has punched a shivered star through the glass of its case. (117)

This suggestion of a road that, starting from 'Bodega Bay, not Whittier, California' (117), curves around the globe until it hits the east coast (therefore subtly reaffirming ideas of American exceptionalism, for America is the country exempt from this globe-encompassing line), builds on Lady Bird's explanation of Johnson's 'great intellectual concept' (115). Namely, 'love, he will say, is a federal highway, lines putting communities … in touch' (115). Given how Wallace has Johnson doubt the Great Society, in 'a reversal of his presidential resolve that the government's *raison* was before all to reduce sum totals of suffering' (111, italics in original), this image of a broken federal highway is apt. For the circle (or in an echo of Allan Bloom's book, the American mind) to close in this analogy implies an overreach of state power, suffocating the creation of future value by removing the possibility of risk. Pat O'Malley explains how, for neoliberals, welfare programmes treat risks 'as pathologies [that] government should eventually (or ideally) eliminate' (1996: 203). Risk for neoliberal thinkers is rather 'a source or condition of opportunity, an avenue for enterprise and the creation of wealth' (204). Like the 'toppled trophy [that] has punched a shivered star through the glass of its case' (Wallace 1989c: 117), risk is essential to reproducing patriarchal American power, which must smash the petrifying tendencies of a state that seeks total security. Yet, as O'Malley also notes, 'this is not to say that *all* risks are so conceived. Clearly, neo-liberalism would regard many *specific* risks as ones that can and should be prevented or minimized' (1996: 204, italics in original). Wallace solicits homosexual risk here not because he thinks all forms of volatility are good, but because this particular risk imbues patriarchal relationships with a manageable and animating sexual uncertainty. Homosexuality is the 'curve that informs *straight* lines' (Wallace 1989c: 117, italics mine), a figurative recursiveness that, though it can be exploited for the benefit of straight men, cannot be allowed to completely close into a 'curved circle' (117).

To recap, Boyd's homosexual risk and Johnson's often hyperbolic heterosexuality combine in the shape of their closeted relationship, which securitizes the former to re-enchant the idea of male pedagogic bonds with a stimulating amount of danger. Despite suggestions that their intimacy is irreducible to sexuality or gender, moreover, it is Boyd's homosexuality that provides the animating risk in this arrangement. Although 'Lyndon' has some basis in the case of Walter Jenkins, an aide to Johnson who resigned after a sex scandal in 1964, Wallace reworks the historical record to make Johnson himself a figure of fresh intrigue, as if mining the legacy of this deceased patriarch for values that have since been lost. The title itself – 'Lyndon' – is significant in this regard, implying an intimacy with the President and forecasting personal revelation. Though, as Boswell notes, 'Wallace deliberately undercuts the piece's principal playful illusion, namely its promise to "get inside" and treat as "real" someone as public and unknowable as Lyndon B. Johnson' (2009: 85). In contrast to *Broom*'s manipulation of Freudian schemas, or the suggestion in 'Luckily' that men share reservoirs of unexplored emotional pain, 'Lyndon' implies that personal interiority is in fact non-existent. In other words, Johnson is merely the conglomeration of the various myths and mediations that intersperse, and indeed constitute, Boyd's narration.

Nevertheless, as the story's fictional eulogist puts it, Johnson 'like all great men, hell, *like all men*, [was] a paradox of mystery' (Wallace 1989c: 108–9, italics mine). The self-correction here is telling. It is not because Johnson was a 'great man' that he will never 'be completely or totally understood' (109), but because he was a man. In this, the story retains the idea of individual straight men as sources of mystery. 'Lyndon' does not present such mystery in psychological terms, but the fact that, in Boswell's words, Johnson 'is a man of feeling turned into an abstraction' (2009: 84) acts a key counterpoint to what Wallace presents as the unfeeling 'medical mystery' (Sedgwick 2008: xv) of AIDS. As Boyd notes of the ailing Duverger, his doctors, 'like Aquinas before God, could think of nothing to do but define his decline via what it was not' (1989c: 110). In fact, they 'could isolate nothing but a pattern in his susceptibility to [disease]' (110). AIDS here is an impenetrable mystery that, unlike the subjective enigmas surrounding who Johnson really was, proceeds instead as an impersonal 'pattern'. Wallace thus suggests that medical understandings of personhood threaten to supplant more humanist concerns with discovering forms of emotional interiority. In the closing scene, for instance, Boyd notes 'the big white Bufferin [a brand of aspirin] of the President's personal master bed' (117). Compounding descriptions of Johnson's head as a 'great big pill' (102), this image implies that pharmaceutical conceptions of selfhood are as dangerously depersonalizing as the illnesses they combat.

Male homosexuality in 'Lyndon' does position straight men (namely, Johnson) as figures of unknowable emotional depths, but in ways that are, first, not psychologized, and second, counterpoised with medical models for examining interiority. That Duverger is a 'frozen skeleton X ray' (117) by the end aligns such medical inspection of interiority with AIDS especially. The tension between individual interiority as being a matter of subjective richness, on the one hand, and as a matter of cold technocratic inspection, on the other, is common throughout Wallace's work, as is perhaps most clear in his satirical depictions of mental-health professionals. However, this tension takes on particular importance in his endeavour to securitize homosexual risk. It is in *Infinite Jest*, moreover, that Wallace most forcefully delineates between images of AIDS that are evocative of biomedical processes, and those that intimate unconscious homosexual cathexes between straight men. As in 'Luckily' and 'Lyndon', these images mainly appear in the context of father–son relationships, the novel sharing those stories' concern with patriarchal influences. Wallace here foregrounds the perceived threat of biomedical ideas of selfhood, and especially in relation to HIV/AIDS, to a far greater extent than in *Girl*. He does so to suggest that male homosexuality's value as a risky asset decreases when it becomes articulable in terms of viral infection and biomolecular science, rather than the subjective experiences of individual men.

Bottom to bottom in *Infinite Jest*

At one point in *Infinite Jest*, in an image that contains suggestions of anal sex, Freudian psychoanalysis and homosexuality as a type of future-negating death, Don Gately relates how two 'pillow-biters from the Fenway were having this involved conversation about some third fag having to go in and get the skeleton of some kind of fucking rodent removed from inside their butthole' (1996: 274). This passage evokes Freud's case history of the 'Rat Man', who suffered from the fear that his father and fiancée would have rats eat into their rectums (1979b). 'Pillow-biters', meanwhile, defines homosexuality in relation to a homophobic understanding of anal intercourse, while the idea of a gay man giving birth to a dead animal from his anus presents it as a danger to reproductive futurism. Anal sex, Freudian thought, and gay men as threats to the future are all central to how Wallace depicts homosexuality as a securitizable asset in *Infinite Jest*. They are also important to how he securitizes it as a means to elucidate male psychic interiority in the face of biomedicine's hollowing out of same. That '*pillow-biter's* a North Shore term, one Gately grew up with, and it and the *f*-term are the only terms for male homosexuals he knows, still' (1003, italics in original) is telling in this regard. By broadcasting an awareness of homophobic prejudice (much as Wallace does to Lipsky), this admission positions homosexual risk as a resource to neutrally manipulate. That it does so by pointing out the reasons for Gately's ignorance, moreover, suggests how such manipulation facilitates insights into the subjective histories of heterosexual men.

It is not Gately, however, through whom Wallace chiefly performs this securitizing process, but Hal. Similar to the dynamics I explored earlier in *Girl*, this works in relation to Hal's father, James. Their relationship, and the paternal history of the Incandenzas generally, is of key importance given Wallace's preoccupation in *Infinite Jest* with how 'fathers impact sons' (32). A particular instance of male intergenerational communication notable for my purposes, though, is Hal's account of his father's meta-gay porn film, 'Accomplice!' This is one of the novel's many ekphrastic vignettes, in which the description of an audio-visual text becomes so thorough that it momentarily supplants the main narrative frame. As Hal recounts, the film follows 'a beautifully sad young bus-station male prostitute' (945), who is picked up by a 'dissipated-looking old specimen with grey teeth' (945). The older man takes offence at how the boy 'size[s] him up as a health risk. The obvious health risk here is referred to … merely as *It* [HIV]' (945, italics in original). Consequently, he decides to scare the boy by cutting his penis with a razor blade while they are having intercourse.

Unknown to the older man, though, is that the boy himself has 'It, the Human Immuno Virus' (945); revealed when he withdraws his penis and notes, 'at the crease of [the boy's] bum' (945), the 'sign of Kaposi's Sarcoma, that most universal symptom of *It*' (945, italics in original). As the boy 'shrieks "*Murderer! Murderer!*" over and over' (946, italics in original), the pun of the film's title becomes clear – if the man is a murderer, then the boy is an accomplice, and vice versa if the boy's shrieks actually refer to himself.

With 'Accomplice!' Wallace self-consciously registers his own manipulation of male anal intercourse and HIV as sources of potentially mortal risk. Carefully placed clues as to James's motivation for making this film, and the emphasis on Hal's jaded response to it, also suggest how 'Accomplice!' works in relation to the novel's wider securitization of such risk. As the age differences between the 'old specimen' (945) and the 'beautiful boy' (945) imply, their roles are evocative of father and son. Wallace compounds this association by relating how the older man, like James's grandfather who smoked 'a long filter' (164), also smokes 'through a long white FDR-style filter' (945).[12] Meanwhile, the boy in this film, 'who is inarticulate' (945) and voices a 'mute howl' (946) after the older man removes his penis, echoes James's delusion in the years before his death that, in Hal's words, 'I'm mute' (31). In these ways, Wallace presents 'Accomplice!' as James's articulation of concerns with paternal inheritance and intergenerational communication similar to those evident in 'Luckily' and 'Lyndon'. The fact that Hal responds to this film with a complete lack of affect – its 'abstract and self-reflexive' (946) nature meaning that 'we end up feeling and thinking not about the characters but about the cartridge itself' (946) – is also significant. For if 'Accomplice!' fails to move Hal because its 'metasilliness' (704) prevents him from becoming emotionally engaged with its characters, then this self-reflexive excess accords with the film's – and indeed the novel's – depiction of HIV/AIDS more generally.

For example, Hal's description of HIV here as 'the Human Immuno Virus' (945) – instead of the Human Immuno*deficiency* Virus – subtly changes its meaning. This truncation mirrors an earlier description of HIV in the novel as a 'Human Immuno-Virus' (202), implying that it is not the case that Hal has stated it inaccurately. By removing 'deficiency' from this phrase, Wallace implies the virus is risky not because it depletes a subject's resilience to infection, but because it makes one immune to being 'Human'. As in 'Lyndon', therefore, Wallace suggests that HIV as a biomedical epidemic is dangerous because it endangers humanist conceptions of personhood; here broadly defined as the ability Hal outlines to feel and think 'about the characters' (946) in a film, rather than just about the film itself. Wallace develops this point in endnote 238, which is appended to an explanation of annular fusion given by Hal's classmate, Pemulis. Annular fusion is a self-replenishing energy creation process that evolved out of a 'micromedical model ... [of] bombarding highly toxic radioactive particles with massive doses of stuff even more toxic than the radioactive particles' (572). The endnote goes on to relate that 'while the annular meta-disease treatment is highly effective on metastatic cancers, it proved a disappointment on the HIV-spectrum viri, since AIDS is itself a meta-disease' (1044). Putting to one side the inaccurate description of AIDS here as a disease, this comment suggests that its status as a meta-virus, and hence one that works self-reflexively, is what makes it so virulent.

By unpacking this image further, one can see how the novel positions HIV/AIDS as being indicative of biomedicine's threat to traditional ideas of heterosexual male interiority. In the sense that AIDS can arise from HIV, and is therefore a collection of second-order diseases that result after the original viral infection, then it can be considered a 'meta-disease' (1044) of sorts. However, the endnote relates that it is 'the HIV-spectrum viri' (1044) in particular that proves so resistant to Wallace's fanciful medical treatment. Waldby observes how HIV's '"strategic" status as a kind of metavirus within biomedicine, derives from a lack of proper, singular viral identity' (118). As a virus that infects healthy host cells in order to mimic their processes, HIV works recursively; indeed, it is a *retro*virus. This term refers to how, after having infected the body's CD4 cells (by targeting specific proteins found on the surface of immune cells), HIV begins a process of reverse transcription. This process allows HIV's genetic material to convert into DNA, which is essential to allowing HIV to enter the CD4 cell's nucleus. From here, HIV controls a CD4 cell's mechanisms in order to reproduce itself, acting in the words of one commentator 'like a broken copying machine' (Kolata 1993, cited in Kruger 1996: 7), and in doing so, destroying further host CD4 cells.[13] In this light, annular fusion is an ineffective way to treat HIV because it aggravates one self-replicating process through the application of another.[14]

Scientific explanations of these cellular processes also tend to be marked in ways that align the virus with homophobic ideas of gay sex. Steven F. Kruger explains how, in 'the phallic imagination at work in visualizing viral activity' (1996: 36), the invading virus, 'like sperm ... is conceived as a package put together primarily to introduce genetic material into a cell' (35). However, given that in the dominant biomedical imaginary the host cell 'already represents a "marriage" of male and female, nucleus and cytoplasm' (37), this sperm-like virus is actually envisaged as 'a debased but also threatening homosexual masculinity' (38). Thus, as Kruger explains further, while HIV's genetic information

> can be 'convert[ed]...into DNA', and incorporated seamlessly into the cell's 'proper' genome, it remains essentially different from and foreign to its 'host' ... in its challenge to the ... 'properly' unidirectional flow of information in the cell, the retrovirus – directing information *backward* – represents a perverse threat to the coherence of linguistic process imagined at the cellular level. ... In a geometry that evokes anal sex, cellular DNA is made to 'bend over' so that the virus can 'sneakily' insert itself into the host chromosome. (38–9, italics in original)

Wallace's suggestion that HIV is a 'meta-disease' (1996: 1044), and his presentation of anal intercourse as an abject source for its transmission, follows these associations of retroviral processes and homosexuality as being risks to heterosexual men. What is most significant here, though, is that Wallace only hints at this biomedical backdrop. Similar to the mysterious pattern that is killing Duverger in 'Lyndon', Wallace evokes HIV as an unknown biomolecular process occurring inside the (heterosexual, male) body.

Wallace hints at these mysterious molecular activities, and particularly in relation to anal sex, to highlight by contrast the idea that homosexuality forms part of individual men's psychic lives. In doing so, he suggests that the former understanding of interiority endangers the latter, and in turn, the closeted homoeroticism that he implies is essential to securing patrilineal bonds. In fact, Wallace manipulates Freud's account of the primal scene, particularly as Freud explains it in his case history of the Wolf Man, to establish this juxtaposition in connection to Hal and his forbears. Of course, the Incandenza family is a dense knot of neuroses and repressions, and is therefore hugely generative of psychoanalytic investigation. Andrew Warren, for instance, focuses on the same relationships I do, but he emphasizes the applicability of Freud's *Totem and Taboo* instead (2018: 183–4). By tracking the novel's many references to the Wolf Man in particular, though, it becomes apparent how Wallace mobilizes psychoanalytical understandings of homosexuality in order to renew intimacies between interiorized straight men. As such, the financial logic that is evident in *Broom* and *Girl*, where the closet works to securitize homosexuality in order to speculate on the return of intimacy between such men, serves a slightly more specific goal here. Wallace modulates his presentation of homosexual risk to compel men to invest in the 'right' models of interiority; models which position them as sources of a rich and engaging psychic life, rather than what are, apparently, dehumanizing biomolecular processes.

Wallace reworks Freud's primal scene in the tale of how James, as a boy, started to think about the possibilities of annular fusion. This section of the novel is presented as an excerpted chapter from *'The Chill of Inspiration: Spontaneous Reminiscences by Seventeen Pioneers of DT-Cycle Lithiumized Annular Fusion'* (1034, italics in original). Far from spontaneous, though, this chapter is artfully crafted by James, and we only learn in its final paragraphs of how he first thought about the recursive process of energy-creation-via-waste-consumption mentioned earlier. The preceding eleven pages relate how James once helped his parents take their bed apart to locate the source of a squeaking noise. The image of a boy in the presence of his parents' bed is reminiscent of Freud's most detailed account of the primal scene in relation to the Wolf Man. At the age of one and a half, this patient saw his father having sex with his mother from behind, 'the man upright, and the woman bent down like an animal' (1979a: 270). This experience instigated the patient's identification with his mother, and therefore a wish to be loved by his father. After a later dream reactivated this wish, 'The result was terror, horror of the fulfilment of the wish, the repression of the impulse' (267), and 'fear of his father appeared in its place in the shape of the wolf phobia' (279). The cause of horror was the revelation that, to be loved by his father, he must undergo castration; a fact that his 'libido ... in the form of concern for his male organ' (279) resisted.

These details are important to how James's reminiscence rebounds upon Hal, and indeed upon the closeted homosexual wishes Wallace securitizes in their relationship. Yet James's chapter also alters the primal scene as related by Freud to suggest the collapse of paternal authority augmenting it. This chapter's many references to how James's father is dressed in white (in his capacity as an actor playing a corporate mascot) echoes 'the *white* wolves' (Freud 1979a: 269, italics in original) of the Wolf Man's phobia. But, far from being a figure of intimidation, James's father ends the chapter emasculated, and in the position of the Wolf Man's mother. Falling ill, his father collapses over the bedframe, 'face-down, with his bottom high in the air ... [his] crack all the way down to the anus itself was now visible' (Wallace 1996: 501). In Freud's words, 'The wolf that he [the Wolf Man] was afraid of was undoubtedly his father; but his fear of the wolf was conditional upon the creature being in an upright posture' (1979a: 272). With his anus vulnerable to penetration, James's father is the inverse of such intimidation. James then runs to his bedroom and, jumping onto his bed, dislodges his closet door knob, whose peculiar roll when it hits the floor inspires him to think about annulation – in a neatly literal sense, then, this dangerously recursive idea 'comes out of the closet'. With the collapse of the father comes the discovery of the same recursive system that gives rise to annular fusion. If 'Accomplice!' presents male–male intercourse as a source of meta-disease, the potential anal eroticism in this scene similarly figures as the cause of a harmfully self-referential process.

That the father's initial 'bearing-down action [on the mattress] looked very much like emergency compression of a heart patient's chest' (Wallace 1996: 491) is suggestive of how Wallace aligns paternal weakness here with the fragility of psychoanalytical frameworks. Reiterating the trope of defective hearts as symbols for deficiency, Wallace has James craft this chapter to imply that the rise of annular fusion corresponds with the decline of models of psychic interiority organized around fatherly authority. For instance, the mattress on which a possible primal scene would occur is 'flaccid and floppy as [James and his father] tried to jockey it' (495) out of the room. The need to apply CPR to such frameworks, and so to male psychic interiority, also informs how the anal intercourse depicted in 'Accomplice!' affects Hal. Before we receive his account of the film, his encounter with the Enfield Tennis Academy janitors Kenkle and Brandt contains another reference to Freud's Wolf Man. Kenkle, talking to Brandt as Hal approaches, asks 'what is the essence of Christmas morning but the childish co-eval of venereal interface, for a child?' (874). Kenkle's remarks refer to how the Wolf Man equated 'Christmas with its presents [with] the deeper wish ... for sexual satisfaction from [his] father' (Freud 1979a: 277).[15] This reference places Hal within his father's psychic history. Indeed, Kenkle inveighs against anal intercourse, as it is a '*hunched* way to have interface' (Wallace 1996: 875, italics in original), but he 'will wager [that Hal] rar-e-ly hunches' (875). The word 'hunch' in relation to anal sex then lodges in Hal's narration, occurring several times in his description of 'Accomplice!' and the 'hunched, homosubmissive position' (945) of its male prostitute. By establishing this string of references to Freud's account of the primal scene, and the significance of anal sex within it, Wallace places Hal in a patrilineal line of unconscious homosexual wishes.

The point of all this detective work is that, by tracking the novel's various references to the Wolf Man, one can see how Wallace uses the image of male anal intercourse as a generator of HIV to facilitate what he suggests is its opposite; namely, homosexual desire as an animating but repressed element of straight male psychic life. Moreover, unpacking these references shows how Wallace orchestrates them – notably by placing clues at the novel's beginning and end – in a way that urges the reader to invest in the 'right' form of homosexual risk. For as the novel moves towards its conclusion, references to Hal and same-sex desire increase. As well as his synopsis of 'Accomplice!', and his encounter with Kenkle and Brandt, we receive Hal's reaction to the possibility that two male friends are sharing a bed. Despite the fact that 'the universe seemed to have aligned itself so that even acknowledging it would violate some tacit law' (872), Hal cannot help but reflect on such 'unthinkable possibilities' (872). These references ensure that we leave Hal with the question of his possible homosexual wishes at the forefront of his and our minds. In fact, the last we hear from his first person narration are details about how 'it was impossible for me to imagine Himself [i.e. James] and the Moms being explicitly sexual together' (957). Like James in his reconstruction of the circumstances that led him to discover annular fusion, Hal cannot imagine a primal scene as Freud describes it with the Wolf Man, but only its failure; it is no coincidence, then, that his final paragraph as narrator focuses on his mother's cuckolding of James.

The novel closes not with Hal, though, but with Gately, hospitalized with a gunshot wound and remembering the murder of his crime partner, Gene Fackelmann. Precipitating this final section, Gately hears somebody laugh at how 'it was getting harder these days to tell the homosexuals from the people who beat up homosexuals. ... He remembered two of his Beverly High teammates beating up a so-called homosexual kid while Gately walked away, wanting no part of either side. Disgusted by both sides of the conflict' (973). The first remark implies that Gately has possibly contracted HIV, the virus's association with homosexuality at odds, from this suggested homophobic perspective (which given the context is most likely that of a doctor), with Gately's macho physique. The following memory, which registers Gately's disgust at homophobic violence as well as with homosexuality, evinces how the novel generally positions the latter in relation to heterosexual men. By having Gately walk away from this conflict (or rather, this homophobic attack), while stressing his disgust with gay men, Wallace positions homosexuality as a source of abjection that is still undeserving of violent renunciation. Instead, homosexuality as I have shown throughout this chapter is a useful form of risk which, once securitized, will facilitate insights into the emotional lives of straight men such as Gately. The way in which these final intimations of homosexuality in Gately's narrative loop backwards to the beginning, moreover, also serves this purpose on the larger scale of the novel's structure.

Drawing on archival materials and letters between Wallace and his editor, Casey Michael Henry explains how *Infinite Jest*'s end is designed to circle back to its start. Furthermore, the beginning and end respectively concern 'Hal and Gately's two final transformations and bottoms' (2015: 481). 'Bottom' is an Alcoholics Anonymous term for the 'cliffish nexus of exactly two total choices' (Wallace 1996: 349) which works as an epiphanic moment of decision for the addict – to surrender to AA or die from their addictions. Reaching Gately's bottom, we are compelled to turn back to Hal's bottom, in a process mimicking the fatally entrapping 'Infinite Jest' film. If we consider how 'bottom' here puns on buttocks, though, then this recursive looping back is evocative of how the novel presents male anal intercourse as the source of HIV's meta-disease. Before the novel's final sequence begins, Gately 'felt an upward movement deep inside that was so personal and horrible he woke up [into his recollection of Fackelmann's murder]' (974). Though this remark implies that Gately is lifted onto a gurney, its proximity to details concerning his possibly having HIV means it resonates with a suggestion of penetration. In this sense, the novel's looping back mimics the actions of a retrovirus, which in Kruger's words affronts the 'unidirectional flow of information … [by] directing information *backward*' (1996: 38, italics in original), as well as the image of male anal intercourse as working from behind.

By encouraging us to return to Hal's bottom, Wallace sends us back to another scene of homosexual intrigue. As he is interviewed by a university admissions board, in a scenario reminiscent of Boyd's interview by Johnson in 'Lyndon', Hal is subject to what he suspects is a come-on. The Director of Composition 'emerged as both the Alpha of the pack here and way more effeminate that he'd seemed at first, standing hip-shot with a hand on his waist, walking with a roll to his shoulders … cupping what I feel to be a hand over my sportcoat's biceps (surely not)' (1996: 9). This echoes how a flange patron in *Broom* tries to pick up Lang, 'gauging the man's bicep under his sportcoat' (1987: 224). The Director of Composition though also disturbs Hal's sense of Alpha and effeminate (and in Wallace's imagining here, heterosexual and homosexual) men. His come-on in this way troubles the security of a distinction between the two, as Hal's parenthetical 'surely not' (1996: 9) suggests. What Henry describes as 'the psychological reverberations of these polarized bottoms' (2015: 491) therefore are distinctly sexualized in terms of Hal's and Gately's subjective estimations of homosexuality. Both men's encounter with possible same-sex desire – Hal's with a potential come-on, but also in the novel's Wolf Man references, and Gately's intermittent homophobia with closing suggestions that he has HIV – stresses their status as interiorized men. Wallace loops the novel in such a way so that the intimation of HIV and anal intercourse as similarly recursive processes situates the two male protagonists as sources of psychic depth. To the extent that this circularity mimics HIV's reverse transcription, then a bio-scientific understanding of interiority secures what Wallace presents as its opposite: Hal and Gately as subjects formed by personal psychological histories.

Moreover, this securitizing process draws in the reader, for Wallace compels us to carry on securitizing homosexuality envisaged as a kind of deadly narcissistic recursion so that straight men can figure as sources of mystery. As Henry notes, the novel's 'narrative system [is] a circle of self-enclosed thought, broken only with a disruptive and reflexive insight' (2015: 481). Therefore, 'breaking the self-enclosed annular rings that we might understand the novel's arrangement prompts' (2015: 483) involves speculating on the missing year between Gately's recollection and Hal's interview, and particularly in order to better understand the fates of both men. This gap allows for multiple interpretations, encouraging one to go over the various clues that Wallace provides so that we can try and reconstruct what happened – indeed, the enigma continues to entice and perplex fans of the novel. As such, the missing year functions as a closet of sorts. Though it does not tease sexual knowledge per se, it works like the closet as seen in *Broom* and *Girl* to render heterosexual men (Hal and Gately) mysterious. Given Hal's come-on and Gately's possible contraction of HIV at the novel's separate bottoms, an encounter with same-sex desire can be said to instigate this elision. What interrupts *Infinite Jest*'s recursive loop, and thus aims to save us from dangerously recursive systems, are questions surrounding men whose self-understanding as heterosexuals Wallace productively troubles.[16]

An encouragement to break from the novel's self-enclosed loops, however, does not necessarily mean a call to renounce them, in what Hering argues is the novel's 'rejection of solipsistic and claustrophobic closed systems' (2015: 141). This reading falls short of accounting for how these recursive structures, despite Wallace's general denigration of such, are key to effecting the 'way out' (Wallace 1996: 981) that is so ostensibly needed. Like the 'curve that informs straight lines' (1989c: 117) with which 'Lyndon' ends, *Infinite Jest*'s missing year only registers as an escape from the novel's recursive loop if said loop still presents the threat of closure. If we consider this loop as the recursion of HIV and anal sex between men, which if unchecked will flow from bottom to bottom, then Wallace securitizes this risk by making it productive of the excised or 'closeted' year whose enabling mysteries centre upon Hal and Gately. In the same way that Wallace presents homosexual abjection as an asset to be manipulated, so too does he figure the novel's recursive yet punctured narrative structure – as the appropriate amount of risk required for creating its absent temporal keystone. That the task falls to us as readers to fill in this missing year means that, by doing so, we legitimate the securitization Wallace performs to create it. It is our labour that facilitates the future value that the novel's securitized narrative loop endeavours to spark.

The criticism can be made that this argument rests too heavily on comparing *Infinite Jest*'s circular narrative with its depiction of homosexuality as dangerously recursive, and particularly because of its perceived association with anal intercourse and HIV. It is certainly the case that annularity as a motif does not pertain to same-sex desire exclusively. Meta-fiction, drug abuse and ecological damage are just a few of the many phenomena the novel critiques for their recursive inwardness. That said, honing in on Wallace's association of annular processes with homosexuality sheds light on his investment in male heterosexuality as the 'higher quality' asset to be capitalized on, and in a way that these other factors, arguably, do not. Pursuing this line of enquiry has shown how the novel securitizes male homosexuality as a specifically (in light of HIV) biomedical risk to the 'human', and to reaffirm straight men as subjects of interior mystery. References to Freud's primal scene work in conjunction with the novel's presentation of HIV as a meta-disease to propose such inner mystery, which if not strictly Freudian, retains that discourse's emphasis on the individual as a source of inner psychic life. The novel's securitization of homosexual risk to effect such mystery informs its organization as a loop broken primarily by the withheld experiences of two heterosexual men. Speculating on this aporia perpetuates the sexual and financial dynamics at play, in which homosexuality is – indeed, *has* to be – an immutably toxic risk to the novel's heroes.

Conclusion

Writing on the intersections of credit markets, race, gender and non-normative sexuality, Melinda Cooper relates how 'the AIDS crisis … represented a turning point in the historical relationship between gay men and American capital' (2017: 158). When the introduction of antiretroviral drugs meant that HIV was no longer an automatic death sentence, 'financial service brokers and consumer lenders embarked on an extraordinary quest to capture the "gay market"' (2017: 159). As a result, American 'gay men who at the height of the AIDS crisis had been defined as uninsurable were now counted as exceptionally good credit risks and ideal consumers of financial services' (159). This shift in attitudes towards homosexual men and capital is a prime example of what Lisa Duggan describes as '*the new homonormativity*' (2003: 50, italics in original). In Duggan's words, homonormativity allows for 'the possibility of a demobilized gay constituency and a privatized, depoliticized gay culture anchored in domesticity and consumption' (50). From the perspective of the late 2010s, this situation proceeds as strong as ever, as is most notable in the number of Western banks – such as Lloyds, HSBC, Bank of America and Deutsche Bank – that now broadcast their support for Pride. Within the broader context of homonationalism, in which queers can enjoy convivial relations with some of the most oppressive branches and activities of the nation state,[17] such neoliberal pinkwashing implies that historical stigmatization has given way to the inclusive recognition of LGBTQ communities as just another market to tap.

The relative absence of AIDS and male homosexuality in Wallace's work after *Infinite Jest* implies that as the risk attendant on both decreased in light of medical advances and greater tolerance, so too did their attractiveness to Wallace's project. In the short story 'Good Old Neon', collected in *Oblivion*, we can in fact witness Wallace try to relinquish links between male homosexuality, risk and the closet. The protagonist, Neal, has realized that psychoanalysis is a dead-end when it comes to tackling the feelings of fraudulence that eventually lead to his suicide. Key to this realization is how he finds himself able to outwit his analyst, Dr Gustafson, not least on the basis of the latter's repressed same-sex desires. Reflecting on Gustafson's terminal colon cancer from what Wallace implies is the afterlife, Neal notes how the idea of 'using your rectum or colon to secretly *harbor an alien growth* was a blatant symbol both of homosexuality and of the repressive belief that its open acknowledgment would equal disease and death' (2004b: 163, italics in original). This awareness of homophobic ideas is qualitatively different from that evident in a story such as 'Lyndon', as it implies that to read the story in question with these ideas in mind is hopelessly banal. Whether 'Good Old Neon' escapes said homophobia is debatable; Neil's statement that Gustafson should 'just go over to Garfield Park and blow somebody in the bushes and try honestly to decide if he liked it or not' (170), at least, seems purposely crass. Most significant for my purposes is how, by the time of *Oblivion*, and amid more liberal attitudes to gay men, Wallace no longer found homosexuality a risky enough asset to securitize.

Nevertheless, it remains that from *Broom* to *Infinite Jest* Wallace's securitization of male homosexuality helps further the idea that it is not only a toxic risk, but that it is useful by virtue of being so. Wallace does this by depicting homosexuality as an animating yet unacknowledged desire inhering in straight men. A psychologized idea of the closet works like a financial security to bundle together notionally distinct forms of desire: specifically, a low-risk enervated heterosexuality with a high risk, abjectly active homosexuality. The prospected benefit of such securitization is that same-sex desire will replenish heterosexuality with the risk needed to facilitate intimacy between straight men.

That this process gestures to the future, and by affirming the importance of patriarchal lines of inheritance, presents male sexuality as useful to the extent that it confirms a reproductively futurist ethos. Importantly, for the securitizing processes I have identified to work, one must accept that homosexuality is a 'shameful, dirty, secret' (2004b: 163) to begin with. Indeed, Wallace's refusal to question the idea that male homosexuality is toxic entrenches the homophobic perspective from which he makes such judgements. The self-awareness Wallace displays of homophobia is a front, invested as he is in casting gays in positions of abjection and disease. The next two chapters alter my focus from negativity to violence, but there too I show how Wallace forecloses the idea that male sexuality can be anything other than toxic.

3

Contract

Gazing within masochism

'It's OK to hate Jonathan Franzen. Everybody else is doing it' (2019), says Kevin Power, in his review of said hate-figure's *The End of the End of the Earth: Essays* (2018). Franzen certainly has a knack for angering writers, reviewers, critics and general readers. As Power observes in his review, though, the ire that meets this National Book Award winner (for 2001's *The Corrections*) has a tendency to be reductive, however flawed his novels and essays are. Furthermore, Franzen's comments on literature and cultural worth have still provoked some fascinating if no doubt heated debates. This is particularly the case with his essay 'Mr Difficult', in which he proposes two opposing models for literary value. On the one hand, Franzen suggests that there exists the 'Status model' (2002: 100), where an author prizes formal difficulty as a sign of how their work is above the lay reader, and so 'invites a discourse of genius and art-historical importance' (100). On the other hand, though, is the 'Contract model' (100), where 'the deepest purpose of reading and writing fiction is to sustain a sense of connectedness' (100). Franzen is aware that this model, if 'taken to its free-market extreme' (100), positions the reader as a consumer and the author as a kind of service provider, but he supports it nonetheless. He values the Contract model's ability to create connections between text and reader, even if 'the Contract sometimes calls for work' (111) from the latter – a stipulation that implies he has something akin to an employment contract in mind. Wallace complicates Franzen's dichotomy; in Severs's words, he is 'disdaining [of] Contract models of reading' (2017a: 220), displaying the difficulties that Franzen associates with the Status model.[1] Yet Wallace's disdain for contracts, whether as a metaphor for the relationship between reader and text, or as a general means of capitalist organization, does not arise from his hostility to connectedness. It arises from the suspicion that contracts create a power relationship in which one party is subservient to another.

As Walter Benn Michaels explains, neoliberal thinkers such as Friedrich Hayek and Ludwig von Mises object to contracts on similar grounds. For them and their followers, contracts are 'too constraining, or, at least, constraining in the wrong way' (2017: 29). Whereas traditional employment contracts are 'binding in a way that necessarily limits the will' (29), neoliberals promote contracts that will protect individual self-determination. One result of this, as Ted Schrecker and Clare Bambra note, is that since the rise of neoliberal policies in the United Kingdom and the United States 'more and more people are working on either temporary contracts or no contracts' (2015: 45). As they note, 'The once standard full-time, permanent contract with benefits has been superseded' (45) by temporary employment 'which tend[s] to be characterized by lower levels of security and poorer working conditions' (45). Quoting Andrew Hoberek, Michaels writes that 'in this world ... contract begins to look (but only for the worker) like "a site of nostalgia"' (30). There is no such nostalgia in Wallace's depictions of contracts.[2] Severs is right to say that his texts show an 'anticontract stance' (2017a: 219), whether out of a belief that contracts inflict 'second-order rules' (45) onto more authentic connections, or because they mean – to use his example of Lenore in *The Broom of the System* – 'loss of individual efficacy of will' (45). Wallace suggests that the contract between reader and text needs to be reformed, and out of a neoliberal concern with protecting the former's agency.[3]

That this agency pertains, in part, to their ability to feel what Franzen describes as a 'sense of connectedness' (2002: 100) with a text chimes with my previous analyses of Wallace's interest in emotional intimacy. However, there are two important ways in which my readings here differ. First, Wallace's hostility to contracts expresses less a desire for intimacy than it does for a sense of unmediated reality. One of the problems with thinking of the relationship between reader and text as a contract, for Wallace, is that it buffers the reader's ability to connect with something 'real'. This points to the second difference: Wallace associates this unmediated reality with ideas of male sexual violence. In *Infinite Jest* scenes of rape, torture and suicide work *within but against* the contract between reader and text to remind the latter of an apparently male pleasure in inflicting harm. This chapter therefore marks a shift in my reading of Wallace's depictions of male toxicity, from the Edelman-inspired notion of a tamed or securitized sexual negativity, to what Sally Bachner (2011) describes as the prestige of violence. To recap, for Bachner an influential strand of contemporary American fiction figures violence as an extra-linguistic reality, one whose resistance to representation affords those who try to write about it a degree of literary-cultural prestige. In *Infinite Jest* male sexual violence plays this extra-linguistic role, the prestige in question arising from the struggle to depict said 'reality' in defiance of contractual constraints. Wallace prioritizes one activity especially here: men's capability, and ostensibly their desire, for sadistic gazing.

This brings to mind Laura Mulvey's theories of gender and spectatorship, especially in her influential essay 'Visual Pleasure and Narrative Cinema'. Here Mulvey explores 'the way the unconscious of patriarchal society has structured film form' (2009: 14). Working in a generally Lacanian framework, she argues that cinema replicates formative psychic processes for male spectators. In particular, 'the woman as icon, displayed for the gaze and enjoyment of men' (22) in classical narrative film instigates castration anxiety, to which men can respond either by 're-enactment of the original trauma ... counter-balanced by the devaluation, punishment or saving of the guilty object' (22) or 'disavowal of castration by the substitution of a fetish object' (22). Significantly, for Mulvey 'the first avenue, voyeurism ... has associations with sadism' (22). Wallace's texts are invested in this notion of specifically male sadistic looking. However, this is not to suggest that he follows Mulvey's work to the letter. What I describe as the male gaze in relation to his texts, in fact, shows little sign of the psychoanalytic ideas or the feminist politics driving her theories. Consequently, although I will use the phrase 'male gaze' throughout this chapter to evoke the understanding of spectatorship that Mulvey's work gives rise to, I do not try to evaluate its analytical accuracy. In my usage the male gaze refers to a mode of spectatorship, coded as heterosexual and male, that positions the subject in a sadistic relationship to that which he gazes at.

In fact, to understand how this gaze functions in Wallace's texts, it is necessary to consider how those writing in Mulvey's wake have challenged her work. As Michele Aaron argues, Mulvey's theories of spectatorship suggest that cinema is 'an institution that inflicts and allows to dominate, if not to triumph, the gaze of the aggressor' (2007: 52). In this sense, male spectators are helpless before cinema's ability to turn them into voyeurs; forcing them to comply with this position, it grants men the illusion of mastery over the events onscreen. Following in the footsteps of Gaylyn Studlar (1993), however, Aaron proposes that it is more useful to think of spectatorship as a masochistic activity. For Aaron, 'sadism cannot characterize spectatorship for it opposes complicity, where spectatorship, like masochism, is by nature contractual' (2007: 90). Central to Studlar and Aaron's readings is Gilles Deleuze's argument, in his study *Masochism: Coldness and Cruelty* (1989), that 'the masochistic contract implies not only the necessity of the victim's consent, but his ability ... to train his torturer' (Deleuze 1989: 75). The spectator enters a consensual, masochistic contract with a film, which allows them to disavow their complicity (namely, in deciding to suspend disbelief) in upholding the fantasy taking place on-screen. To enjoy the illusion that a film affords, the spectator pretends they are being 'done to' against their will. In reality, though, the film is a pseudo-sadist, for it depends on the spectator's active disavowal of its fakery to run smoothly.

In *Infinite Jest*, Wallace tries to problematize these dynamics by soliciting the male gaze. The focus on contract in Deleuzian-inspired theories of spectatorship, not to mention how such masochistic models legitimate what Aaron calls 'activity-in-passivity' (2007: 62), runs counter to his desire to remind readers of their own 'male' capability for gazing. As my reading of his essay 'E Unibus Pluram: Television and U.S. Fiction' will demonstrate, for Wallace the spread of meta-fiction in popular culture undercuts the enjoyment to be had from masochistic contracts. This is because (in what has become an old chestnut in accounts of Wallace's aversion to postmodernism) television shows and films now highlight their own fakery, thus compromising the spectator's ability to suspend disbelief. Such self-awareness, for Wallace, has important implications for how spectators engage with images of violence and suffering in particular. He suggests that spectatorial self-reflexivity disenchants these images, specifically by encouraging the entertainment industries to treat 'shock, grotesquerie, or irreverence' (1997b: 40) as little more than 'PR techniques' (40), and by presenting violence itself as a source of irony. Examples of such neutering can be seen in *Infinite Jest*'s account of the demise of television advertising, and in Wallace's criticism, in 'David Lynch Keeps His Head', of film director Quentin Tarantino. Indeed, given the importance of male sexuality to these dynamics, 'neutering' is a very suitable term.

Such images for Wallace do little to undermine the self-reflexivity his texts diagnose; as the example of 'Accomplice!' in the last chapter shows, they can actually reinforce it. In contrast he creates scenes that, by trying to subject readers to 'real' extra-linguistic violence, aspire to break through the textual self-reflexivity that the idea of contract perpetuates. That said, my priority is not to assess how successful Wallace's texts are in achieving this goal. The force of Deleuzian inflected readings of spectatorial sadism, in fact, arises from how they render such a goal impossible. In other words, Wallace cannot subject readers to the fate of Gene Fackelmann at the end of *Infinite Jest*, held to a chair with his eyelids sewn open and forced to watch his own imminent torture. I am interested, rather, in what the endeavour to inflict and solicit sadism implies about his attitudes to male sexuality, the gaze and contract. Moreover, throughout this chapter I approach Wallace's texts through theories first deployed in film studies. In doing so, I concur with Philip Sayers that Wallace pursues 'a semiotically hybrid project, in which novel and film are shown to be fundamentally intertwined' (2014: 108). Sayers is referring to *Infinite Jest* here, but his observation is applicable to other areas of Wallace's oeuvre. Indeed, for Stephen J. Burn 'his fiction – indeed his very theory of fiction – is profoundly visual' (2014b: 86). Though I am careful not to conflate literature with film, therefore, I draw on accounts of the latter in the conviction that they are appropriate tools with which to assess Wallace's use of the male gaze.

The idea that sadistic gazing challenges the subservience that, for Wallace, contracts impose, also points to the spermatic metaphors underpinning my readings in this chapter. In Chapters 1 and 2 my metaphors derived from spermatic economy – hence notions of waste and investment. The current chapter, by contrast, works with ideas of blockage and release. As Sally Robinson observes, male liberationist discourse since the 1970s has often conflated 'emotional, sexual, and violent "release" (2000: 154). In fact, the assumption 'that emotional and sexual forces *must* be released constructs a blocked masculinity in order to legitimize various forms of release' (130, italics in original). My next chapter considers Wallace's self-aware engagement with notions of male 'liberation' in more detail. For now, I wish to emphasize how the dynamics Robinson spotlights, whereby a need for release retroactively legitimates the idea that male sexuality is blocked, informs their depictions of the male gaze. Wallace uses the male gaze to suggest the possibility of release from masochistic contracts that hamper a reader's ability to access – and acknowledge their capacity for carrying out – 'real' violence. The possibility of such release, though, is more important than its actuality, for in *Infinite Jest* especially Wallace works within masochistic dynamics to resist them.

The presumption here that men's desire to gaze stems from a sadism they harbour *as men*, moreover, furthers Wallace's suggestion that male sexual toxicity is immutable. Chapter 1 argued that for Wallace men must manage, rather than challenge, their sexual negativity, chiefly envisaged as their desire for casual sex and masturbation. In Chapter 2 I showed how this management extends to the more abject negativity of male homosexuality, whether in relation to its presence in the psychic life of heterosexual men, or in relation to male–male anal intercourse. In the current chapter I explore how Wallace's attempt to cultivate the male gaze in response to images of violence and suffering implies that sadism is an inevitable characteristic of male sexuality. True to the performative logic that characterizes his writing on this topic, Wallace's effort to reform the contract between reader and text on the basis of a (seeming) equality constructs the desire to gaze that he seeks to protect. If Chapter 3 acts as a pivot point in this book – from a concern with emotional intimacy to unmediated reality; from spermatic metaphors of investment and waste to those of blockage and release; from non-reproductivity to the prestige of violence – my interest in male sexual toxicity in Wallace's texts remains constant. The story 'B.I. #48', concerned as it is with an apparent sexual sadist, offers a good starting point for this investigation.

'B.I. #48' and the masochistic contract

Although 'B.I. #48' does not focus on spectatorship or visual culture, it is Wallace's most concentrated treatment of male sexuality in relation to ideas of masochism and contract. Indeed, this story articulates the same dissatisfaction with contracts – that they prevent access to 'real' experience and undermine individual will – that inform his attachment to male gazing. Like many (but not all) of the stories in the 'Brief Interviews' cycle, 'B.I. #48' takes the form of a one-sided conversation, in which the female interviewer Q – whose dialogue Wallace withholds from the reader – questions a man about sex. In 'B.I. #48', the interviewee explains the process by which he asks his female dates '"How would you feel about my tying you up?"' (1999h: 86). In addition, he analyses his motivations for this ostensibly sadistic activity, which he attributes primarily to an emotionally abusive mother. The details that he gives Q come to evoke the constraints Wallace suggests contracts pose, especially to ideas of male sexual violence. Reading this story closely, therefore, can help to illuminate the conceptual context in which Wallace mobilizes the male gaze. To the extent that he does so in opposition to Deleuzian ideas of masochistic contract, moreover, 'B.I. #48' is even more illuminating. Although Boswell reads this story as a parody of Lacanian psychoanalysis (2009: 192), it is more accurate, I believe, to interpret 'B.I. #48' as an oblique but precise response to Deleuze's arguments in his study *Masochism: Coldness and Cruelty*.

Through a critical reappraisal of the work of Leopold von Sacher-Masoch, most famously the author of *Venus in Furs*, Deleuze questions the idea of sadomasochism. Describing the conjunction of sadism and masochism as 'a semiological howler' (1989: 134), he seeks to emphasize their irreconcilability. Most significant for my purposes, and a central part of the theories put forth by Aaron that I outlined earlier, is Deleuze's argument that 'the masochist draws up contracts while the sadist abominates and destroys them' (20). In fact, 'a genuine sadist could never tolerate a masochistic victim. ... Neither would the masochist tolerate a truly sadistic torturer' (40–1). While a genuine sadist requires that their victim be non-consenting, masochistic fantasies require a torturer who is willing to play along with the *illusion* of such non-consent. The man of 'B.I. #48' has internalized such arguments. For example, he stresses that 'it is not ... S and M, and I am not a ... *sadist*, and I am not interested in subjects who wish to be ... *hurt*' (1999h: 88, italics in original). Moreover, he refers to his desires 'in the phrase of Marchesani and Van Slyke's theory of masochistic symbolism, as *proposing a contractual scenario*' (88, italics in original). In place of Marchesani and Van Slyke – who are theorists of Wallace's invention – one can read Deleuze, and specifically his argument that masochism involves a 'world of fantasy and symbols' (1989: 65) which rests on the contractual agreement to disavow its own fictitiousness.

If the interviewee of 'B.I. #48' is thus a pseudo-sadist – to the extent of binding his dates to 'bedposts [that] are decorative and not at all sturdy and could no doubt be snapped by a determined effort to free themselves' (Wallace 1999h: 96) – then his 'victims' are seemingly in control. As he explains further, 'The play is in ... freely and autonomously submitting to being tied up ... the contract ensures that all abdications of power are freely chosen' (90). This resonates with Michaels's discussion. The neoliberal objection to employment contracts, for Michaels, can be understood as an objection to 'the relation between a "Dominant" and a "Submissive" [which] would seem like the exemplary instance of asymmetry' (2017: 29). Reading masochism in the terms derived from Sacher-Masoch, however, reconfigures 'that relation as one that the Submissive desires and to which she consents' (29), and so 'renders them [i.e. Dominant and Submissive] symmetrical' (29). What makes this reconfiguration conducive to neoliberal thought is that it denies material inequalities in favour of the idea that we are all independent contractors, free to invest our human capital. Thus, to argue that the interviewee's 'victims' approach the erotic activity with the same (if not more) power as the man who ties them up downplays the fact that he is still the one who authors the scenario. Deleuze's masochist may enjoy the psychic power of knowing *they* control the fantasy, but they lack a material power that would afford them more determinate forms of social agency.

One could thus read 'B.I. #48' alongside Michaels's essay as critiquing neoliberal masochism, in that the story aligns the speaker's orchestration of a contractual scenario in which no one is actually bound with what turns out to be his psychological damage. There is a subtle difference between the two, however, that undercuts this reading. For Michaels the activity-in-passivity to be derived from masochistic contracts is questionable because, when applied to the employer-employee relationship, it masks capital's exploitation of labour by suggesting that the latter's willingness to work is a sign of its empowered self-determination. This is the belief that 'what workers really want is to be fucked' (2017: 31). By contrast, Wallace's objection to such activity-in-passivity is that the empowerment it produces is not empowering *enough*; to use Michaels' metaphor, instead of wanting to be fucked, the reader should be fucking.[4] The task for the reader is not what Michaels implicitly suggests it is for the worker – to realize the capital–labour relationship is exploitative, and so demolish it – but, rather, to seek forms of agency that activate their potential as bearers of (human) capital themselves. As I argue later on in this chapter in relation to *Infinite Jest*, this does not mean that Wallace escapes Michaels's objection, so much as that he proves its pertinence at a further remove. In other words, the activity that the novel tries to stoke in readers as male gazers itself comes to mask power disparities between the two. For now, it is enough to say that in 'B.I. #48' the closing revelation that the speaker occupies the role of masochist affirms this apparent need for a more empowering, because violent, individual agency.

Having explained to Q the process of tying up his dates, and of then asking them to assure him that they know he will not 'betray or abuse the power I've been ceded' (1999h: 97), the scenario reaches 'a sustained climax which persists for exactly as long as it takes me to extract these assurances from her' (97). If this language is suggestive of an orgasmic build-up, not only does its consummation – in the form of his 'victim's' assurances – counter any sense of phallic aggression, but so does the fact that 'I weep. It is then that I weep' (97). Despite being 'restricted … by the bonds [he's] made' (97), his dates ultimately occupy the role of (pseudo-) sadist rather than masochist – for it is they, in their solicited assurance, who allow the speaker to indulge in his suffering. Wallace hints at this in an earlier slip-of-the-tongue – the man's psychological complexes force him into 'contracted rituals where … control [is] ceded and then returned of my own free will. [Laughter.] Of the subject's, rather. Will' (94, third brackets in the original). Hence Severs is inaccurate to read 'B.I. #48' as an example of how Wallace makes 'contracts' mastery the province of sadists, characters who inflict pain and call it pleasure' (2017a: 149).[5] Far from being proof of his sadism, the speaker's need to form contracts is part of a convoluted attempt to surrender his will to partners who, though immobilized, can stand in judgement of his suffering.

Convolution is indeed the key term here, as it points to an aspect of the neoliberal objection to contracts that eludes Michaels's focus, but which is important to 'B.I. #48'. This is the constraint that arises less from the disciplinary nature of contracts, and more from their excessive obfuscation. As Gerard Hanlon observes, 'A dominant neo-liberal motif has been to burn red tape' (2016: 179), understood as bureaucracy and regulation that reduces efficiency. In 'B.I. #48' the speaker's use of 'sustained and increasingly annoying f.f.' (1999h: 91), that is, the 'flexion of upraised fingers to signify tone quotes' (85), is evocative of a form of interpersonal red tape. The phrase 'flexion of upraised fingers' (85), and variations or abbreviations upon it, appear fifty-seven times in this thirteen-page story, suggesting the contractual mesh in which its speaker resides. At first sight, this constant self-reference indicates the speaker's attempt to control the interpretation of his speech, hence Severs's suggestion that he exemplifies the 'legalistic tyrants, even fascists' (2017a: 221) in Wallace's texts who use contract language. Yet, given how the speaker is in fact a masochist in the guise of a (pseudo) sadist, it is more accurate to read his finger flexions as a sign of his subservience to scenarios that, though of his own making, undercut his individual agency. Hence the irony of his and the story's final sentence – 'sometimes one just has to go with the mood' (Wallace 1999h: 97). The contractual red tape with which he surrounds himself makes any such impassioned action unlikely.

Moreover, Wallace suggests that breaking the contract by demystifying its mechanics does little to cut through said tape. 'B.I. #48' is one long demystification of the processes that masochistic fantasies normally keep in the dark – chiefly, the fact that the pain inflicted is with a victim's consent, who is a complicit party in the fantasy's unfolding. As the interviewee puts it, 'I know precisely what the whole thing is about' (1999h: 88). This echoes Wallace's complaint that metafiction only offers a faux transcendence of textual mediation, in what he argues is the misguided notion 'that revelation of imprisonment led to freedom' (1997b: 67). The speaker's knowledge of his desire to form masochistic contracts cannot free him from what Wallace implies are its debilitating effects. The need arises, therefore, for a more effective means of challenging such contracts, which as I will show soon, Wallace explores through the male gaze. When issues of vision do appear in 'B.I. #48', they reiterate the speaker's inability to act sadistically. He explains how, as his dates process his proposal, 'I answer their intense gaze with a bland gaze of my own. … But again please note I am in no way aggressive or threatening about it. This is what I meant by [f.f.] *bland gaze*' (1999h: 92, italics and brackets in original). For Wallace, contemporary American culture makes the male gaze bland on account of how the same self-reflexivity the man in 'B.I.

#48' exhibits has spread throughout popular media. Wallace directs most of his blame for this state of affairs at television.

Tongue scrapers and born oglers

In 'E Unibus Pluram: Television and U.S. Fiction' Wallace discusses the effect that television has on spectatorship. Though his chief focus is on writers – 'oglers' who 'lurk and stare' (1997b: 22) and about whom there is 'something creepy, somehow. Almost predatory' (22) – his arguments also aim for a broader cultural relevance. For 'Joe Briefcase', Wallace's 'average U.S. lonely person' (22), television is 'almost like voyeurism' (23) because it allows for the illusion of 'espial on the forbidden' (45). However, in contrast to 'genuine Peeping Tomism' (23), 'television is performance' (23), so what appears to be a forbidden reality is in fact pre-fabricated. In this light, Wallace describes television in ways that imply a masochistic relationship between audience and screen, as 'illusions of voyeurism and privileged access require serious *complicity* from the viewer' (24, italics mine). Thus, the illusion of true voyeurism rests on a complicit understanding of how this voyeurism is fake; we are only a 'pseudo-spy, when we watch', but 'we choose to ignore' (24) this fact in order to enjoy the illusion. Wallace's descriptions evoke the masochistic contracts that Aaron argues characterize spectatorship. As my analysis of 'B.I. #48' suggested, his suspicion of these dynamics arises from a belief that they hamper an individual's ability to experience – and feel as though they can perpetuate and enjoy – an authentic male sexual violence. In 'E Unibus Pluram' Wallace argues that this problem is exacerbated by a phenomenon he calls 'meta-watching' (33).

He uses this term to refer to a culture of self-aware spectatorship. Television has helped to create this culture, Wallace argues, by incorporating the self-referential techniques of postmodern fiction. Consequently, meta-watching forestalls a spectator's ability to believe that what they see on television is real – or, at the very least, that it points to 'versions of "real life" made prettier, sweeter, livelier' (33). Indeed, television 'has become immune to charges that it lacks any meaningful connection to the world outside it' (33). The meta-watching that this self-referentiality encourages, for Wallace, is a 'disease from which ... watchers, and readers all suffer' (49). This is because such a 'metastasis of self-conscious watching' (34) has led – in what is now a commonplace in Wallace Studies – to an emotionally alienating hyper-reflexivity. Most important for my purposes is how Wallace envisages this process in terms that are suggestive of masochistic contracts. For 'we are responsible [for this suffering] basically because nobody is holding any weapons on us forcing us to spend amounts of time second only to sleep' (37) watching television. Spectators are not subject to sadism – no one forces them to watch at gun point – but willing victims of the emotional suffering that meta-watching creates. Hence 'the very idea of pleasure', understood as the ability to suspend disbelief in illusions, 'has been undercut' (59), and in its place has arisen the substitute (and for Wallace, paltry) satisfaction of knowing one is not being fooled.

In this respect, the 'quiet psychic intercourse between images and oglers' (53) that spectatorship depends upon is no longer quiet. Instead spectators for Wallace now occupy a position similar to that of the interviewee in 'B.I. #48'; they are thoroughly aware that passivity before screen media is the result of a consensual decision. Further, if masochistic theories of spectatorship stress how, in Aaron's words, masochism 'is an active desire played out through passivity' (2007: 52), then spectators' awareness of this fact allows them to manipulate their own activity-in-passivity as a form of capital. In other words, spectators will not watch texts that do not promise a return on their spectatorial investment. As a result, for Wallace when 'networks do occasionally abandon time-tested formulas the Audience usually punishes them for it by not watching the shows' (1997b: 40). This is important because it suggests how his objection to masochistic modes of spectatorship is, in part, indicative of his suspicion that entrepreneurial logics have crept into the relationship between texts and spectators. There is thus room to read Wallace's descriptions of spectatorship as being anti-neoliberal, as he scorns the entrepreneurial approach to texts that, in Rachel Greenwald Smith's words, posit that 'investment of energy needs to be justified by the return of readerly reward or pleasure' (2015: 36). That said, his problem with the faux nature of this agency – that it is acted out through passivity – trumps his problem with its entrepreneurial implications.

One can see this in his discussion, towards the end of 'E Unibus Pluram', of George Gilder's *Life After Television: The Coming Transformation of Media and American Life* (1990). Ostensibly, the scepticism that Wallace shows for Gilder's arguments suggests his distance from the idea that contracts suppress individual agency. Indeed, he quotes Gilder's belief that the technological limitations of television means that it relies on 'a "master-slave" architecture' (Wallace 1997b: 71). Gilder's solution – technological advancements that will give viewers more control over what they watch – accords with the idea of making them more entrepreneurial. As their 'own manipulator of video-bits' (73), spectators can choose to invest their attention only in those texts which provide a pleasurable return. Yet this solution strikes Wallace as 'wildly unrealistic' (74): Gilder's 'new tech would end "the passivity of mere reception"' (74), but it would not end 'the dependency that is part of my relation to TV or the impotent irony I must use to pretend I'm not dependent' (75). Thus, though Wallace is sceptical of Gilder's desire to allow spectators to 'break from the coffle and choose freely' (74), he still subscribes to the idea that television *does* dominate audiences – albeit, in ways that convince them that their dependency is a sign of their empowerment. A more genuine agency that will challenge screen media's domination of spectators is possible for Wallace, one that, as I will demonstrate, he associates with sadistic male gazing.

Wallace sees the possibility of such agency in the films of David Lynch, which in their depictions of sexual violence try to remind male spectators of their propensity for same. Before I explore how this works, though, it is important to consider the role of images of violence and suffering in his work more generally. For the violence that Wallace lauds in Lynch's films, and which I argue he tries to replicate in *Infinite Jest*, is an exception to his otherwise pessimistic estimation of extreme visual content. His most sustained focus on this is in *Oblivion*'s closing story, 'The Suffering Channel'. In part about a television channel showing 'real life still and moving images of [the] most intense available moments of human anguish' (2004d: 291), the story suggests how 'shock, grotesquerie, or irreverence' (Wallace 1997b: 40) lose their power to affect spectators when they become implicated in the marketing strategies of entertainment industries. However, a more productive example of this process appears in *Infinite Jest* itself, namely in Hal's account, in one of his school assignments, on 'the fall and rise of millennial U.S. advertising' (1996: 411).[6] This vignette relates the circumstances in which television in *Infinite Jest* comes to be replaced by a technology much like Gilder's proposed 'telecomputer' (Gilder 1990, cited in Wallace 1997b: 72). Here the most disturbing images of suffering only lubricate forms of spectatorship that, in their focus upon a spectator's agency-in-passivity in a consensual framework, follow the logic of masochistic contract.

The disturbing images in question appear in commercials for aspirin, liposuction and tongue scrapers, and all utilize bodily suffering that spectators find 'so excruciating that they were buying the product but recoiling from the ads' (1996: 412). Adverts for 'NoCoat Inc.' (413), in particular, with their 'close-up on an extended tongue that must be seen to be believed' (414), 'crossed some kind of psychoaesthetic line' (413). Seemingly, then, these images of suffering sadistically affect spectators, for they are 'so violently unpleasing to look at that they … awakened legions of these suddenly violently repelled and disturbed viewers to the power and agency their thumbs actually afforded them' (413). The irony that such agency amounts to changing the channel is compounded by how cable providers launch a campaign attacking 'the "passivity" of ... pussified Network broadcasters', by 'extoll[ing] the "empoweringly American choice" of 500-plus esoteric cable options' (412). Not only does spectators' power to change the channel make them active in their passivity, but cable providers manipulate this power to sell products. Wallace's critique of Gilder's idea that better technology will end the spectator's passivity applies here, locked as audiences are into the '*appearance of freedom*' (1031, italics in original). Hence 'violently unpleasing' (413) images in this scenario, rather than reminding spectators of their ability to perpetuate violence, only further implicate them in a masochistic subservience to their screens.

The result of this use of images like tongue scrapers is the rise of InterLace, the Gilder-esque televisual technology behind which stands Lace-Forche – a 'woman called by Microsoft's Gates "The Killer-App Queen" and by Blockbuster's Huizenga "The only woman I personally fear"' (415). After teaming up with 'ad-maestro P. Tom Veals' (415), Lace-Forche sets out a vision for empowering the 'vox- and digitus-populi' (416) in a way that highlights her gender. For 'what if, Veals's spokeswoman ruminated aloud, what if the viewer could become her/his own programming director; what if s/he could define the very entertainment-happiness it was her/his right to pursue?' (416, italics in original) The idea that Lace-Forche is merely Veals's 'spokeswoman' is misleading given that she has had InterLace 'idling ever since she'd first foreseen broadcast apocalypse in the Nunhagen ads' (415) for aspirin, and that it is she who 'ruminate[s] aloud' here undercuts Veals's apparent seniority. One can attribute 'her/his' and 's/he' to her, the repetition of the former implying that these terms signal more than just gender parity. By pointedly prioritizing a feminine pronoun, they signal how Wallace links the intensified passivity that arises from InterLace with women. In addition to its gender traditionalism, this link implies that treating images of violence as little more than a way to sell products emasculates male spectators.

These dynamics echo my investigation of pornification in Chapter 1, notably in how Wallace urges readers to question women's consumerism. Moreover, his comment in 'Big Red Son' that pornography's need to retain an aura of unacceptability despite its cultural prominence means that 'the real horizon late-'90s porn is heading towards is the Snuff Film' (2005a: 28) resonates with my current discussion. One can indeed interpret Wallace's concern with visual extremes in the context of his treatment of pornification; it is no accident that the broadcast proposals for the Suffering Channel mention 'MCI Premium's Adult

Film Channel rate variance per prorate' (2004d: 291) as a model. A difference here, of course, is that pornification as I have examined it previously pertained to texts that solicit literal sexual expenditures. By contrast, with advertisements for tongue scrapers and liposuction it is a case of soliciting a more general prurience. Helen Hester argues that, with the rise of genres such as torture porn, ideas of the pornographic have started to refer to 'a realm of representation that not only sporadically eschews or displaces sex, but that *need not be sexually explicit at all*' (2014: 15, italics in original). Wallace's notion that hardcore pornography will naturally lead to snuff films of the kind that appear on the Suffering Channel supports Hester's argument. Still, that he approaches these images via a concern for men's threatened capability for sadistic gazing confirms how male sexuality remains a key reference point.

Indeed, the sadistic gazing that Wallace suggests televisual culture inhibits in 'E Unibus Pluram' is distinctly reminiscent of the male gaze. As the earlier descriptions of a lost ability to 'ogle' in a 'creepy' and 'almost predatory' way imply, the voyeurism that television endangers is a stereotypically male form of sadistic looking. Though Wallace notes that 'born oglers' (1997b: 81) include those worried about 'whether their shirttail might be hanging out of their fly, [or] whether there's maybe lipstick on their teeth' (21), this (heteronormative) gender parity does not bear out. In fact, alongside his comment that television has hold of 'my generation's cojones' (41), his invocation of the parodically banal Joe Briefcase, and his recourse to the phrase 'Peeping-Tomism' (23), it is clear that the ogling that Wallace presents as under threat is specifically male. That it is also heterosexual, moreover, is implied in the image he uses to warn against Gilder's interactive technologies; namely, he wonders 'who's going to want to take such stuff [i.e. guides for aesthetic worth] seriously in ecstatic post-TV life, with Kim Basinger waiting to be interacted with?' (76) From the perspective of 1993 (the publication year of 'E Unibus Pluram' in *The Review of Contemporary Fiction*), Basinger's fame rested on her status as a sex symbol in films such as the erotic thriller *9 ½ Weeks* (1986) or the spoof comedy *Wayne's World 2* (1993), where she plays a character named Honey Hornée. Wallace's mention of her, then, reaffirms how the 'erotically charged' (23) voyeurism he believes television undercuts is a characteristic of heterosexual men in particular.

Too much might seem to rest here on comments that appear incidental to Wallace's central arguments in 'E Unibus Pluram' concerning irony, meta-fiction and television. His at times cartoonish expressions – for example, complaining that television has 'a hold on my generation's cojones' (41) – also encourage one to take these comments as mere slapstick flourishes. Nevertheless, they indicate the specifically hetero-masculine frameworks through which Wallace advances his arguments, frameworks, I argue, that fundamentally colour his understanding of spectatorship. By focusing on similar aspects in 'David Lynch Keeps his Head', it becomes even more apparent how important male sexuality is in this regard. For Wallace, Lynch's films hold out the promise of challenging the masochistic contracts that, he suggests, undermine the power of violent images to remind spectators of their own potential sadism. Reading this essay in light of 'E Unibus Pluram', as well as alongside his comments elsewhere on mainstream cinema, allows me to better coordinate Wallace's own attempts to solicit male gazes in *Infinite Jest*. As will become clear, Wallace draws energy from what he considers to be Lynch's disregard for spectatorial contracts. He does so, however, in order to appropriate those aspects that gel best with the neoliberal desire to make contracts between film and spectator, or reader and novel, ones of seeming equality.

Gazing with David Lynch

In 'David Lynch Keeps His Head', Wallace explores spectatorship in ways that are reminiscent of his arguments in 'E Unibus Pluram', albeit in relation to cinema rather than television. Indeed, Wallace's descriptions of spectatorship here suggest that both mediums share similar masochistic dynamics. Ostensibly, 'movies are an authoritarian medium. They vulnerabilize you and then dominate you' (1997d: 169). This seems to conflict with his suggestions in 'E Unibus Pluram' that nothing forces people to watch so much television. Yet, the fact that 'part of the magic of going to a movie is surrendering to it, *letting it* dominate you' (1997d: 169, italics mine), implies that a spectator's consent is vital to such domination taking place. In this light, Wallace conceives of cinema and television as both depending upon the spectator's ability to pretend they are being 'done to' against their will. This is not to say that Wallace simply equates the two. Hering is arguably overgenerous in describing Wallace's criticisms of television as being 'rather reductive' (2016: 176). Although Wallace displays similar disapproval for certain films (as I will show shortly in relation to *Terminator 2: Judgement Day* (1991)), his texts also allow for the idea, as Sayers points out, that art film in particular can 'reverse the sleep-inducing effect of [commercial] entertainment' (2014: 112). Wallace is attracted to Lynch's work because it complicates the distinctions between 'art film and commercial film' (Wallace 1997d: 170), but he values its ability to wake spectators up to realities they would rather not face. Chiefly, his films remind them of their propensity for male gazing.

Discussing the relationship between Jeffrey (Kyle Maclachlan) and Frank Booth (Dennis Hopper) in *Blue Velvet* (1986), Wallace suggests that with Jeffrey 'we too peeked through those closet vents at Frank's feast of sexual fascism' (207), as the latter rapes Isabella Rossellini's character, Dorothy. When Frank turns to Jeffrey in a later scene to tell him that '"*You're like me*"', Wallace 'just ha[s] to sit there and be uncomfortable' in his awareness that Frank is also talking to him (207, italics in original). In a footnote he then states that 'I don't think it's an accident that of the grad-school friends I first saw *Blue Velvet* with ... the two who said they felt like either the movie was really sick or they were really sick or both they and the movie were really sick ... were both *male*' (207, italics in original). *Blue Velvet*'s depiction of sexual violence, Wallace implies, resonates with men in particular, who find 'the sadism and degeneracy he [i.e. Jeffrey] witnesses compelling and somehow erotic' (167). That he does not entertain that men might identify with Dorothy – and so with a suffering, masochistic position – compounds how his interest lies in the film's power to force men into acknowledging their capability and desire for sadism. Indeed, 'nothing sickens me like seeing on-screen some of the very parts of myself I've gone to the movies to try to forget about' (166). Film spectatorship may work within a masochistic dynamic, but *Blue Velvet*, for Wallace, shows how an artist can challenge this in order to sadistically affect spectators; in this instance, men whom Lynch forces to confront their own desire to gaze.

Wallace attributes this sadistic power to the fact that Lynch's depictions of violence are 'qualitatively different from Hollywood or even anti-Hollywood's hip cartoon-violence. Lynch's violence always tries to *mean* something' (165, italics in original). Wallace points to the films of Quentin Tarantino as exemplifying the 'violently ironic' (165) character of anti-Hollywood in particular. For 'unlike Tarantino, D. Lynch knows that an act of violence in an American film has, through repetition and desensitization, lost the ability to refer to anything but itself' (165). By implication Lynch's violence refers outside of itself, and refuses to flatter the spectator's knowledge of 'hip cartoon-violence', so that it can '*mean* something' for men especially. In this regard Tarantino's 'hip' violence, by affirming the spectator's ability to get the joke or understand a reference, has much the same effect as the meta-watching Wallace describes in 'E Unibus Pluram'. To reuse a line from that essay, Tarantino's violence 'lacks any meaningful connection to the world outside it' (33). This suggests that, by forestalling the spectator's ability to believe that such violence is real, or at least points to the real, films like Tarantino's *Reservoir Dogs* (1992) flatter the spectator's awareness of being within cinematic conventions. As a result, for Wallace the scene in said film 'where Michael Madsen, dancing to a cheesy '70s tune, *cuts off a hostage's ear*' (164, italics in original) can only register as an ironic intertextual reference (indeed, to the severed ear in *Blue Velvet*). Tarantino leaves the spectator's own possible desire to cut off people's ears unprovoked.

Wallace goes on to write in 'David Lynch Keeps His Head' that 'if we know on some level what a movie *wants* from us, we can erect certain internal defenses that let us choose how much of ourselves we give away to it' (170–1, italics in original). With Lynch's films, by contrast, 'you don't feel like you're entering into any of the standard unspoken/unconscious contracts you normally enter into' (170). Apparently, then, Lynch bypasses the masochistic contracts that underpin spectatorship and sadistically affects male spectators as a result. Yet the qualifying phrase '*you don't feel like* you're entering' (170, italics mine) these contracts forestalls the idea that Lynch contravenes the spectator's consent entirely, implying as it does that the contract is still at work but without the spectator's knowledge. This contrasts with the speaker's self-awareness in 'B.I. #48', and Wallace's arguments in 'E Unibus Pluram' that spectators only invest in texts which promise them a satisfying return. If Lynch's films create the impression of an unmediated connection between film and spectator, they do so in ways that deny spectators the ability to manage their own consent in being 'dominated'. In this sense, his films, for Wallace, work within masochistic contracts to resist them. Frank's rape of Dorothy in *Blue Velvet*, then, confronts male spectators with a seemingly genuine sadism, unhampered by the psychic defences that contracts allow for.

It is not just anti-Hollywood, however, against which Wallace contrasts Lynch's films. He also critiques mainstream Hollywood for pandering to audience expectations. This is most evident in his comments on how 'most U.S. mystery and suspense and crime and horror films … massage … our moral certainties' (210). Consequently, 'when a filmmaker fails to wrap his product up in the appropriate verity-confirming fashion … we feel an unspoken but very important covenant has been violated' (210). This implies that masochistic modes of spectatorship are conducive to genre film – indeed, as it is 'inarguable, axiomatic' (209) that these kind of films conclude in forms of 'commercial catharsis' (203), 'the discomfort we feel at [for example] "suspense" movies is perceived as a pleasant discomfort' (210). For the film scholar Thomas Schatz, if 'genre exists as a sort of tacit "contract" between filmmakers and audience, the genre film is an actual event that honors such a contract' (1981: 16). The applicability of this observation to the masochistic contract is clear: the spectator disavows their knowledge that what they see is not real in the expectation that a film will fulfil what Schatz calls a 'system of conventions' (6). Notably, Wallace's complaint lies with the conventionality of these processes, not with the creation of suspense or 'pleasant discomfort' (1997d: 210) itself. To see how this informs his desire to solicit the male gaze, it is useful to turn to his reading of James Cameron's *Terminator 2*.

In 'The (As It Were) Seminal Importance of *Terminator 2*', Wallace argues that this film is responsible for 'inaugurating what's become this decade's new genre of big-budget film: Special Effects Porn' (2012d: 177). This is because such films consist of 'half a dozen or so isolated, spectacular scenes ... of riveting, sensuous payoff – strung together via ... often hilariously insipid narrative' (177). Wallace's analogy supports Hester's notion that '"porn" has become attached to a surprisingly diverse set of texts and affects, few of which actually put the sexual body front and center' (14). In place of the violence that Wallace conceptually links to hardcore porn in 'Big Red Son' or 'The Suffering Channel', though, the payoff here pertains to computer-generated spectacles. Most notable for my purposes is that he describes these spectacles as payoffs, in the sense of the film industry's desire for profit, but also in the sense of the genre film's expected pleasures. Yet for Wallace, the pre-sell in 'the popular entertainment media before *T2* even goes into production' (183) means that 'one of the few things that keep us on the edge of our seats during the movie is our suspense about whether James Cameron can possibly weave a plausible, non-cheesy narrative' (183). If Hollywood's reliance on lucrative genre conventions inhibits its power to challenge spectators, the meta-watchful context of *Terminator 2* further ameliorates this power to the point that, for Wallace, its products follow the same formulas as 'hardcore cheapies' (177).

Wallace's spermatic puns in this essay – namely, why *Terminator 2* is *seminally* important – are also significant. He concludes by noting that 'popular entertainment media report that Cameron's new *Titanic*, currently in post-production, is (once again) the most expensive and technically ambitious film of all time. A nation is even now pricing trenchcoats and lubricants in anticipation of its release' (188–9). This image of a stereotypical male porn consumer compounds Wallace's idea of 'the F/X Porn genre' (182), whereby male orgasm figures as a metaphor for Hollywood's generic pleasures. Further to this, the more oblique pun here – that these consumers wait in 'anticipation of its release' (189) – is telling of how male orgasm, masochistic/generic contracts and suspense intertwine. *Titanic* promises the same meta-watchful awareness as *Terminator 2* did, where an abundance of industry pre-sell reduces the suspense available for male spectators to the level of routinized ejaculation. Hence the irony of Wallace's parting remark: the release of coming has little value when the anticipation involved is so dependable that spectators can prepare for it in advance. Echoing the dynamics I explored in Chapter 1 concerning how pornification's easy gratifications devalue male sexuality, Wallace suggests that F/X Porn undermines the tension and suspense that – for him, at least – makes ejaculation worthwhile.

By contrast, Wallace asserts that *Blue Velvet*'s 'real climax, and its point … comes unusually early' (207), a remark he footnotes with the single word '(prematurely!)' (207). This climax pertains to the aforementioned moment when Frank tells Jeffrey '"*You're like me*"' (207, italics in original). By describing what he believes is the film's central point – forcing spectators to recognize how, like Jeffrey, they have a propensity for sadistic gazing – through an image of premature ejaculation, Wallace distinguishes Lynch's violence from mainstream Hollywood's generic pleasures. Further, this image also undercuts the figurative value of male ejaculation to the narrative's progress, and so to the catharsis that a spectator would expect from a less challenging film. As Wallace goes on to note, Jeffrey's response to Frank's statement is to punch him 'in the nose. … In the film's audience, I, to whom Frank has also just claimed kinship, have no such luxury of *violent release*; I pretty much just have to sit there and be uncomfortable' (207, italics mine). Having prematurely climaxed, *Blue Velvet* denies spectators what films such as *Terminator 2* cater for: an ejaculatory, aesthetic satisfaction that confirms their preconceptions, in this instance, that they are different 'from sadists and fascists and voyeurs' (207). That Wallace must sit and feel uncomfortable signals how this furthers the film's power to implicate him in its sexual violence.

In *Infinite Jest*'s scenes of rape, suicide and torture, Wallace pursues many of the same effects that he lauds in Lynch's films; chiefly, their attempt to remind spectators, as he puts in the Lynch essay, of 'the psychic spaces in which [straight, male] people are capable of evil' (203). More specifically, these scenes manipulate the masochistic contract between an imagined male spectator/reader and text to remind the former of their propensity for sadistic gazing. But there are important differences between Lynch's methods and those deployed in *Infinite Jest*. Wallace leavens his enthusiasm for what he describes as the 'sick' (166) nature of Lynch's films with an awareness that, while 'some of them are brilliant and unforgettable; others are jejune and incoherent and bad' (166). Beyond this explicit equivocation a more important difference arises from the fact that, although Lynch can remind male spectators of their capacity for sadistic gazing, he does not remind them of their contractedness. The effect of feeling 'like you're

[not] entering into any of the standard unspoken/unconscious contracts' (170) with Lynch may be positive for helping to remind men of their sadism, but it does not assist in reforming contracts so much as (providing an impression of) doing without them. In the passages of *Infinite Jest* I examine shortly, the point is not just to remind a male reader of their sadism, but in doing so, to transform the masochistic contract between reader and text from one of dominance-submission to one of seeming equality.

To return to Michaels, neoliberalism 'won't just let contract go … because it's only employment contracts that it really wants to get rid of' (2017: 31). The point is to replace a 'liberal relation between employer and employee' (31) with 'the neoliberal relationship between independent contractors' (31), because in doing so, 'real capital saves itself a lot of money' (31). *Infinite Jest*'s reasons for transforming contract in this way do not arise from a desire to save resources (the scenes I look at are some of the novel's most descriptively rich), but out of an ideological conviction that Michaels's readiness to ascribe blame to 'real capital' elides. Wallace tries to remind male readers of their propensity for sadistic gazing because contracts in which no party dominates are, ostensibly, more respectful of individual will. Additionally, by placing text and reader on a seemingly equal footing when it comes to such gazing, Wallace implies that reformulating contracts thus facilitates a greater intimacy with an unmediated, 'real' violence. For whereas *Blue Velvet* depicts sexual violence so that 'the colors are so lush and the *mise en scene* so detailed and sensual' (1997d: 206), similar scenes in *Infinite Jest* – despite their lushness – figure violence as a reality that escapes representation. By looking at an AA speaker's tale of her sister's rape, Joelle's suicide attempt, and Gene Fackelmann's torture, one can see how Wallace works within but against masochistic contracts to position a male reader and the text as equally humbled in the face of elusive depravities.

'*Cruel* is spelled with a *u*, he remembered'

What Bachner describes as the prestige of violence in contemporary American fiction is based on something of a paradox. Violence in the texts she examines is 'the extralinguistic ontological order' (2011: 4) which said texts 'gesture [toward] but insist they cannot reach' (4). Hence, 'violence remains outside, above, or below the reach of language' (3), but we only know this because writers keep insisting on its inviolability through language. The scenes from *Infinite Jest* that I look at here illustrate this paradox. Despite their linguistic density, they represent the violence in question as – to borrow a cinematic image from Wallace's description of the end of *Infinite Jest* – 'projected by the reader somewhere beyond the right frame' (Wallace, cited in Max 2012a: 319). Wallace uses this elusiveness to suggest that reader and text are therefore equally frustrated in their attempt to access such violence. Reminding them of their propensity for sadistic male gazing, these scenes reconfigure the contract between reader and text along the neoliberal lines of a seeming equality. That this means reforming rather than voiding said contract, moreover, is evident in how the rape, suicide and torture that I explore mobilize a masochistic suspense of the kind, in fact, that Wallace argues F/X Porn films like *Terminator 2* neuter. In the spermatic imagery of these passages, Wallace gestures towards orgasmic climaxes he never provides, compounding the impression of a figurative impotence before unmediated realities that *Infinite Jest* shares with its reader-cum-male gazer.

To understand what makes this suspense masochistic, one has to return to Deleuze. Dissatisfied with attempts to explain masochism in terms of its content (chiefly, the apparent reversal of pain into pleasure), Deleuze proposes that one can consider it more accurately in formal terms. Paramount here is the idea that 'masochism is a state of waiting' (1989: 71), whether for 'the whip or the sword that never strikes, the fur that never discloses the flesh, the heel that is forever descending on the victim' (70), or so on. Such waiting, says Deleuze, can be divided into two currents: that which is *awaited*, 'something essentially tardy, always late and always postponed' (71), and that which is *expected*, 'on which depends the speeding up of the awaited object' (71). Consequently, 'the masochist waits for pleasure as something that is bound to be late, and expects pain as the condition that will finally ensure … the advent of pleasure' (71). As Aaron explains, 'Rather than pleasure being achieved and enhanced by the wait being over … pleasure is heightened through anticipation itself (excitement grows with expectation of the desired object's arrival … having it could only be disappointing)' (60). The scenes from *Infinite Jest* that I will now analyse illuminate this dynamic. Their accumulating violence figures the expectation of pain as an anticipatory prerequisite for awaited pleasure, which – and the following pun is significant – never actually comes.

This is clear in an AA speaker's tale of how she witnessed, and became complicit in, her stepfather's repeated rape of her paralysed stepsister. Wallace moves from descriptions of the sister's formlessness, to the revelation that the father forces her to wear a Raquel Welch mask, to how the speaker hides evidence of the abuse from her stepmother, to how the sister enjoys being raped, and so on. Delivered in one paragraph over four and a half pages, this gradual increase of information subjects readers to the expectation of ever greater depravities. That the speaker removes the mask from her stepsister after each rape, moreover, makes her complicit in the abuse: the father 'never once acknowledged the adopted daughter's little post-incestuous tidyings-up. It's the kind of sick unspoken complicity characteristic of wildly dysfunctional families' (1996: 372). This 'sick unspoken complicity' also extends to the reader, whom Wallace positions as gazing at the events in question. Before she begins her tale, the speaker's admission that she was 'a stripper and semi-whore at the infamous Naked I Club' (370) causes 'a number of male eyes in the audience [to] flash with sudden recognition, and despite all willed restraint automatically do that crawly north-to-south thing down her body' (370). Wallace frames the story from the start, then, in the context of the male gaze. This diegetic recognition of being implicated in her suffering, and the subsequent compulsion to gaze regardless, models a similar response for the reader.[7]

If the passage's breakneck delivery and proliferative detail (the sister does not just wear a mask, but 'a cheesy rubber Raquel Welch full-head pull-on mask' (371)) urges the reader to become caught up in the suspense of what fresh indignity Wallace will relate next, this expectation does not result in any final payoff. In fact, echoing the way in which *Blue Velvet* climaxes prematurely, Wallace includes an image of male orgasm that suggests a lack of release. When the speaker realizes her sister has enjoyed being raped, we are told that her 'face looked post-coital sort of the way you'd imagine the vacuole and optica of a protozoan looking post-coital after it's shuddered and shot its mono-cellular load into the cold waters of some really old sea' (373). Far from signalling escape, where the pain the speaker's auditors endure in listening to her would give way to the pleasure of relief from such, this prehistoric ejaculation is just another step in the unfolding description of her suffering. For the passage does not end with this 'climax', but continues with more revelations. She relates, for instance, how her stepmother tasks her with lifting the stepsister from a 'never-mentioned wheelchair' (373) so they can worship a photo of Bernini's statue *The Ecstasy of St Theresa*. Affirming the masochistic suspense, then, this protozoan orgasm forestalls the possibility that awaited pleasure will eventually succeed the suffering being related.

It is from within this masochism, however, that Wallace implicates the reader into gazing at a male sexual violence beyond representation. In the speaker's telling, her sister's expression of 'carnal bliss' (373) is the same expression as that found on Bernini's statue, 'that exact same shuddering-protozoan look beyond pleasure or pain' (373). Given that Wallace genders this protozoan as being male (shooting its 'mono-cellular load' (373)), one can conclude that the text interprets St Theresa's ecstasy in terms of *male* pleasure. This is significant because Wallace's mention of Bernini's statue recalls Jacques Lacan's invocation of it in his essay 'God and the *Jouissance* of T̶h̶e̶ Woman' (1985). Notoriously, Lacan argues the statue epitomizes a feminine pleasure that cannot be grasped by a masculine signifying economy.[8] By focalizing this non-representable feminine bliss in terms of a male protozoan ejaculation, and one that emerges as the result of the stepfather's abuse, Wallace suggests that what actually eludes grasp here are the effects of male sexual violence. For the novel, and the interpolated reader-as-gazer, this sadism is beyond comprehension. In turn, both the text and reader can only look on at an 'unspeakably, unforgettably ghastly and horrid and scarring' (1996: 373) scene, aware of their own inability to fully experience it but compelled to gaze at its intimation of unmediated, 'real' violence nonetheless.

Accordingly, this scene places readers on the same level as the text. The masochistic contract between them does not entail the former's subservience to the latter, but rather their equal standing. That the speaker's story reforms rather than cancels this contract, moreover, is evident in how the scene prevents readers from forgetting (as Wallace argues that Lynch's films do) that they are still within a contract with what they are reading. For in the midst of the speaker's story of how 'she was forced to gaze … on Its lit-up paralytic post-diddle face' (373), endnote 142 interrupts the heretofore continuous prose with the fact that 'the speaker doesn't actually use the terms *thereon, most assuredly*, or *operant limbic system*, though she really had, before, said *chordate phylum*' (1026, italics in original). This endnote compounds the free indirect discourse, the speaker's voice blurring with that of the implied narrator. More than this, though, such seemingly incidental information momentarily takes the reader out of the speaker's immersive tale. Consequently, this endnote acts as a reminder of the fact that, not only is the violence here mediated, but by continuing to consume it, one does so voluntarily. The passage foregrounds a reader's contracted position at the same time as its intimation of unrepresentable male sexual violence suggests 'he' is not bound to the text; he is, rather, a complicit participant, gazing of his own free will.

This is what it means to say that Wallace works within but against the masochistic contract between reader and text. The scene I have just unpacked is thoroughly masochistic in the way that it subjects readers to a suspenseful suffering that lacks payoff. When the novel breaks from the speaker's tale, in fact, her AA audience can only sit in 'empathetic distress' (374). Significantly, by positioning the reader as a complicit male gazer on the scene, and with reference to a violence that 'he' and the text are unable to fathom, Wallace reworks the masochistic contract from one of subservience (where the reader passively receives details of the speaker's suffering, no matter the supposed activity-in-passivity this might entail) to one of seeming equality (where a reader, though contracted to the text, actively tries to gaze at a sadism that eludes them both). I say 'seeming' because, for this to signify as equality, one has to ignore the overwhelming descriptive arsenal that Wallace, unlike the reader, has recourse to in describing the sister's abuse. If the neoliberal logic of contract is to suggest that an unequal relationship between capital and labour is an equal relationship between independent human capitals, this maps on to how the speaker's tale figures the relationship between a maximalist, encyclopaedic novel and a reader as one of shared epistemological limits – and in regards to a knowledge of violence, moreover, that Wallace determines access to.

One can refine these points further, and show how the dynamics I identify signal a sustained rather than anomalous aesthetic strategy, by turning to two other scenes of violence and suffering in the novel. The first is Joelle's suicide attempt, which presents a range of interlinking images for the male gaze. Before Joelle moves to the bathroom where she tries to kill herself, 'she lets herself slide forward from Méliès' lap' (231). That she sits in a chair moulded into the shape of George Méliès evokes the iconic image of his film *A Trip to the Moon* (1902), which in light of her concern with how 'the moon never looked away' (222), positions it as a symbol for the gaze. Wallace reiterates this equation between gazing and light with the scene's closing sentence: 'bladed vessels aloft in the night to monitor flow, searchlit helicopters, fat fingers of blue light from one sky, searching' (240). With moonlight, blades, searchlights and fingers, Wallace overdetermines the scene with phallic gazes. 'Fingers' is particularly significant in how the only other experience she can compare to taking cocaine is going to the cinema with her father, with 'his hand in her lap her hand in the [Crackerjack] box and rooting down past candy for the Prize' (239). Given revelations later on in *Infinite Jest* that her father harbours incestuous desires for Joelle, one can detect intimations of past sexual abuse. As the recipient of so many male gazes, her suicide attempt works intra- and extra-diegetically as an invitation for men to gaze at her suffering.

As with the AA speaker's tale, the suspenseful expectation of pain that quickens an awaited pleasure, but which ultimately never arrives, characterizes Joelle's suicide attempt. For instance, the 'party-noise' (240) around her reaches a 'precipice of volume to teeter on just before the speakers blow' (240) as the cocaine reaches its 'highest spiked prick, peak, the arrow's best descent' (240).

The slip and subsequent correction of 'prick, peak' here figures this sense of imminent yet foreclosed release in terms of a frustrated male orgasm. Taking 'prick' as a colloquialism for penis, which is in keeping with descriptions of the cocaine as a 'lover' (237) that makes Joelle 'feel about to be entered by something … all about making her feel good' (237), Wallace frames the violence of her attempted suicide via reference to (a heteronormative understanding of) male sexual pleasure. Significantly, that Joelle 'sees, after inhaling, right at the apex, at the graph's spiked tip, Bernini's "Ecstasy of St Theresa"' (235) again implies that this violence is beyond representation. If the effect here is to suggest that reader and text are therefore both limited in their ability to access this violence – which, as the expression of so many male gazes, Wallace codes as being distinctly heterosexual and male – this only makes sense if one again ignores how the novel controls and delimits the parameters within which this seeming equality becomes apparent.

Furthermore, Wallace stresses how this scene relies upon a reader's contracted complicity; not, as with the AA speaker, in the use of an endnote, but through how Joelle meta-watches her own efforts to kill herself. For instance, she reflects on how cheap horror films usually finish 'by putting *?* after *THE END*, [and this] is what pops into her head: *THE END?* amid the odors of mildew and dicky academic digestion?' (235, italics in original). This savviness to generic convention shows how Joelle refuses to be taken in by the pathos of her situation. Aware of how 'sentimental and banal' (239) it is to think about those that she will leave behind, she is conscious of the volitional nature of her actions throughout; as, in turn, is the passage's projected reader. For insofar as these indications of the scene's banality inform the narrative voice, notably in how Wallace's free indirect discourse aligns said voice with Joelle, then Wallace forestalls one's ability to disavow complicity in gazing at her pain. Even the passage's final paragraphs, which are the most suspenseful in their lyrical, flowing descriptions of Joelle's potential overdose, are interrupted by a partygoer's knock and 'Look here then who's that in there?' (240) Her suicide attempt may suggest that reader and text are equally limited in comprehending male sexual violence, but it does so by foregrounding how the need to 'look here then' (240) is contractually mediated.

My examples thus far have hinged upon women as the objects of male sadistic gazing. In this regard, Mulvey's understanding of the gaze as something that men actively inflict on passive women holds true for Wallace's scenes of violence and suffering. However, there is enough in these passages to suggest that Wallace is aware of this feminist critique. Though he uses Lacan's invocation of *Ecstasy* to suggest a realm beyond representation, he stresses the phallic constitution of this idea that Lacan's critics have objected to. Luce Irigaray, as Tom Hayes relates, argued Lacan 'had failed to understand that he was referring to a statue made by a man who was a master deployer of what she called "the phallic gaze" … by which she meant the way men look at women as objects' (1999: 333).[9] Wallace descriptions of *Ecstasy* stress the presence of phallic aggression in Bernini's own artistry, namely in the 'psychotic-looking cherub-type angel standing on the lady's open thighs and pointing a bare arrow' (373). The difference, of course, is that where Irigaray's objection queries Lacan's use of the feminine as a sign of unrepresentability, Wallace uses it in order to position male sexual violence as the source of such instead. Furthermore, my last example – Gene Fackelmann's torture as seen by an immobilized Gately – demonstrates how the processes I have been exploring also work independently of explicit references to women and femininity.

Incapacitated after a drug binge, Gately watches as crime boss Whitey Sorkin's underlings torture his partner Gene Fackelmann by sewing his eyelids open. Burn suggests that 'Fackelmann's bloody end (with which Wallace significantly decides to close *Infinite Jest*) is presumably intended to prophesize the violence that reconfiguration [of the United States, Mexico, and Canada into ONAN] will bring' (2012: 39). I agree that this scene forecasts violence even greater than that which it already depicts. The impenetrability of such violence though – projected as it is 'somewhere beyond the right frame' (Wallace, cited in Max 2012a: 29) – is, I believe, more significant than how it evokes specifically geopolitical strife. Similar to Wallace's use of Bernini's *Ecstasy* in relation to Joelle's suicide attempt and the AA's speaker's tale, the violence which *Infinite Jest*'s final scene leads up to, but does not fulfil, figures as an unmediated 'real' that reader and novel are seemingly equally limited in accessing. Indeed, as Gately realizes that those who are torturing Fackelmann have given him a drug to make his torture all the more sharply felt, he reflects that '*Cruel* is spelled with a *u*, he remembered' (1996: 980, italics in original). As a homonym for 'you', this italicized 'u' not only refers to Gately, but also to the reader. In this regard, Wallace endeavours to remind readers of their own complicity in viewing the violence at hand.

That he does so through reference to male gazing is evident in Wallace's descriptions of Gately. His vision takes on the characteristics of a camera: 'only one of his eyes would open because the floor's impact had shut the other up plump' (974), and he 'could focus best when he squinted' with 'one eye still swollen shut' (976). Added to how he receives a 'rotary view of the whole room in almost untakable focus' (980), these descriptions position Gately as having a camera's monocular, mechanical viewpoint. Wallace genders this viewpoint as male; after being kicked in the groin, Gately wonders, 'Why is it you feel it in your gut and not your nuts per se, when you get brodied?' (977) The free indirect discourse here means that this rhetorical question, in addition to signifying Gately's query to himself, also works as the narrator's question to the reader, assuming a knowledge between men. Indeed, though the absence of a feminine object would seem to undermine the sexual nature of the male gaze, Wallace notes how 'Gately was trying to think. Too they wouldn't have got him. Him. Got him off' (980). Sorkin's men have injected Gately with a powerful type of heroin called Sunshine, and on one level the sentence's fragmentation represents his struggle to maintain consciousness. Wallace's isolation of 'Him' and 'Got him off', however, not only highlights the scene's preoccupation with a male subject ('him' includes Gately, the narrator, and the imagined reader), but is also suggestive of orgasmic build-up.

That Wallace forestalls Gately's 'getting off', though, and so works within the same masochistic dynamic as is present with Joelle and the AA speaker, is evident in how he uses the imagery of growing light in this scene. After relating that 'it felt like a sun in [Gately's] head' (973) (he either remembers or hallucinates this scene while in hospital), Wallace notes 'the rising sun' (974), that 'it was dawn outside' (974), and 'the room brightened as the sun climbed' (975). In this 'sunny room' (978) he is injected with 'pharm-grade Sunshine' (979), and as a result 'the air in the room got overclear, a glycerine shine' (980), 'the arterial roar of the Sun' (980) meaning the 'window exploded with light' (980). By associating the scene's escalating horrors with the growing s/Sunshine, Wallace not only employs a kind of pathetic fallacy for Gately's near death condition – he is, in a sense, on the verge of 'walking towards the light' – but also evokes a sense of imminent climax. That he denies such consummation compounds the masochistic suspense that animates this scene's solicitation of the male gaze. Of course, the novel's final phrase, 'way out' (981), seems to imply that the awaited pleasure of relief *does* break the expectation of further suffering. Yet the fact that Wallace leaves one ignorant of Gately's fate, and indeed with an abundance of unsolved mysteries, suggests that a suspended climax, and the continuation of suffering, is the point. In stark contrast to how a genre film sets out to fulfil a system of conventions, Wallace leaves the reader aware of how the contract they are in with *Infinite Jest* lacks any such resolution.

This distinction from texts like *Terminator 2*, in fact, speaks to how the *prestige* of violence is at work. Bachner accounts for this prestige through Pierre Bourdieu's theory of cultural capital, where '"taste" – in this case, taste in particular subjects by authors and critics – participates in the legitimation and replication of class values, positions, and interests' (4). To the extent that *Infinite Jest*'s handling of the subject of violence works to distinguish the novel from more formally generic texts, then my examples confirm Bachner's point. However, I have been less concerned with this sociocultural use of the term 'prestige' than I have been with the common sense understanding of it as signifying authority and power. In other words, the AA speaker's tale, Joelle's suicide attempt, and Gene Fackelmann's torture figure male sexual violence as harbouring an authority and power, before which both reader and text are epistemologically humbled. The consequences of this humbling, as I have traced them, are twofold. First, and my most explicit object of inquiry, has been how it works within masochistic contracts between reader and text in order to resist power imbalances, fulfilling Wallace's neoliberal desire for contracts that protect a – seeming – equality. Second, by using the imagined reader's propensity for male gazing, these dynamics help to construct the idea that sadistic gazing is, in and of itself, a naturally heterosexual male trait.

Conclusion

An interest in looking is evident throughout Wallace's texts. My focus on the male gaze in relation to masochism and contract can only account for one specific aspect of this. Burn's (2014b) investigation of the physiology of eyes in *The Pale King*, for instance, is a testament to how deeply Wallace engaged with issues of looking. Indeed, discussing the ways in which critics can assess the role of vision in literary texts, Burn notes how, in one approach, 'an imported theoretical framework allows a critic to address the more abstract dimensions of vision. With this approach, power structures typically become visible' (2014b: 87). I have followed this approach, concerned as I have been with how Wallace uses the male gaze as theorized in film studies to remind projected readers of their 'male' capacity for sadism. *Infinite Jest*'s scenes of violence and suffering have been my key examples in this regard. Yet, by tracing how similar concerns preoccupy 'B.I. #48', 'E Unibus Pluram', and 'David Lynch Keeps His Head', I have also shown how Wallace's texts more generally display a desire for sadistic gazing. Hering's 'theory of the mirror and reflection in Wallace's fiction' (2016: 83) comes close to my reading in what he describes as 'a motif of *refraction*' (87, italics in original) by which Wallace 'reframe[s] looking and watching as a communicative, dialogic gesture' (87). Whereas Hering leaves the exact character of this looking untheorized, though, I have argued that one can account for Wallace's desire for such through recourse to the male gaze.

Furthermore, if Hering interprets refractive looking as a potentially dialogic gesture, my reading of the male gaze stresses how Wallace's texts control and delimit such seeming reciprocity. I have argued that they do so in order to push against the masochistic contract between reader and text from within, and out of the conviction that such contracts put readers in positions of subservience. Connecting this to the neoliberal desire for contracts that protect individual self-determination, I showed how the resulting equality between reader and text that arises from *Infinite Jest*'s scenes of violence and suffering is false. For these scenes only register a humbled equality before unrepresentable male sexual violence if one elides how it is the novel that sets the parameters for, defines access to, and (paradoxically) represents, in exhausting detail, the violence in question. Extrapolating from this point, one can tentatively posit that analyses supporting the idea that Wallace empowers readers – like Hayes-Brady's notion that he 'prevents the closure of the system of interpretation' (2016: 107), or Adam Kelly's belief that his texts are 'structured and informed by this dialogic appeal to the reader's attestation and judgement' (2010: 145) – exemplify such elision. In short, if with *Infinite Jest* in particular Wallace 'employs' us to work towards meanings that 'break with representation' (Kelly 2010: 143), he does so via the disingenuous idea that the novel, like readers, can only try and fail to penetrate such unfathomableness.

This, of course, goes to the heart of Bachner's notion of the prestige of violence, animating as it does texts 'that announce the persistence of something real most powerfully through their failure to record it' (2011: 54). There is an important aspect of her argument, though, that I have yet to consider in detail. As noted in my Introduction, for Bachner this focus on seemingly unrepresentable violence 'enables a deeply therapeutic and illusory reckoning with that violence' (5). Thus, the texts she examines try to resolve the anxiety of being implicated in violence by foregrounding their incapacity to account for it. Applied to Wallace's texts as I have explored them in Chapter 3, the anxiety of being complicit in patriarchal violence (after all, *Infinite Jest* does stress how *Ecstasy* is the object of Bernini's phallic gazing) leads them to present such violence as the intransigent 'real' of masculinity. Reckoning with male sexual violence *as* something unrepresentable, in other words, allows Wallace to both acknowledge its disturbing power and to reaffirm its intractability. Turning to Chapter 4, this dynamic is especially notable in his depictions of feminism. The 'Brief Interviews' story cycle implies that only by facing up to a failure to definitively represent male sexual violence can one hope to articulate an efficient feminist critique of same.

4

Property

Privatizing feminist critique

In the climactic scene of Steven Soderbergh's 1989 film *Sex, Lies, and Videotape*, Ann (Andie MacDowell) confronts her husband's old friend, Graham (James Spader), about his hobby of interviewing women on camera about their sex lives. 'You've got a problem', Ann tells him, and despite Soderbergh's non-judgemental depiction of Graham, most audiences would probably agree. After the end of a previous relationship, Graham has suffered from erectile dysfunction for nine years, and can only attain sexual satisfaction by masturbating to his collection of video interviews. Graham's response however is not remorseful. Rather, with a small chuckle followed by a growing look of conviction, he confirms to Ann that 'you're right … I've got a lot of problems. … But they belong to me'. Wallace's short story cycle 'Brief Interviews with Hideous Men' can be said to rework Graham's peculiar hobby, so that it is an unnamed female interviewer – Q – asking the (redacted) questions, and of men rather than women. Much like Graham, though, these men all have various sexual problems; moreover, they are also decisively sexually problematic. Among the eighteen interviews, which appear as selections from a series of at least seventy-two, are those of a man who argues that surviving gang rape can be character building; another who manipulates women into sex by exploiting their sympathy for his withered arm; and a man who cannot help but shout 'Victory for the Forces of Democratic Freedom!' (1999c: 14) when he ejaculates. Q's questions may lack Graham's masturbatory motives, but as in Soderbergh's film, their effect is to position heterosexual men as the bearers of repulsive desires and behaviours.

A comparison with Graham though is only useful to some extent, as his sensitive demeanour is the inverse of Wallace's hideous men. A productive counterpoint to him can be found in Paul Thomas Anderson's 1999 film *Magnolia*, specifically in the character of Frank T. J. Mackey (Tom Cruise). Through his self-help programme 'Seduce and Destroy', Frank preaches a mantra of 'Respect the Cock and Tame the Cunt' to men who want to pick up women. Significantly, he tells his male audience at one point:

> Men. Are. Shit. What? Men. Are. Shit! Well isn't that what *they* say? Isn't that – because we do bad things don't we, we do horrible, heinious [sic]… *heinous*, terrible things. Things that no woman would ever do. … I will not apologize for who I am. I will not apologize for what I need. I will not apologize for what I want!

Like Graham, Mackey asserts a proprietary relationship to his own status as a male 'shit'. More pronounced here, however, is how the shittiness that Mackey embraces – the ability to do 'horrible … *heinous*, terrible things' – stems precisely from the perceived accusation of such from a female (and implied feminist) other. By embracing 'what *they* say' about men and, given the context of Seduce and Destroy, as it pertains to straight male sexuality in particular, Mackey claims this idea of shittiness for himself. A similar dynamic plays out in 'Brief Interviews'. When they are not anticipating charges, as one interviewee puts it, of being the type of man that 'you … bra-burners can see coming a mile away' (Wallace 1999n: 259), and thus their own potential interpolation into pre-set narratives of male chauvinism, the men that Q questions are all to various degrees aware of their own hideousness. In some cases, as with the aforementioned 'Johnny One-Arm' (1999g: 69), this self-awareness serves Mackey's goal of emotionally manipulative seduction.

If these stories present men who 'own' their hideousness then, they also position it as the property of male heterosexuality more broadly, and particularly as it has been outlined by (a perceived) feminist critique. As D. T. Max suggests, with the 'Brief Interviews' 'it was as if he [Wallace] were challenging women, saying, You [sic] think men are disgusting? I'll show you disgusting men' (2012a: 247). Max's attempt to account for why Wallace wrote these stories says more about his goals as a biographer than as a literary critic. Nevertheless, his identification of a challenge at work in the 'Brief Interviews' – and a challenge specifically aimed at feminist women – is astute. Scholars have certainly picked up on the collection's attempt to provoke with its depictions of such odious characters. In his early consideration of these stories, Boswell argued that they 'test the boundaries of our willingness to "empathize"' with men who are 'sexist, self-protective, self-absorbed, objectifying, and most of all, cruel' (2009: 189). David Coughlan has also suggested that in a book as 'disquieting, challenging, provocative, and dark' (2015: 163) as *Brief Interviews*, 'Wallace's desire [is] to make us aware of, and question, who and why we are judging' (2015: 173). What

Max acknowledges, however, and what Boswell and Coughlan skirt around, is how this desire to provoke is aimed at the apparent pieties of a feminist critique of male heterosexuality. Moreover, the collection's attempt to challenge such pieties – like the idea, caricatured by Mackey, that 'what *they* say' is men are shit – reasserts men's claim to own such hideousness in ways that, I argue, are comparable to reasserting private property rights.

The notion that such rights need *re*asserting, of course, implies a prior attenuation. Ann's response to Graham's belief that his problems 'belong to me' is illustrative in this regard: 'You think they're yours, but they're not. Everybody that walks in that door becomes part of your problem' (1989). Soderbergh's fairly conventional denouement positions Ann as a healing feminine influence, bringing Graham back into the fold of heteronormative romance by convincing him of the necessity – indeed, the inevitability – of relinquishing individual control over his (formerly) private problems. Wallace's reassertion of male hideousness as a form of private property proceeds from the notion that women like Ann deprive men of the ability to speak about their own sexuality. In this, the 'Brief Interviews' articulate through sexual relations one of the cardinal beliefs of thinkers who are now often labelled neoliberal. Simply put, this is the notion that Western welfare states, through an excess of government intervention, have weakened the freedoms attendant on a strong system of private property rights. One can see the significance of such rights to neoliberal thinkers in the response Friedrich Hayek once gave when asked to sum up 'everything that was meaningful and significant' to his work: 'If we destroy … the recognition of private property, I think it will destroy the sources which nourish present day mankind and create a catastrophe of starvation beyond anything mankind has yet experienced' (*The Hayek Prophecies*, 2010). The 'Brief Interviews' may not match Hayek's histrionics here concerning the importance of private property, but their depictions of male hideousness rest on similar grounds. Namely, feminists' supposed newfound authority over what can be said about straight male sexuality solicits a complex attempt to reassert men's right to speak about it themselves.

Rights to private property, however, are a hallmark of liberal capitalism as much as they are of its neoliberal reboot. John Gray observes the 'vital role, theorized in the classical liberal intellectual tradition, that the institution of private property and its corollary, the free market, play in constituting and protecting the basic liberties of the individual' (1995: 61). What makes Hayek's defence of private property neoliberal, in this sense, is its reactive stance in the face of an attempt to dilute such. Furthermore, Matthew Eagleton-Pierce explains how 'if private property is a foundational principle within capitalism, then the movement towards the privatization of state-owned assets or services carries a more distinctive neoliberal edge' (2016: 147). To the extent that the 'Brief Interviews' remove charges of male hideousness from the anonymous Q, and so that individual men can embody such hideousness themselves, then these stories follow such a privatizing logic. Indeed, accusations that Q's line of enquiry is 'full of knee-jerk politics' (1999i: 105) and eager to 'have everything tied up all nice and tight and tidy' (1999d: 16), suggests that this privatizing manoeuvre protects those 'basic liberties of the individual' that Gray identifies, and in ways that will allow for a complexity that her ideological questioning apparently suffocates.

However, it is too easy to argue that the 'Brief Interviews' are wholly symptomatic of a pushback against feminism during the closing decades of the twentieth century, of the kind Susan Faludi documents in *Backlash: The Undeclared War Against American Women* (1991). As Rachel Haley Himmelheber notes, '*Wallace means for the reader to both feel implicated by their* [i.e. the men Q questions] *hideousness and separate enough from it to judge it*' (2014: 522, italics in original). At the same time as these stories implicate readers in their defence of male hideousness as a form of private property, they also encourage them to simultaneously judge these men. Their privatization of hideousness takes on an added resonance in this regard. For by allowing men to speak of their own hideousness, and in doing so, having them damn themselves through unintentional revelations of their own repugnancy, the 'Brief Interviews' imply that feminism is best served by privatizing its critique. In other words, if justifications for privatization centre on the inefficiencies, in Lisa Duggan's words, of 'coercive, plodding, incompetent, intrusive' (2003: 13) governments in achieving their goals, then a similar logic drives these stories' depictions of feminism. Rather than imposing a one-size-fits-all idea of male hideousness on these men, the stories suggest that feminist critique will work more efficiently if it allows individual men to articulate their own sexual problems.

Given Wallace's focus elsewhere on community building and civic engagement, it may seem odd to suggest that the 'Brief Interviews' stories advocate a neoliberal logic of privatization. One need only look to *Infinite Jest*'s system of 'Subsidized Time' (1996: 234), where the ONAN government allows corporations to compete for advertising rights to each year, to get a sense of how Wallace's satire is aimed at capitalism's erosion of the commons. Nevertheless, there is much to be gained here from pursuing what might at first appear to be a counter-intuitive argument. By doing so, one can see how the 'Brief Interviews' privatize feminist critique in the pursuit of a more effective anti-masculinist politics. The stories pursue such privatization not only in order to delegate more control to individual men, but because it is ostensibly more efficient and productive than the feminist methodologies that Q is taken to represent. In what follows, I explore how the 'Brief Interviews' stories – and to a lesser extent, *Infinite Jest* and Wallace's late non-fiction – endorse these privatizing manoeuvres. I show how a feminist interrogation of male hideousness gives way, first, to men's reassertion of such as private property, and second, to a privatization of that initial feminist critique. These manoeuvres suggest that, because of its narrow mindedness, feminist critique as practised by Q blocks a true comprehension of her interviewee's toxicity. Though seminal metaphors are less pronounced here than they were in my previous chapters, the reclamation of hideousness I explore works as a possible release from this blockage.[1]

'Men mostly are shit, you're right, heh heh'

As my recourse to *Sex, Lies, and Videotape* and *Magnolia* implies, reclaiming straight male hideousness as a form of private property is not exclusive to Wallace's texts. These films' respective release dates – 1989 and 1999 – bracket the 1990s as a decade in which images of sexually problematized and problematic straight men enjoyed a heightened cultural visibility. The classic account of this phenomenon is Sally Robinson's *Marked Men: White Masculinity in Crisis* (2000). In this study Robinson looks at a range of literary, popular and academic texts produced since the 1960s to argue that American men in the closing years of the twentieth century were invested in 'an identity politics of the dominant' (2000: 3). In other words, for Robinson, 'announcements of a crisis in white masculinity, and a widely evidenced interest in wounded white men, themselves perform the cultural work of *re*centering white masculinity by *de*centering it' (12, italics in original). Hamilton Carroll has updated Robinson's arguments for millennial American culture through his notion of white male '*lability*' (2011: 10, italics in original). This refers to those 'strategies by which white masculinity has transformed the universal into the particular as a means of restaging [its] universality' (10). Wallace's texts often self-consciously exhibit this marking of white masculinity. 'Westward the Course of Empire Takes its Way', for instance, is plaintively concerned with 'nameless faceless Great White Male' (1989d: 303) experience, while in 'Good Old Neon', the protagonist Neal coolly apprises his analyst's suggestion that 'America's culture had a uniquely brutal and alienating way of brainwashing its males' (2004b: 163). Wallace's treatment of such marking may not remain the same from text to text, but its persistence as a topic speaks to its importance in understanding his depictions of masculinity.

However, while Robison and Carroll investigate a broad cultural marking of white masculinity during this period, I wish to isolate a specific strand of this process in the 'Brief Interviews'. Namely, these stories are indicative of how, as David Greven usefully puts it, 'the late 1990s prognosticated a new form of depraved masculinity' (2013: 143), and one in which the reprehensibility of straight male sexual behaviour figured prominently. Greven's focus is on millennial Hollywood, and cinema from that time is again illuminating. When Lorin Stein interviewed Wallace about the publication of *Brief Interviews* in 1999, she titled her piece 'In the Company of Creeps' (2012: 89–93), thus, one can assume, playing upon the title of Neil Labute's 1997 debut *In the Company of Men*. In this film two male middle managers seduce a deaf female co-worker, waiting until she has fallen in love with one of them so that they can end the relationship in the most damaging way possible. Prefiguring the conscious amorality that characterizes some of the men in Wallace's 'Brief Interviews' (and as the pun on 'company' implies, also how these stories present late capitalism as being conducive to such amorality), Labute's film explores the idea that hideousness may indeed be a property of male sexuality.[2] As was perhaps to be expected given this context, in 2009 John Krasinski adapted the 'Brief Interviews' into a film, suggesting if nothing else that representations of sexually problematized and problematic men continue to appeal into the early years of the new century.[3]

Given the above, it is useful to see the male sexual hideousness that Wallace writes about in the 'Brief Interviews' stories as forming part of a wider discourse in 1990s US culture. For Foucault, one can 'call discourse a group of statements in so far as they belong to the same discursive formation' (2002: 131); in other words, the same field of relations between dispersed 'objects, types of statement, concepts, or thematic choices, [where] one can define a regularity' (2002: 41). Wallace's 'Brief Interviews' belong to the same discourse of male sexual hideousness as the aforementioned films, insofar as they all exhibit a common discursive regularity. Specifically, this is their shared depiction of male sexuality as being amoral, narcissistic, manipulative, or in short, toxic, and of straight men who articulate such hideousness in manners that evoke ideas of private property. In fact, these men's attempts to reclaim a hideousness whose definitional contours arise precisely *from* feminist critique is suggestive of what

Foucault calls a '"reverse" discourse' (1998a: 101). Foucault expands on this idea in a 1977 interview with Bernard-Henri Lévy:

> Take the case of homosexuality. Psychiatrists began a medical analysis of it in the 1870s: a point of departure certainly for a whole series of new inventions and controls. ... But taking such discourses literally, and thereby turning them around, we see responses arising in the form of defiance: "All right, we are ... sick or perverse, whichever you want. And so if we are, let us be so, and if you want to know what we are, we can tell you better than you can". (1988: 115)

Homosexuals thus began to assert their own legitimacy through the same discourse that had constructed them as abnormal – 'in the same vocabulary, using the same categories by which [homosexuality] was medically disqualified' (Foucault 1998a: 101). This is what Wallace's hideous men (and, indeed, the stories they appear in) do, whether explicitly or not. They reverse a feminist discourse that positions them as 'sick or perverse' (1988: 115) in order to elucidate such sickness and perversity themselves. Significantly, this 'feminist discourse' is a homogenized caricature, in line with Wallace's tendency in *Infinite Jest* to reduce feminist politics to a reductive idea of 'Dworkinite' (1996: 929) anti-male critique.

Indeed, the idea that Wallace's hideous men, like homosexuals around the *fin de siècle*, are on the receiving end of a discourse that they resist by reversing, rests on two very questionable assumptions. First is the notion that a popular pathologization of straight male sexuality in 1990s American culture is somehow akin to the historical persecution of gay men. Wallace's reported comments to Jonathan Franzen that 'it's not an accident that so many of the writers "in the shadows" are straight white males' (Franzen 1996: 51) implies his sympathy for this opinion; the phrase 'in the shadows', in fact, is redolent of the homosexual closet. Secondly, the assumption that American culture marginalizes heterosexual men for their sexual desires, itself confirming Robinson's 'identity politics of the dominant' (2000: 3), positions feminist critique of the same period as enjoying an oppressive, hegemonic influence. These ideas are difficult to sustain, if not outright false. Still, frustration on the behalf of white male novelists with feminism's apparent excesses is detectable in Wallace's key contemporaries. As well as Franzen's own notorious baiting of feminist readers, most notably in his novel *Purity* (2015b),[4] Jeffrey Eugenides's *The Marriage Plot* (2011) (which includes a character loosely based on Wallace) displays similar resentments (2011: 157–63). By arguing that Wallace's men reverse feminist discourse, I explore power relations which, though they have a questionable correspondence to sociological realities, are integral to how the 'Brief Interviews' present men reclaiming their hideousness as private property.

Two further concepts from Foucault's thought on the regulation of discourse offer a useful way to unpack this dynamic: the author and the discipline. The idea of the author for Foucault constitutes one of the internal 'procedures for controlling and delimiting discourse' (1981: 56). This is not 'of course, in the sense of the speaking individual who pronounced or wrote a text, but in the sense of a principle of grouping of discourses, conceived as the unity and origin of their meanings' (1981: 58). Indeed, he describes this procedure elsewhere as the 'author function' (1998b: 211). Most notably for my purposes, however, Foucault suggests that 'the author has played the role of the regulator of the fictive, a role quite characteristic of our era ... of individualism and private property' (1998b: 222). As Carla Hesse explains, he suggests therefore that the author 'emerged historically as the cultural incarnation of a new axis of sociopolitical discourse: the inviolable relation between the rights-bearing individual and private property' (1991: 109). Additionally, Foucault observes how ideas of the discipline also work to regulate discourse:

> [The discipline] is opposed to the principle of the author because a discipline is defined by a domain of objects, a set of methods, a corpus of propositions considered to be true, a play of rules and definitions, of techniques and instruments: all this constitutes a sort of anonymous system at the disposal of anyone who wants to or is able to use it. (Foucault 1981: 59)

In this light, one can understand attempts to reclaim hideousness in the 'Brief Interviews' as reasserting individual men's authorship of said discourse as a form of private property – so that, in the words of the interviewee in 'B.I. #59', 'I alone have any rights to speak of it' (1999l: 191). This is opposed to Wallace's caricature of a feminist politics which, as an anonymous discipline with 'a set of methods, a corpus of propositions' (Foucault 1981: 59), opposes the relationship between an author and the texts he produces.

One last caveat is needed, though, before proceeding with this reading. The pure authorship that Foucault dismisses – 'the speaking individual who pronounced or wrote a text' (1981: 58) – is an ideal that Wallace never relinquishes. In fact, as John Roache (2017) demonstrates, Wallace was sceptical of Foucault's arguments on authorship,[5] an antipathy that is also clear in his gloss of post-structuralism in 'Greatly Exaggerated'. In this review of H. L. Hix's *Morte d'Author: An Autopsy* (1987), Wallace displays a general enthusiasm for Hix's interrogation of 'one of the true clarion-calls that marked the shift from New Criticism to structuralism to deconstruction, Roland Barthes' 1968 announcement of "The Death of the Author"' (1997c: 138). After summarizing post-structural attempts to show that the 'author-as-owner is not just superfluous but contradictory' (141), Wallace ends with a guarded withdrawal into sentimental biologism: 'For those of us civilians who know in our gut that writing is an act of communication between one human being and another, the whole question seems sort of arcane' (144). What is most interesting for my argument here is that Wallace focuses on the author's '*ownership* of meaning' (140, italics mine). By presenting post-structural critique as being levelled at authorial property, and ultimately (if surreptitiously) siding against Foucault and co.'s interrogation of such,[6] Wallace sets up a dynamic that particularly comes to the fore in the 'Brief Interviews'. His depiction of men reclaiming 'author-ity' (143) over their hideous sexuality, though by no means endorsing a simplistic one-to-one relation between an individual and 'his' text, attempts to bolster men's property rights to such. Central to this process is Wallace's suggestion that feminist critique makes public what is otherwise men's private sexual hideousness.

The monthly diddlecheck

Krasinski's film adaptation of the 'Brief Interviews', by presenting Q as a graduate student (named as Sara Quinn, and played by Julianne Nicholson) interviewing men to understand their hideousness, makes explicit various dynamics the stories themselves only hint at. As Himmelheber observes, throughout these stories 'Wallace uses single quotation marks around the men's speech, indicating that these partial transcripts are not only of a larger piece, which is contextually obvious, but are of a *constructed piece*' (2014: 525, italics in original). In other words, it is not only the men Q interrogates that Wallace presents for our consideration but, more obliquely, Q's project itself. As Himmelheber also goes on to suggest, 'Because this implied narrator is constructing a narrative arc through the beginning, middle, and end of each interview ... there is ample evidence that the narrator(s) is critiquing the interviewee characters' (525). Rather than a neutral and yet muted interlocutor presenting freely given information, Q proceeds from a predetermined ideological objective – identifying and documenting examples of straight male hideousness. As someone 'interested in critiquing gender relations' (Himmelheber 2014: 525) on the basis of straight male behaviour, she starts from the broadly feminist project of bringing to light the hidden ways in which men sexually oppress women. As such, Q's project accords with what Antony Easthope, writing in 1990, described as the main goal of feminist masculinity studies: to expose how, traditionally, 'masculinity has stayed pretty well concealed. This has always been its ruse to hold on to its power' (1992: 1). The confessional interview format that Q uses, in fact, attests to how her attempt to serve this public good works precisely by depriving straight men of their ability to practice such power in private. Such expropriation shifts author-ity over what can be said about this hideousness from individual men to an anonymous feminist discipline.

It is in *Infinite Jest* though, rather than the 'Brief Interviews', where Wallace first aligns this process with the expropriation of private property. This is evident in the scene where Hal and a few other students are sitting outside the principal's office, waiting to be reprimanded for their inaction during an event that leaves several younger students injured. As they are waiting, in a nearby office Avril is 'with pretty much every E.T.A. female under thirteen' (1996: 510), covering for academy counsellor Dr Dolores Rusk's duties in carrying out 'administrative diddle-checks' (510). That she is standing in for Rusk here implies how Avril is carrying out an impersonal task, the diddle-check furthering a discipline in Foucault's sense that it is 'at the disposal of anyone ... able to use it (1981: 59). These checks are of young women considered 'to be potential diddlees' (Wallace 1996: 511) and are 'required at all North American tennis academies since the infamous case of coach R. Bill ('Touchy') Phiely' (510). Echoing Humbert Humbert in Vladimir Nabokov's *Lolita* (1955), Phiely's 'hair-raising diary and collection of telephotos and tiny panties – discovered only after his disappearance into the Humboldt County hill country with a thirteen-year-old' (510) – mean that these meetings are designed to 'nip any potential Phielyisms in the bud. Monthly diddle-checks are in Rusk's contract because they're in E.T.A's O.N.A.N.T.A. accreditation-charter' (511). Identification of one man's hideous behaviour leads to government attempts to manage such. This hideousness, once privately embodied in a diary and secret collection of photos and panties, is brought into the open as a result of the diddle-check to serve a public good – to make young women more aware of sexual predators.

Wallace emphasizes the diddle-check's distinctly public orientation through the scene's descriptions of Avril. We know by this point in the novel that she has 'a black phobic dread of hiding or secrecy in all possible forms with respects to her sons' (51), but this phobia also manifests outside of her maternal role. 'It's impossible not to overhear' (514) the diddle-check, as 'the absence of a door to the Moms' office means you might as well be in there' (511). Though we are told 'she has little sense of spatial privacy or boundary' (511) due to 'having been so much alone when a child' (511), it is also 'simply [for] enclosure-reasons' (512) – 'she's in there unenclosed right now' (510), 'serv[ing] (pro bono) as E.T.A.'s Dean of Academic Affairs and Dean of Females' (510). The term 'enclosure' has special resonances in the history of capitalism. As David Bollier explains, 'The English enclosure movement, which flourished ... from 1750 to 1860 ... allow[ed] the ruthless seizure of millions of acres of commonly used forests, meadows, and game' (2003: 5), therefore 'lead[ing] to the creation of modern industrial markets' (5). By pointing out how Avril is anti-enclosure, this scene presents her diddle-check as working as an obstruction to private property. That she performs her task pro bono, moreover, reiterates how, as a representative of the state via 'E.T.A.'s O.N.A.N.T.A. accreditation charter' (511), Avril furthers a public good by helping to deny men like Phiely the privacy to carry out their nefarious activities.

In these regards, Avril can be said to represent the kind of state intervention that, as my earlier reference to Hayek demonstrates, so disturbs neoliberal thinkers. One of the most cogent expressions of the neoliberal opposition to such intervention is clear in the founding statement of Mont Pelerin Society; the 'thought collective' (2009: 4), to use Dieter Plehwe's phrase, that would prove so influential to what Harvey describes as neoliberalism's '"long march"' (2007: 40) to dominance in the later twentieth century. For those associated with this society, freedom was under threat 'by the spread of creeds which, claiming the privilege of tolerance when in the position of a minority, seek only to establish a position of power' ('Statement of Aims' 1947). The creeds in question, as Ben Jackson explains in his overview of the origins of neoliberal thought, were those that espoused 'socialist central planning' (2010: 133). In the founding statement's terms, such planning fostered 'a decline of belief in private property and the competitive market'. The notion that planners who, though 'claiming a privilege of tolerance' ('Statement of Aims' 1947), are actually working to destroy private property rights, resonates with how Wallace presents Avril's activities in the diddle-check scene. For, if nothing else, these diddle-checks have occurred 'monthly' (Wallace 1996: 511) 'for the last four years' (511) at ETA, and therefore exemplify planning.

To be more precise, though, the type of planning that early neoliberals objected to was, in Hayek's words, the 'central direction of all economic activity according to a single plan, laying down how the resources of society should be "consciously directed" to serve particular ends in a definite way' (2001: 36). Avril's attempt to find evidence of abuse among her female charges accords with this idea. Although she 'gives them verbal space, [she] tried gently to steer the topic close to true Phielyism' (Wallace 1996: 514), thus directing the available data to confirm her pre-set goals. For instance, she asks the girls 'have any of you been kissed or nuzzled or hugged or rubbed or pinched or probed or fondled or in any way touched by a tall person in a way that's made you uncomfortable?' (513). The proliferation of different forms of potential physical abuse here, which by the end of the sentence Avril has subsumed under the single rubric of feeling uncomfortable, enacts syntactically the logic that motivates her diddle-check. In other words, the object in question – a private propertied idea of male sexual hideousness – loses its variety in the process of Avril's attempt to identify it. She expropriates such private idiosyncrasy from these girls' possible testimonies to serve a public good (namely, diddle-prevention) whose overt ideological objectives suffocate nuance. Indeed, Wallace's salacious slapstick in naming this molester 'R. Bill ('Touchy') Phiely' (510) evokes a vibrancy that is missing from the anonymous bureaucratize of 'E.T.A.'s O.N.A.N.T.A. accreditation charter' (511). That 'Phiely' is a near homonym for 'freely' (this former noun's absent 'r' isolated and capitalized at the name's beginning) also reiterates how Avril's actions here work against the freedoms supposedly attendant on private property. For Wallace, those left with the 'Bill' in this regard are heterosexual men, charged with bearing hideous desires they must pay for in manners that deny their individuality.[7]

Notably, however, Wallace counters the expropriation Avril's diddle-check performs in this scene through his description of how another student, Trevor Axford, objectifies her. As Avril talks 'In full if kind of oblique-angled view of the people in the waiting room' (510), we learn that she has 'legs whose taper you can see T. Axford is appraising with the frankness of adolescence' (510). The novel then sends readers to endnote 210, relating how 'Hal and Mario have long since had to accept[a] the fact that Avril, at 50+, is still endocrinologically compelling to males' (1035). In a footnote to the word 'accept', we are told that '"accept" isn't the same as "be crazy about," of course' (1035). As Avril encourages the girls to give examples that confirm male sexuality's toxicity, and to put them on guard against the dangers of such, Axford's gaze subtly undercuts her endeavour. The obstinately hormonal here affronts a loosely feminist (the diddle-check is designed to be 'nurturingly empowering' (511)) attempt to mark and prevent straight men's hideous desires. In fact, the endnote implies that Avril works against biology – against what is 'endocrinologically compelling' (1035), something that like Hal and Mario we may not 'be crazy about' (1035) but which it is best to 'accept' (1035) as inevitable. That these remarks appear in an endnote within an endnote suitably positions their sentiments as marginalized yet persistent. The diddle-check may expose men's predatory desires to serve the goal of their prevention, but Axford's objectification of Avril, which Wallace presents as being inevitable, suggests this project runs against a male sexual hideousness that however critiqued, cannot be denied.[8]

Nonetheless, if feminist critique here works as a form of expropriation, and is thus in conflict with an obdurately individual male sexual hideousness, the scene also complicates the purity of a public versus private binary that this conflict seems to imply. That it is with 'the *frankness* of adolescence' (510, italics mine) that Axford objectifies Avril undermines the idea that there is anything necessarily private about his licentiousness. Also, despite the fact that the diddle-check takes place 'in full if kind of oblique-angled view' (510) of those in the next room, it remains exclusively geared to the young girls in her charge. As public as it is, the diddle-check remains, at least notionally, a private affair. In these ways, the scene blurs what is otherwise a clash between private male hideousness and an expropriating feminism. One could make a similar point about the relationship between Q and her interviewees in the 'Brief Interviews'. Indeed, these stories are an assemblage of the men's private experiences and what Wallace implies are Q's public-minded methods and intentions. However, to stop here would be to miss how the imbrication of private and public in this story cycle, as in the diddle-check scene, is still weighted towards a need to bolster the former. In the face of Q's implied attempt to critique her subjects, these stories reassert individual men's property rights over a hideousness that, ostensibly, they are best placed to talk about.

Reclaiming hideousness as private property

David Hering argues that Wallace's attempts to resuscitate authorial presence in the wake of post-structural critique often centres upon the figure of the ghost. He observes that such figures develop from the '"absent possessor"' (2016: 20) to a '"companion ghost"' (29), and as a means for Wallace to address 'problems of authorial monologism' (19). The absent possessor exemplifies 'the prescriptive authority of unseen forces' (20), while the companion ghost, by contrast, 'makes plain its desire for *interaction*, rather than a kind of remote orchestration' (29, italics in original). This reading chimes with dynamics at work in the 'Brief Interviews'. Such movement away from what Hering calls 'being externally controlled or possessed' (2016: 21), and '*towards* an engagement with dialogism … through awareness of … monologic tendenc[ies]' (35, italics in original) captures well how these stories present men reclaiming hideousness as private property. The expropriating manoeuvres of an assumed feminism that Q, in part, represents, works as the absent possessor in this equation. These men's attempts to reclaim 'their' hideousness though puts her project more in the role of the companion ghost – as a co-creator of the discourse that results, but one whose implied monologism is potentially transformed by refraining to speak *for* her male subjects.

It is thus important not to see the men's reclamation of hideousness as rejecting all forms of control or 'remote orchestration' (Hering 2016: 29). Wallace in fact parodies such an absolutist idea of private property in *Brief Interviews'* second story, 'Death is Not the End'. As Mary K. Holland helpfully summarizes, 'Running three and a half pages but comprising one paragraph and only three sentences, the story merely describes a man lying motionless outside' (2013: 114). He is an 'accomplished poet, reading his magazine in his chair on his deck by his pool behind his home' (Wallace 1999a: 3). This chain of possessives echo the opening page's long list of national awards this poet has received (at least a dozen), reiterating how he is completely ensconced by forms of property. Notably, Wallace describes the scene as an '*enclosed* tableau ... wholly still and composed and *enclosed* ... the silent living *enclosing* flora's motionless green vivid' (1999a: 3, italics mine). If Avril, particularly during the diddle-check scene, is anti-private property to the extent that she is anti-enclosure, then this poet is the obverse. Indeed, 'the trees and shrubbery ... are densely interwoven and tangled and serve the same essential function as a red-wood privacy fence or a wall of stone' (1999a: 3). This quite literal enclosure, Wallace implies, is suited to such a grotesque figure; wearing 'a black Speedo swimsuit' (1), middle-aged, overweight, and with a 'hairline unevenly recessed' (1) due to various hair transplants, this author is not so much resting on his laurels as he is wilfully being smothered by them.

Despite the story's cloistered atmosphere, however, there is as Hering observes 'an implicit counterforce ... that incorporates a recognition of a world outside the protective sealed space' (2016: 70). This is 'the final, gnomic footnoted pronouncement ... [that] seems to defy the hermetically sealed space of the story both by its contrarianism and physical placement outside the body of the main narrative' (70). Hering then compares this footnote to 'the entry of an interviewer' (70) in 'B.I. #59', who 'brings his story into the environment outside' (70). This is in fact Q's role throughout the 'Brief Interviews' – she is the expropriating force without whom these men's testimonies could not be communicated to us. Nonetheless, if her project forestalls the kind of static hiddenness that the reclining poet in 'Death Is Not the End' evokes, it still allows her subjects to reclaim hideousness as a form of private property. Q may be the mediator of these interviews, in other words, but in contrast to Avril's diddle-check, her project stokes these men's expressions of hideousness. As a reverse discourse, then, these expressions affront what Wallace caricatures as feminist endeavours to speak with author-ity on men's toxic sexual behaviours.

Brief Interviews #14 and #40 offer compelling examples of these dynamics at work. Before proceeding to show this, however, a clearer idea of what private property means is needed. The multifarious approaches to this topic means that there is, in Jeremy Waldron's words, a 'lack of a generally accepted account of what private property is and how it is to be contrasted with alternative systems of property rights' (1991: 26). My interpretation of private property in the 'Brief Interviews' is accordingly heuristic rather than definitional. I aim to demonstrate how the reclamation they carry out accords with a neoliberal desire to defend and reassert private property against supposed attempts to undermine it. Paul H. Rubin and Tilman Klump offer a useful framework through which to conceive of property, and in turn to unpack its significance to these stories. They suggest that

> in its idealized form, a property right entitles its holder to a strong form of authority over an asset, called ownership. Ownership can be viewed as a "bundle of sticks," composed of the following rights:
>
> *C*: The right to *control* the asset and decide on its use.
> *V*: A claim to the *value* the asset generates.
> *E*: The right to *exclude* others from using the asset.
> *T*: The right to *transfer* the bundle *C, V, E, T* to another holder.
>
> (2012: 205, italics in original)

The third of these, 'the right to *exclude* others from using the asset' (205), resonates with how the 'Brief Interviews' stories reverse a perceived feminist discourse in order to strengthen men's '*control* [of] the asset' (205) – their hideousness – as private property. Furthermore, Rubin and Klump point out that 'rarely, if ever, does one encounter the bundle of sticks *C, V, E, T* in its entirety' (205), and a complex mixture of these rights are evident in 'Brief Interviews'. Indeed, Q's role as the overarching mediator of these men's testimonies implies how such rights to exclude or control cannot be individually self-sufficient.

In fact, the coprolalia-afflicted interviewee's admission that he shouts 'Victory for the Forces of Democratic Freedom!' (1999c: 14) as he ejaculates suggests his powerlessness; it is 'uncontrolled. It's like it comes out the way the spooge comes out … I'm not even thinking it until it comes out and I hear it' (14).

Seminal discharge as a result of 'some girl, it doesn't matter who' (14) limns not only with the interviewee's inability to control his speech, moreover, but with Q's expropriating measures as well. The fact that 'I just about die of the embarrassment' (14) in the sexual scenario, and that 'god, now I'm embarrassed as hell' (15) after admitting such to Q, suggests this correspondence. Additionally, his admission confirms a commonplace in feminist interpretations of male sexuality: namely, that it is characterized by violence. As Ken Plummer explains, 'Certain themes consistently reappear in feminist discussions of male sexuality, and accounts of male sexuality as prone to violence, pressure, coercion, and objectification abound' (2005: 182). The phrase 'Victory for the Forces of Democratic Freedom!' (Wallace 1999c: 14), like Mackey's 'Seduce and Destroy', confirms the male hideousness that Q's project sets out to document – specifically, the idea that men's 'shooting off' (1999c: 15) is a form of violence. In these ways, this man's ownership of 'his' sexuality is compromised from the very beginning. Not only does he lack the right to control the meaning of his orgasm, he confirms meanings produced by feminist others. In turn, this shows his inability to exclude said feminist interpretations from speaking with authority over the nature and significance of his sexual problems.

If perceived feminist discourse thoroughly constitutes this interviewee, it is from this position of subjection that his account can be seen to 'talk back' to the critique Q stands for. This process is more complex than the self-conscious embrace of 'shittiness' that Mackey's programme exemplifies, even though there are elements of such elsewhere in the story cycle. As David M. Halperin explains, for Foucault a reverse discourse does not have to 'simply produce a mirror reversal – a pure one-to-one inversion of the existing terms of the discourse it reverses' (1995: 59). This interviewee does not embrace his coprolalia and 'recapitulate [it] in an affirmative vein' (Halperin 1995: 59) – he notes that 'it's so fucking weird' (1999c: 15). Rather, by the end of the story he has reproduced the hideousness his orgasmic outbursts imply, but, in Halperin's words, 'in a new direction' (1995: 59). Commenting that 'it's the ones that'll act all understanding' (Wallace 1999c: 15) that ultimately get him 'pissed off' (15) – 'those are the ones ... the ones that say "I think I could love you anyway"' (5) – the interviewee ends in a position of greater rhetorical authority. Rather than being spoken for, he is now speaking for, contemptuously mimicking a woman's attempt to understand his problems. The repetition of the phrase 'the ones' here implies how this process inverts the power dynamics at play. Q's attempt to categorize men as hideous, and so to subject them to a typology of pre-set actions, rebounds into this man's misogynistic grouping of women into certain types.

David P. Rando, in his reading of male hideousness in Wallace's texts as a form of affective lovelessness, suggests that this 'persistent "typological" imagination of women' (2013: 581) is one of the ways in which 'B.I. #20' and 'Good Old Neon' present revelations of men's inability to love. Notably, he also argues that 'B.I. #20' undermines the interviewee's endeavour to 'preempt the feminist interpretation to which he imagines the interviewer will subject his story by formulating it himself' (2013: 581) – his attempt, in a sense, to reverse her discourse. It does so when the woman whose anecdote he is relating to Q speaks 'with [a] devastating power' (582) that proves to be life-changing for him. This focus on an attempted male appropriation of women, which in turn fails when said women 'speak' from within the male voice that is appropriating them, is prevalent elsewhere in Wallace criticism. Hayes-Brady calls this 'the appropriative power of the reported feminine' (2013: 148) in Wallace's texts, while Holland notes that 'Wallace explored the bestial male appropriation of the female other' (2017: 7) throughout his career. These readings are compelling, but they miss how such male appropriation of women, and said women's ability to 'subvert the controlling power of the narratively articulate men by taking control of the masculine voice' (Hayes-Brady 2013: 143), still position the men in question *as* hideous; indeed, they compound the link between male sexuality and toxic attitudes and behaviours.[9]

This is evident in 'B.I. #40', in which Johnny One-Arm recounts how he exploits women's responses to his withered appendage in order to sleep with them. Several passages of his testimony report how these women react to seeing 'the Asset' (Wallace 1999g: 69). For instance, they say 'how I'm such a nice young fella and it breaks their heart to see me talk about my own part of me that way' (70), or 'how I'm such a good listener and sensitive ... and she can't believe there's any way the arm's as bad as I'm making out' (71). When Johnny has cornered his subjects – ensuring his arm is so ugly that for them to leave would confirm that 'It Was Because Of The Arm' (71), and in turn the shallowness of their compassion – these women 'just cry and cry. Sometimes they get me crying too' (72). Reported feminine voice and expression plays a significant role in this story, and even lead to the protagonist's admission of occasional emotional breakdown. As a consequence, however, Johnny simply reaffirms his hideousness in manipulating women into sex. In response to Q's last question, which we can imply is along the lines of 'how often are your tactics successful?' he responds 'more pussy than a toilet seat, man. I shit you not' (72). Feminine appropriation of Johnny's voice thus strengthens rather than undercuts his author-ity over hideousness. This complicates the idea that women's infiltration of these men's communication, in and of itself, weakens said men's reclamation of control over what is said about their hideousness.

Indeed, as noted earlier, reverse discourse works precisely by redeploying received expressions towards counter-oppressive goals. In comparison to 'B.I. #14', the connection between Johnny's testimony and a reversal of perceived feminist pieties is less apparent. Yet, as with the coprolalia-afflicted ejaculator, Johnny's narrative duplicates the sexual scenario, in modified form, at the level of Q's interview. As he recounts, 'I show it [his arm] to her just like I just did you' (71). In fact, Johnny's seduction stages the appropriative process by which Q makes these men's hideousness public. By positioning his sexual conquests as liberating him, professing that 'Don't You See You Have Set Me Free of Being Shameful Of The Arm Thank You Thank You' (72, *sic*), Johnny controls the breaking of his privacy these women ostensibly carry out. Furthermore, the story's excremental imagery suggests how this author-ity also works as a right to exclude. By getting 'more pussy than a toilet seat' (72), Wallace implies Johnny's embrace of 'shittiness', an association the near pun on *ass*et reiterates. This shittiness works as self-demarcation in the face of Q's attempt to document his hideousness, as the phrase 'I shit you not' (72) subtly evokes. If 'I shit' signifies 'Johnny is a shit', and 'you not' that 'Q is not a shit', then the testimony Q has expropriated from Johnny ultimately affirms the latter's distinctly male hideousness. Consequently, the 'my own part of me' (72) Johnny reclaims in this story is more than his withered arm. It is a renewed author-ity to speak on his hideousness and which arises from a complex manipulation and reversal of women's attempts – whether in his sexual partners' compassion, or, far more obliquely, in Q's potentially ameliorative feminist goals – to do so for him.

The testimonies in 'B.I. #14' and 'B.I. #40', then, reclaim hideousness as these men's private property. They do so through their complex reversal of feminist discourse, reasserting their rights to control what can be said about their hideousness and to exclude said feminists from similar authority. Significantly, the perceived feminist discourse in question here varies in terms of its specificity. If the ejaculator's outburst risibly confirms feminist commonplaces about male sexuality and violence, Johnny's manipulation of his partners' self-perceptions as compassionate people is more indirect. His testimony affronts rather the (apparent) general assumption that women can talk about male hideousness, whether to help 'cure' said men (as Soderbergh's Ann does for Graham), or in order to condemn it (as is implied, if only by these men's paranoid pre-emptions, that Q's project attempts to do). Reclaiming such hideousness as private property, moreover, does not entail a rejection of all control in favour of unfettered individualism. Q is essential to the cycle, its necessary mediator and instigator – the companion ghost whose 'absent opacity' (2013: 148), to use Hayes-Brady's description of femininity in Wallace's texts, co-ordinates the various testimonies we receive while minimizing her own influence.

This minimization of control is important to how, by reasserting private property, the 'Brief Interviews' also work to privatize feminist critique. The reluctance to speak *for* these men, and thus, in Hering's words, a movement '*towards* an engagement with dialogism … through awareness of … monologic tendenc[ies]' (2016: 35, italics in original), implies judgements about the value of individual voice (created, but not dominated, through dialogic means) over being 'told' by an anonymous other. Such judgements inform how the story cycle endeavours to 'improve' the feminism that we can imply motivates Q's questions. What needs improving, as intimated earlier, is feminism's apparent reduction of these men's attitudes and behaviours to overly restrictive ideas of hideousness. Wallace suggests, then, that attempts to know and transform male hideousness through feminism used as a discipline fail to the extent that they neglect men's position as authors. By respecting this position, and in turn allowing men to reclaim author-ity over hideousness, the anti-masculinist politics that Q pursues can ostensibly be more effective. What Wallace designated his 'parody (a feminist parody) of feminism' (Wallace, cited in Max 2012a: 247), in this respect, accords with some of the central justifications that neoliberal governments often give for privatization. These are that services can be improved, and particularly in ways that increase efficiency and reduce waste, if ownership moves from public to private hands.

Privatizing Q

Avril's diddle-check proves to be comically inefficient in identifying examples of abuse. After asking 'about being touched by a tall person in an uncomfortable way' (Wallace 1996: 513), one girl notes that '"Gramma pinches my cheek"' (513), another that '"I hate it when some adult pats my head like I'm a schnauzer"' (514). Ultimately, the session degenerates into the girls 'exchanging data on what kinds of animals members of their own biologic families either imitate or physically resemble' (526). The only instance of potential abuse is slight – one girl's complaint that 'my daddy gives me these small little shoves in the small of the back when he wants me to go into rooms' (514). Avril's response – 'Mmmmmm-hmm' (514) – however, implies that such information is conducive to her goals. Wallace not only presents the diddle-check as inefficient, then, but also as unduly biased towards finding examples of male hideousness, however innocuous the evidence. The inefficiency of disciplines that set out to confirm pre-set assumptions appear throughout Wallace's corpus, most often embodied by psychotherapists and medical professionals. Feminism in Wallace's texts, imagined as a group of ideas about male hideousness, is part of this dynamic. As well as the diddle-check, for instance, Rusk's attempt to diagnose male students with various sexual pathologies (437, 550) shows her disciplinary short-sightedness. Elsewhere, the novel's parodic feminist group – the 'Female Objectification Prevention and Protest Phalanx' (929), or 'FOPPP' (929) – is suggestive of similar faults. As well as being risibly militant, to the extent of assaulting and kidnapping cheerleaders (929), their abbreviation implies inefficiency. The misogynistic irony of naming them 'fop', a term that designates male dandies and thus vain ineffectuality, is compounded by the unnecessary and wasteful extra 'P's.[10]

Cutting waste and boosting efficiency is one of the major justifications, in neoliberal thought, for privatization. As Duggan notes, this 'primary strategy of turn-of-the-millennium neoliberalism' (2003: 12) equates 'economic activity with voluntary, uncoerced, private freedom, and with productivity, efficiency and wealth expansion' (12). It is the Reagan and Thatcher governments of the 1980s, though, that most famously implemented privatization in pursuit of these goals. Significantly, privatization for these governments was intimately associated with property rights. For Thatcher, state ownership entailed 'ownership by an impersonal legal entity: it amounts to control by politicians and civil servants. ... Through privatization – particularly the kind of privatization which leads to the widest possible share ownership by members of the public – the state's power is reduced and the power of the people enhanced' (Thatcher, cited in Evans 2004: 35). Privatization, in this sense, means reasserting private property against the state's overreach, and out of the conviction that private control is morally and logically preferable to delegating such, in Hering's phrase, to an 'absent possessor' (2016: 20). Paul Starr explains how, from this angle, the efficiency benefits of privatization lie in how 'the more individuals stand to gain from tending to their property, the better will it be tended' (1988: 21). Conversely, 'The more attenuated and diluted their property rights, the less motivated individuals will be to use property under their control efficiently' (21). This logic informs how the 'Brief Interviews' stories privatize feminist critique. By reasserting men's author-ity over their hideousness, these stories imply that men can gain an individuality that overly broad feminist methodologies elide. This in turn implies that a feminist project of identifying and explicating hideous male behaviour is most efficiently achieved if men speak for themselves.

Significantly, this does not mean that Q's feminist goals are completely delegated to individual men, any more so than privatization means complete state withdrawal in favour of private enterprise alone. Indeed, the supposed efficiency that Wallace implies feminism can gain by not talking 'for' these men at times occurs without their consent. In other words, Q's subjects often inadvertently damn themselves, thus advancing a critique of male hideousness without suppressing their individual voices. The ejaculator of 'B.I. #14', for instance, in his attempt to distinguish his outburst from any political position, states that 'I'm not one of these America First, read the newspaper, will Buchanan get the nod people' (1999c: 14). The 'America First Committee' was a 1940-1 pressure group that urged against involvement in the Second World War.[11] Pat Buchanan, meanwhile, is a conservative politician and celebrity, notable for his non-interventionism and indeed for using the phrase 'American First' during his campaigns. That the ejaculator anxiously avows his dissimilarity to both undercuts his denial that 'Victory for the Forces of Democratic Freedom!' (14) is a political statement. By stressing his difference from non-interventionist political groups and figures, he ends up inadvertently confirming the militaristic connotations of his orgasm. The feminist objective of identifying male hideousness has proceeded without weakening the ejaculator's author-ity over such, and in a way that is more efficiently precise than the blanket statements to which – as Wallace presents them – feminist estimations of men subscribe.

Foucault's description of the author is suggestive of this emphasis on efficiency. For when 'one is thrifty not only with one's resources and riches but also with one's discourses ... the author is the principle of thrift in the proliferation of meaning' (1998b: 221). Wallace's reassertion of these men's author-ity over hideousness is thus suggestive of privatization's focus on thrift over perceived largesse. The latter characterizes feminism as a discipline in Wallace's texts, and this inefficiency indeed dovetails with how feminism, as he presents it, fails to adequately engage with the male hideousness it tries to critique. Foucault suggests that 'in a discipline ... what is supposed at the outset is not a meaning which has to be rediscovered ... but the requisites for the construction of new statements' (1981: 60); indeed, 'there must be the possibility of formulating new propositions' (60). In Wallace's depiction, feminism as a discipline has calcified into positions that can only rediscover established meanings. This is clear in the classes that FOPPP member Mary Esther Thode teaches, which have included 'The Toothless Predator: Breast Feeding as Sexual Assault' (Wallace 1996: 307).

When Ted Schact easily answers her exam question on double binds with '*mail fraud*' (308, italics in original) – thus punning on 'male fraud' – the implication is that Thode is so 'politically rabid' (307) that even in notionally non-feminist contexts she can only regurgitate an unthinking antipathy towards men.

Foucault goes on to argue that a 'discipline recognises true and false propositions; but it pushes back a whole teratology of knowledge beyond its margins ... there are monsters on the prowl whose form changes with the history of knowledge' (1981: 60). Taking the example of botanist Gregor Mendel, the significance of whose work was not truly appreciated until the twentieth century, Foucault suggests 'it is always possible that one might speak the truth in the space of a wild exteriority, but one is "in the true" only by obeying the rules of a discursive "policing"' (1981: 61). As Mendel's findings did not accord with the disciplinary conditions that were prevalent during his lifetime, he 'spoke the truth, but he was not "within the true"' (1981: 61). A similar dynamic is evident in how Wallace presents his hideous men, whose behaviours and attitudes, if nothing else, make them prowling monsters. Wallace implies that these men speak the truth of male sexual hideousness, but are not 'within the true' of feminist discourses of such. By privatizing the disciplinary methods Avril, Rusk, Thode, or Q represent, Wallace reaffirms men's author-ity over hideousness as a form of private property in a way that, ostensibly, allows feminists to better engage with these monsters. Consequently, with the 'Brief Interviews' he suggests that feminism can more efficiently advance an anti-masculinist politics that will be able, *qua* Foucault, to formulate new propositions, rather than reproducing commonplaces about male shittiness.

'B.I. #28' is the perhaps most pointed example of this. One of the two interviews that follows a pair of men in conversation, this story concerns E and K's discussion of 'what does today's woman want. ... In terms of the old mating dance' (Wallace 1999m: 192). E and K are students savvy to feminism; like the women whom they claim are in a double bind of postfeminist pressure and pre-feminist expectations, both 'have the empowerment-lingo down pat, that's for sure' (192). Indeed, 'whether it sounds Neanderthal or not' (192), they posit that 'today's women' (192) only espouse feminist ideas as a coded plea for men to rescue them from the pressures of such. Their misogynistic remarks that women 'do make great moms' (199) and that '*No* doesn't meant yes, but it doesn't mean no, either' (199, italics in original) encourages us to doubt their ideas. At the same time, however, their colloquy offers an incisive take on how consumer culture co-opts female empowerment to reaffirm traditional gender roles, thus bolstering women's supposed need for 'just-another-Neanderthal-male' (197). In this, E and K speak truths that are seemingly not 'within the true' of a perceived feminist discipline. Their hideousness contravenes the discursive policing of a feminism that works against misogyny, while implying that this feminism should expand its disciplinary parameters to accommodate E and K's analysis. If letting E and K speak confirms their hideousness with (ostensibly) a greater precision than an impersonal feminist discipline would allow, such privatization will also urge said discipline to develop its otherwise stale modes of analysis. Listening to the monsters who currently lie outside of its disciplinary comprehension, Wallace suggests, will spur feminist critique into more nuanced estimations of male hideousness.

The need to engage with ideas and opinions that one may find reprehensible marks much of Wallace's writing around the time of *Brief Interviews*. For instance, in 1997 *New York Observer* published Wallace's review of John Updike's *Toward the End of Time*, in which he skewers Updike's sexual chauvinism while still professing to be 'one of the very few actual subforty [*sic*] Updike *fans*' (2005b: 52, italics in original). The following year would also see the first appearance of 'Big Red Son', albeit under its original title of 'Neither Adult Nor Entertainment'. Most pertinently for my present discussion, in 1999 Wallace published 'Tense Present: Democracy, English, and the Wars over Usage' in *Harper's Magazine*, later collected in extended form as 'Authority and American Usage' in *Consider the Lobster* (2005d). This review of Bryan Garner's *A Dictionary of Modern American Usage* moves from asking, 'Whence the authority of dictionary-makers to decide what's OK and what isn't?' (Wallace 2005d: 75), to broader meditations on the political impasse between liberals and conservatives. Relating how he forces his black students not to write in an African American vernacular, or of how his pro-life convictions entail a pro-choice recognition that he should not interfere with others' lives, Wallace comes across as a self-aware conservative frustrated with 'Politically Correct English' (2005d: 110). For him, this language 'burke[s] the sorts of painful, unpretty, and sometimes offensive discourse that in a pluralistic democracy lead to actual political change' (112). The validity or otherwise of this idea aside, the implication that 'PC progressives' (111) undermine their own causes by 'pussyfooting around these [tough] realities with euphemistic doublespeak' (109) accords with how the 'Brief Interviews' stories suggest that feminism, if it privatizes its methods and so supports men's author-ity over their hideousness, can achieve its goals more effectively.

'B.I. #20', the longest interview of the entire cycle, closes with a provocative confirmation of this idea. The interviewee, concluding his story of how he fell in love with a woman after she tells him about being brutally raped and almost murdered, informs Q that

> I know how this sounds, trust me. I know your type and I know what you're bound to ask. Ask it now. This is your chance. I felt she could save me I said. Ask me now. Say it. I stand here naked before you. Judge me, you chilly cunt. You dyke, you bitch, cooze, cunt, slut, gash. Happy now? All borne out? Be happy. I don't care. I knew she could. I knew I loved. End of story. (1999n: 271)

Critics have tended to read these parting remarks as the interviewee – whom Wallace hints is named Eric (1999n: 266) – falling apart, undermined by Q's questioning and the raped woman's – whom Wallace implies is called Sara (1999n: 266) – implicit manipulation of him. Hayes-Brady, for instance, suggests that Eric's 'incoherent tirade' (2013: 146) signals how 'he loses his control over language altogether' (146). Rando similarly posits that these lines betray 'Eric's own inability to control the interpretation of his narrative' (2013: 582). Given that Eric's insults are perfectly coherent, as well as coldly measured in their deliberateness, it is more accurate to read them as a final assertion of author-ity over his own hideousness. This passage presents us with the kind of 'painful, unpretty, and sometimes offensive' (2005d: 112) language that, for Wallace, politically correct forces censor. Notably, when *The Paris Review* originally published this story, the question 'all borne out?' appeared as 'all judgements confirmed?' (Wallace 1997a), suggesting Eric's remarks are indeed intended as one last affront to Q's ideas about male hideousness. Wallace implies that privatizing her critique, and so allowing Eric to damn himself in ways that are more efficient and precise than apparent feminist judgements, dovetails with airing various abhorrent realties the 'PC left' (2005e: 188) cannot handle.

B.I. #46 offers an extended exploration of this premise. Its interviewee suggests that 'if there wasn't a Holocaust there wouldn't be a *Man's Search for Meaning*' (Wallace 1999i: 98), Viktor Frankl's 'great, great book' (98) about his experiences in Auschwitz. Similarly, there is no reason that being assaulted and raped 'can't have their positive aspects for a human being in the long run' (99); indeed, 'Everybody gets hurt and violated and broken sometimes, why are women so special?' (99). The interviewee takes pains to establish that he is not suggesting such abuse is justifiable, but rather that the 'experience in the human Dark Side' (98) that it affords can be valuable. In this regard, Wallace presents us with another man whose hideous expressions ostensibly speak the truth without being 'within the true' of feminist discourse. This aversion to being 'so smug and knee jerk' (104) about women who survive rape doubles as an antipathy to feminist disciplines, whose frameworks supposedly lack an appreciation of harsh realities. Rape is potentially beneficial, for the interviewee, because it forces proximity to 'the genuine Dark Side' (101): 'Now you really *know*. Now it's not just an idea or cause to get all knee-jerk about' (101, italics in original). This suggestion depoliticizes the issue; ideas or causes, the interviewee suggests, cannot hope to grasp the lived reality of such events. Like a hypothetical 'speechmaker at a school assembly [who] has you all repeat you're Somebody you're Strong over and over' (100), political ideas of female agency and empowerment are at fault for their rote, planned implementation. Such ideas, the story implies, inhibit awareness of the actual experiences of male hideousness they document.

Advocates for privatization tend to suggest that it is unconcerned with politics. For by prioritizing efficiency and reducing waste, privatization in Brown's words 'promulgates a market emphasis on "what works"' (2015: 130). As Duggan notes, this 'is usually presented not as a particular set of interests and political interventions, but as a kind of nonpolitics – a way of being reasonable' (2003: 10). Wallace's antipathy to Politically Correct English in 'Authority and American Usage' is suggestive of how such a reasonable non-politics is, for him, a more productive way to achieve the left's goals. Wallace suggests that the 'ideological principles' (2005d: 110) that informed the rise of PCE have resulted in 'a kind of Lenin-to-Stalinesque irony' (110), whereby egalitarian intentions 'have now actually produced a far more inflexible Prescriptivism' (110). His reference to 'Stalinization' (111) is suggestive of central planning as much as it is of authoritarian dictate. Commenting in particular on the possibility of wealth redistribution, Wallace suggests that 'the type of leftist vanity that informs PCE' (113) means that 'progressives lose the chance to frame their redistributive arguments in terms that are both realistic and realpolitikal' (113).[12] In other words, only by adopting a realistic and realpolitikal ethos of 'what works' can the left escape an ideological narrow mindedness that is 'harmful to its own cause' (111). Privatizing Q's feminist critique in the 'Brief Interviews' stories serves this purpose – it supplants what are apparently 'wacko dogmatic position[s]' (82) with more realistic, because supposedly non-ideological, methods.

Wallace praises Garner's dictionary for these qualities. Garner's style 'kept me from asking … what particular agendas or ideologies were informing what he had admitted right up front were "value judgements"' (119). His dictionary therefore seems '*objective*, but with a little *o*, as in "disinterested," "reasonable"' (119, italics in original). This is because Garner presents 'himself as an authority not in an *autocratic* sense but in a *technocratic* sense … knowledgeable, reasonable, dispassionate, fair' (122, italics in original). As argued, Wallace depicts feminist critiques of male hideousness as lacking such. Indeed, the 'Brief Interviews' privatize such critiques out of a conviction that technocratic approaches to the issue are more effective. However, Garner's technocracy is especially admirable because it also comes from a distinctly personal source. Garner shows the 'enduring passion that helps make someone a credible technocrat – we tend to like and trust experts whose expertise is born of a real love for their speciality instead of just a desire to be [an] expert' (123). As Garner's dictionary is indicative of an impassioned authorial persona – and not of the descriptivist versus prescriptivist disciplines Wallace describes in this essay – his arguments are more convincing than those of 'some established dogmatic camp' (72). Thus Garner's 'real thesis … is that the purposes of the expert authority and the purpose of the lay reader are identical' (125).

The impassioned technocrat's ability to bypass ideological positions, and to access 'lay' truths that said positions apparently fail to grasp, is particularly apparent at the close of 'B.I. #46'. After objecting throughout to Q's 'knee jerk reaction[s] … taking everything I say and taking and filtering it through your own narrow view of the world' (1999i: 101), we learn that his ideas concerning the potential benefits of gang rape derive from what is most likely personal experience: 'What if I said it happened to me?' (105). Though deliberately vague, his mention of 'this cane right here' (104), and his description of 'four guys that knee-jerked you in the balls to make you bend over' (105), intimates that it was he who was treated 'just [like] a hole to shove a Jack Daniel's bottle in so far it blows out your kidneys' (102). He therefore becomes the 'expert' here, affronting Q's 'knee-jerk politics about your ideas about victims' (101) with the particularities of lived experience. That he uses the phrase 'knee-jerked' (105) to describe such assault mirrors his perception of Q's 'knee-jerk politics' (101), provocatively implying that her pre-set estimations of hideous men is a form of rape – a way of conceiving him 'as a thing' (103) rather than a person.[13] The interviewee's final remark, that 'you don't know shit' (105), bears forth the notion that 'men mostly are shit' (Wallace 1999e: 22) that is clear throughout the story cycle. This interviewee knows male shittiness in ways that Q cannot, his expertise working, like Garner's, to stress the shortcomings of her disciplinary approach. His testimony, in turn, renders him an abhorrent if 'credible technocrat' (Wallace 2005d: 123) who is accordingly best suited to advance a critique of male hideousness.

As I have argued more generally, the 'Brief Interviews' present straight men as experts on their hideousness, reclaiming such as a form of private property against feminist critiques that Wallace equates with state ownership. This reclamation privatizes such critique; in other words, it suggests that moving property rights from a public-minded feminism into men's private hands allows for more efficient interrogations of men's sexual behaviour. Part of this process is the notion that, as a discipline, feminism has become ideologically stolid, and therefore at odds with Wallace's conviction that – as he puts it in relation to lexical and political correctness – 'the fundamental questions … involve[d] are ones whose answers have to be literally *worked out* instead of merely found' (2005d: 72, italics in original). The story cycle 'works out' what Wallace suggests are feminist commonplaces about male hideousness. It does so by compelling readers, positioned as Q, to engage with realities that are not 'in the true' of feminism's current disciplinary boundaries. Furthermore, the stories follow this logic to give nuance to what are ostensibly reductive feminist understandings of male hideousness. Despite their implicit focus upon efficiency and the non-politics of 'what works', then, the stories' privatization of Q's critique proceeds by humanizing her subjects, particularly and provocatively when they are at their most monstrous.

Conclusion

An encyclopaedic ambition for discursive mastery characterizes much of Wallace's fiction. Adam Kelly exemplifies a common hagiography when he describes this as 'vintage Wallace, of course: as a writer at home in virtually every discourse imaginable, he understood the specific resonances of each one' (2014a: 17). This impossible ambition for total expertise is arguably at its most brazen in relation to feminism. As I have argued, the 'Brief Interviews' set out not only to challenge feminist ideas about male sexual hideousness, but also to improve its critique of such.[14] For some scholars, such as Himmelheber, Kelly, and Matthew Alexander, this story cycle does offer engaging interrogations of sexism, notably in relation to rape culture. Hungerford takes a different tack; as I noted in my Introduction, she asks if 'one [should] believe that he has anything smart to say about the dynamics between men and women … ?' (2016: 150), and answers firmly in the negative. Indeed, she takes the 'Brief Interviews' as prime examples of Wallace's literary and personal misogyny. I have suggested in previous chapters how Wallace's texts are at times sceptical of feminist politics, and my analysis here of its depiction in both *Infinite Jest* and the 'Brief Interviews' stories furthers this. My interests in this present discussion, however, have not been to assess the value or otherwise of Wallace's paranoid caricature of feminism, but with how these representations follow neoliberal logics concerning property. I have argued that Wallace depicts straight men reclaiming their sexual hideousness as a form of private property. He does so in order to privatize feminist critique, thereby ostensibly making it more efficient.

These manoeuvres position male hideousness as part of a perceived anti-masculinist discourse. Wallace's men reverse this discourse to reclaim it, and in doing so, they strengthen their authorial ownership of such in the face of an apparently stale feminist discipline. With a stronger right to control their toxicity, as well as to exclude feminist others from talking about it, these men's testimonies circulate in ways that stress individual particularity against what they suggest is Q's uniform direction. As in Chapter 3's analysis of contract, therefore, the point here is to protect and empower men against an apparent attempt to suppress their individuality. That the 'Brief Interviews' do this through recourse to examples of male sexual depravity that, though well-intentioned, critiques like Q's cannot hope to ameliorate, furthers my contention that Wallace's texts are invested in the immutability of such sexual toxicity. Furthermore, one should question whether the 'improvement' of feminist critique that these stories proffer is not, in fact, a means of defanging it. In other words, the privatization at work here gestures towards the paradoxical suggestion that feminism, if it wishes to hold the 'Dark Side' (1999i: 98) of male sexuality to account, should surrender its ideological claims and assess misogyny on the basis of individual rather than structural violence. This idea does not give one much hope for the prospect of dismantling patriarchal oppressions which, by their very nature, traverse individual men and women.

As I suggested at the close of Chapter 3, the sense of illusory reckoning with such violence for Bachner allows certain writers to resolve the anxiety of their own implication in perpetuating it. The tension in Wallace's output between being invested in male characters and perspectives, and the awareness that such investments risk supporting patriarchal power relations, is perhaps nowhere more apparent than in the 'Brief Interviews'. By presenting male sexual hideousness as a type of private property, and by reasserting individual men's author-ity over such as a way to privatize Q's feminist critique, these stories endeavour to resolve this tension. Specifically, the process I have outlined in this chapter suggests that male sexual hideousness is best approached as a neutral economic issue: incontestable in itself, but manageable nonetheless. Further to this, although my emphasis here has been less explicitly on male sexual violence as something that defies representation, Bachner's argument on this front has still informed my own. Namely, the 'improved' feminist critique that the 'Brief

Interviews' stories formulate suggests that only by acknowledging her own inability to fully comprehend the sexual hideousness her interviewees embody can Q hope to make her critique more productive. To use Foucault's terms, these men constitute a teratology that an ostensibly inadequate feminist discipline cannot account for.[15]

Additionally, although my references to spermatic metaphors in this chapter have been scant, the dynamics I have outlined still follow ideas of blockage and release. Indeed, testimonies such as those given by the ejaculator of 'B.I. #14' ostensibly break through the ideological blockage of Q's feminist critique and in doing so release this discourse from its apparent tendency to reproduce pre-existing ideas. Despite this chapter's argument that the 'Brief Interviews' seek to protect men's individuality, moreover, the very sexual toxicity that these stories envisage as being in need of reclamation has its genesis in an attempt to brand all men with the same *collective* mark. Put differently, these interviewees reclaim the right to speak about a collective designation as, paradoxically, a sign of their individual hideousness. This uneasy relationship between group identity and the individual in relation to sexuality will be significant in my next chapter. There I will consider the neoliberal logic of austerity, which although it evokes a collective need to tackle debt, places responsibility for this action on individual exemplars of particular groups. To be more specific, in *Oblivion* and *The Pale King*, Wallace looks to the sexual hardships of little men as a means to divert attention away from the need to reform broader ideas of male sexual toxicity.

5

Austerity
Sacrificing and scapegoating little men

During a speech he gave in Michigan on 29 September, 2000, future president George W. Bush declared that 'I know the human being and fish can coexist peacefully' (Weisberg 2000). This surreal ad lib, meant to signal his commitment to not removing energy-producing dams merely because they endangered fish, was a precursor to the many semantic mistakes he would make when in office. Such blunders, and the general ridicule with which they were met in popular culture, also offer a useful entryway into considering a defining trope of Wallace's texts during the same 2001–08 period. Namely, this is Wallace's emphasis on schlemiels, or little men – straight males who, in various ways, are pitiably and comically inadequate. Human–fish relations would of course preoccupy Wallace in his 2005 Kenyon College Commencement Address, in which he spun life lessons from a joke about two goldfish unaware they are in water. Associations between Wallace and this ichthyologic sermon have been hard to break, much to the annoyance of some of his critical interlocutors. Boswell, for instance, regrets the 'unfortunate popular conception of Wallace as a … writer of self-help narratives designed to "save us" (2014: 210), a conception 'calcified by the book publication of his Kenyon graduation speech' (210). Bracketing the speech's content, however, and spotlighting instead the ignorance that these 'two young … boys' (Wallace 2009: 3) display, suggests the importance of little male ineptitude to Wallace's later texts – whether exemplified by goldfish or a president.

Oblivion and *The Pale King* are in fact preoccupied with littleness. In the opening story of the former, 'Mister Squishy', protagonist Terry Schmidt struggles with a sense of 'thoroughgoing *smallness*' (2004a: 31, italics in original) at his marketing job, while in the book's closing novella, 'The Suffering Channel', Skip Atwater ponders how 'the management of insignificance' (2004d: 284) is 'the single great informing conflict of the American psyche' (284). *The Pale King* displays similar concerns in relation to civic duty, and how Americans have apparently lost 'the old sense of being small parts of something larger ... to which we have serious responsibilities' (2012a: 138). Within this general concern with diminution, though, the little man as a figure of sexual ineptitude ironically looms large. In this final chapter, I explore how these ineptitudes are suggestive of a logic of neoliberal austerity. The most recent imposition of austerity measures occurred in the aftermath of the 2008 financial crisis, when, broadly speaking, Western governments shifted responsibility for budget deficits from the banking sector and onto public spending. Reducing deficits by cutting such spending, the thinking went, would better allow societies to tackle high levels of debt. At the same time, what Rebecca Bramall calls 'austerity culture' (2013: 4) – the array of 'discourses, values, [and] ideological elements' (4) that help to legitimate austerity's shifting of responsibility – perpetuated the idea that some behaviours are more conducive to reducing the deficit than others. *Oblivion*'s and *The Pale King*'s depictions of little men work in a similar way. These texts legitimate austerity logic by depicting little men as virtuous avatars of sexual sacrifice, on the one hand, and as sexual profligates to be scapegoated, on the other.

Before exploring how a concern with budgets, deficits and debts relates to Wallace's writing of male sexuality in these texts, it is first necessary to account for the presence of little men themselves. Though they appear elsewhere in Wallace's work – see for instance Rick Vigorous in *Broom*, or the many bumbling personas of Wallace's journalism – little men appear with striking frequency in his later output. Antipathy for Bush offers one possible reason for this. A passing snipe at his 'patrician smirk and mangled cant' (2005e: 187) in Wallace's 2000 essay on John McCain had developed, by the 2007 piece 'Just Asking', into a summary of the ways Bush's government was undermining democracy (2012f: 322). In a simplistic but nonetheless useful estimation of this antipathy, D. T. Max suggests the president enraged Wallace because 'he saw in Bush all the little-man-lost-in-a-big-man's shirt qualities he disliked in himself' (2012b). As a figurative little man, Bush is a contemptible lodestar to the many images of white male ineffectuality that populate Wallace's later texts. In a 2006 interview with Bryan A. Garner, during which he criticized Bush for being 'out of his element' (2013: 110), Wallace suggested that 'we love to laugh at pathetic schlemiels, particularly [those] who are trying to look the opposite of that' (2013: 54). Though he was speaking here about people with poor grammatical skills, 'pathetic schlemiels' (54) are central to *Oblivion*'s and *The Pale King*'s sexual austerities.

That Wallace uses a Yiddish term – schlemiel – to describe such inept men signals his tendency, as explored by Lucas Thompson, to exploit tropes from minority cultures (2016: 199). Wallace's texts indeed appropriate the schlemiel from Yiddish and Jewish-American culture, but they also put the character to their own uses.¹ In an important early theorization of the schlemiel, Hannah Arendt suggests that he (and it is nearly always a 'he') is representative of Jewish experiences of social ostracism. Focusing on the poetry of Heinrich Heine, she argues that this ostracism renders the schlemiel the avatar of a 'natural freedom' (1944: 104), by which he can take a liberatingly askew view of social relations. Later studies, however, tend to emphasize the schlemiel as a tragicomic figure, cynically hopeful in the face of his suffering. Ruth R. Wisse's *The Schlemiel as Modern Hero* (1971) is the most astute analysis in this vein. Wisse suggests that the schlemiel arose as a response to the persecution of Eastern European Jews: 'vulnerable, ineffectual in his efforts at self-advancement and self-preservation, he emerged as the archetypal Jew, especially in his capacity of potential victim' (1971: 4–5). Though Wallace's little men both exemplify and modulate this tradition, more recent work by Brenton J. Malin (2005) and David Buchbinder (2008) has noted the preponderance of white male schlemiels in millennial popular culture. Hence what Stephen Wade describes as a feature that 'goes deep into the literary conventions of Yiddish' (1999: 4) now circulates in media that lack any explicit focus on Jewishness. The presence of this figure in Wallace's texts accords with its mainstream use. I use the phrase 'little man' in this chapter to reflect such mainstreaming, and refer to the schlemiel, mainly in my argument's second half, when it is useful to do so.

That said, the central little man characteristic I wish to explore in these texts – sexual ineffectuality – has a strong lineage in images of Jewish-American masculinity. David Biale describes 'the Jew as sexual schlemiel' (1997: 204) as a stock figure, 'the little man with the big libido and the even bigger sexual neurosis, a character comically unable to consummate his desire' (204). Biale points specifically to Woody Allen, whose performances in films such as *Everything You Always Wanted to Know About Sex* (1972) and *Annie Hall* (1977) arguably epitomize the sexual schlemiel. Wallace's depiction of similar men, such as Terry Schmidt, follows this template. As I argue later on, it is precisely because these men are so neurotically oversexed that Wallace punishes them. Yet little men in *The Pale King* and *Oblivion* who, rather than being punished for hyper-sexuality, are valued for their sexual indifference, bear a different relationship to the precedent Biale outlines. Here Wallace retains the schlemiel's position as both isolated and pathetic, but mutes his sexuality. Two examples from popular film, themselves suggestive of the little man's millennial currency, help to illustrate this. The schlemiels that Wallace punishes resemble Kevin Spacey's character Lester Burnham in *American Beauty* (1999) – a man lusting after his daughter's friend and in conflict with his resulting feelings of shame and social censure. The schlemiels these texts value for their sexual indifference, by contrast, are more like the character Milton Waddams in *Office Space* (1999) – a marginalized office worker whose grotesqueness, and general kookiness, work against any possible sexual characteristics.

Wallace can also be said to torque conventional ideas of the schlemiel through his often bleak worldview in later texts, particularly *Oblivion*. The little man's struggle in the face of various obstacles has traditionally functioned as his saving grace, offering readers and spectators a point of conflicted but redemptive identification. Examining the character in contemporary French literature, Warren F. Motte suggests that 'the schlemiel carnivalizes our struggles and our way of being in the world, holding a funhouse mirror up to us and daring us to recognize ourselves therein. … He is a loser without a doubt; yet he is a beautiful loser' (2003: 79–80). Milton in *Office Space*, or Lester in *American Beauty*, fit this mould rather well – as grotesque and pathetic as they are, both characters also solicit the audience's empathy (though the latter perhaps less so now, given allegations, in 2017, that Spacey has sexually assaulted young men). Wallace's little men are perhaps never completely unlikeable, but he more often than not accentuates their role as losers at the direct expense of their beauty. By the same token, he also downplays what Motte suggests is the schlemiel's carnivalesque or funhouse traits. When little men like Schmidt serve comic functions, it is reminiscent of how Wallace reads Kafka's humour, which he notably values for its lack of 'Pynchonian slapstick … Rothish priapism … or Woody Allen-type kvetching' (2005c: 62–3). Instead of schlemiel comedy, Kafka's humour for Wallace engages with more serious suffering – it relishes the fact that 'the horrific struggle to establish a human self results in a self whose humanity is inseparable from that horrific struggle' (2005c: 64).[2]

Despite these caveats, however, reading various men in *Oblivion* and *The Pale King* in the tradition of the schlemiel is still appropriate. Comparable character types like the fool or the anti-hero are too broad, whereas the schlemiel, or little man, specifies the often pitiable and frustrated nature of male characters in both texts. These traits are also well-matched to how austerity discourses praise the apparent virtues of reduced expectations and necessary hardship. Having described the presence of the schlemiel in Wallace's work, I now turn to an examination of austerity and how it functions in this context. Of chief importance here is to show how austerity's shifting of responsibility for deficit reduction – away from reigning in financial speculation, and towards cuts to public spending – translates into images of male sexuality. It does so, I argue, through how little men's sacrifices and sufferings in *Oblivion* and *The Pale King* transform the problems created by hideous straight male behaviour into the problems of men who are unable to profit from such. Put differently, if austerity deflects attention from capitalism as a force systemically prone to crisis and exploitation, Wallace's sexual austerity does the same for straight male toxicity. With the former, it is the poor who must pay the price; with the latter, it is the little man.

Austerity for little men

Recent studies of the economic justifications for austerity tend to focus on how the concept has developed over time. In *Austerity: The History of a Dangerous Idea* (2013), Mark Blyth examines the thought of Locke, Hume, and Smith to suggest that austerity's 'condition of … appearance – parsimony, frugality, morality, and a pathological fear of the consequences of government debt – lie deep within economic liberalism's fossil record from its very inception' (2013: 115). Florian Schui's *Austerity: The Great Failure* (2014), meanwhile, goes back even further to trace the development of arguments for and against austerity from ancient Greece onwards. As their books' titles suggest, both commentators argue that austerity is misguided, particularly as a path to recovery in the aftermath of the financial crash and the subsequent 2010 Eurozone debt crisis. These events, as Heather Whiteside puts it, have led to austerity being '*en vogue* once again' (2016: 361, italics in original). Blyth's definition is useful in specifying what exactly is now so voguish: austerity is 'a form of voluntary deflation in which the economy adjusts through the reduction of wages, prices and public spending to restore competitiveness, which is (supposedly) best achieved by cutting the state's budget, debts and deficits' (2013: 2). Going forward, I emphasize the latter elements of Blyth's definition – cutting budgets, debts and deficits – as being particularly important to the sexual austerity evident in *Oblivion* and *The Pale King*. For these texts variously mobilize the littleness of their men to stress the apparent benefits of reducing sexual spending.

If the contemporary prevalence of austerity studies is suggestive of commentators making sense of events post-2008 – both the year of the financial crash, and of Wallace's suicide – austerity has nonetheless figured prominently in past neoliberal periods. Whiteside suggests that 'austerity gained prominence in the late 1970s/early 1980s as a solution to the problem of "stagflation"' (2016: 362) – that is, the combined phenomena of high unemployment, high inflation and zero growth. Kim Phillips-Fein, meanwhile, has argued extensively that New York City's 1975 fiscal crisis marks the birth of austerity politics. As she explains, then president Ford, with his advisers Donald Rumsfeld and Alan Greenspan, 'opposed federal help for New York. They were convinced that the city had brought its problems on itself through heedless, profligate spending. Bankruptcy was thus a just punishment for its sins' (2017: 2). The Ford administration's response to New York's out of control spending – immortalized by the *Daily News* headline 'Ford to City: Drop Dead' – prefigures the punitive nature of post-2008 austerity measures. To read sexuality in *Oblivion* and *The Pale King* as being indicative of neoliberal austerity is not, therefore, to apply historical parameters they could in no way foresee. Rather, it is to suggest that they sexually articulate logics that have been internal to neoliberal theory and practice for decades.

Phillips-Fein also observes how, 'paradoxically, the crisis is sometimes noted as a great triumph for New York. … Everyone – labor, business, the banks, ordinary citizens – is thought to have accepted the need for austerity and chipped in' (2017: 4). Comparing this with Democratic House leader Nancy Pelosi's statement, in 2011, that Americans 'must enter an era of austerity; to reduce the deficit through shared sacrifice' (Pelosi, cited in Brown 2015: 275), reiterates how ideas of common hardship are prominent in austerity discourse. Indeed, for austerity's proponents, balancing the budget so that expenditures do not exceed available resources means that everybody needs to bear the burden of reduced spending. If austerity arises, as Lauren Berlant observes, 'out of a sense that *something* was out of control that required a conserving hand' (2011a: 1, italics in original), then its measures for effecting such conservation appeal, as John Clarke and Janet Newman put it, 'to shared sacrifice and suffering, to fairness and freedom, to a sense of collective obligation' (2012: 309). Chapter 1 argued that Wallace's texts responsibilize men into more judiciously expending their individual sexual resources; to realize, as Wallace puts it at the end of 'Back in New Fire', that 'it's not just other people you have to respect' (2012c: 172). In this final chapter I explore the opposite: how *Oblivion* and *The Pale King* follow an austerity logic of conserving sexual resources in the interests of collectivity. This is the notion that, to quote UK prime minister David Cameron (2010–15), when it comes to balancing the budget 'we are all in this together' (Cameron, cited in Clarke and Newman 2012: 303).

As many commentators have pointed out, this discursive emphasis on collectivity does not translate into reality. In fact, in Whiteside's words, 'Austerity has less to do with achieving economic growth (on which its track record is abysmal) than it does with shifting blame for economic conditions … from the wealthy to the already-precarious' (2016: 364). Austerity turns the need to reform (or, abolish) capitalism into making the most vulnerable responsible for its survival. In Marilynne Robinson's words, in the aftermath of 2008,

> the crisis of the private financial system has been transformed into a tale of slovenly and overweening government that perpetuates and is perpetuated by a dependent and demanding population. … For about ten days the crisis was interpreted as a consequence of the ineptitude of the highly paid, and then it transmogrified into a grudge against the populace at large, whose lassitude was bearing the society down to ruin. (2012: 45)

Kim Allen et al., drawing on Stuart Hall, describe this transformation as a kind of 'ideological displacement' (2015: 909), and it is evident in the sexual austerity Wallace prescribes for his little men. In *Oblivion* and *The Pale King* he aligns capitalism, envisaged as the ruthless pursuit of profit, with images of hideous masculinity, implying that both share a drive to accumulate goods – whether monetary or sexual – that is unsustainable. Despite this, it is to little men that both texts look for a solution, suggesting that such figures must sacrifice sexuality, or act as scapegoats to be punished. These processes differ between *Oblivion* and *The Pale King*, but they nonetheless mirror how austerity discourse displaces responsibility for creating and reducing the deficit onto society's most vulnerable.

What does it mean, though, for sexuality to function as a shared budget? Wallace's tendency to depict male sexuality in these terms is in fact most evident in *Infinite Jest*, where James Incandenza, as well as an unnamed 'phalloneurotic New Yorker' (1996: 234), believes 'in a finite world-total of available erections [which] rendered him always either impotent or guilt-ridden' (789).[3] Similarly, when Hal reflects on how 'lifetime virginity is a conscious goal' (634) and 'feels like O.'s [i.e. his brother Orin] having enough acrobatic coitus for all three of them' (634), the suggestion is that his own (and Mario's) lack of expenditure works to offset Orin's satyriasis. Wallace develops this idea of a common sexual budget in *Oblivion* and *The Pale King*, and in turn begs a further question: How can a shared sexual budget accrue a deficit? Or in Michael Tratner's words, 'How can one discharge more libido than one has'? (2001: 29). Discussing *Ulysses*, Tratner reframes this question to ask 'Are there social practices that *increase* libido?' (29, italics in original), and answers that advertising and masturbation are 'a stimulus to consumer demand' (29). Advertising, in particular, 'loans people desires and suggests many new ways of indulging those desires' (29). A similar logic is at work in *The Pale King* and *Oblivion*. Here solicitations for sexual expenditures outside of heteronormative frameworks act as a form of credit, allowing men to spend resources they do not truly have. A deficit arises, then, on the basis that non-reproductive sexuality is a hollow form of expenditure. Based on deferring payment, this spending on credit compels men to engage in activities that, for Wallace, heteronormative sexual budgets cannot cover.

In keeping with the elements of misogyny I have previously identified in Wallace's writing, *Oblivion* and *The Pale King* often align these solicitations for wasteful expenditures with women. Notably, though, they do this through little men's own subjective feelings of powerlessness before them. Though images of malevolently seductive femininity do appear in these texts (see, for instance, Amber Moltke in 'The Suffering Channel'), Wallace focalizes the perils of sexual debt through men themselves. Thus, it is not so much that these men owe something to women, but rather that their ideas of women as bestowing male heterosexual validity has often convinced them that they do. The austerity that these texts endorse, whereby they scapegoat men for their profligacy, or induce them to sacrifice for greater goals, also works through comedic deflations of the same women being idolized. For instance, in 'Mister Squishy', the brief remarks that the woman Schmidt obsesses over has 'thick fingers' (2004a: 26) and a 'great broad back' (55) undercut his outsized desires for her. However, before implying that *Oblivion* and *The Pale King* undermine the misogyny in this dynamic – recycling as it does stereotypical male fears of feminine entrapment – it is important to bear in mind that both texts still envisage debt to women as being objectionable, even as they register how deluded these little men are.

Wendy Brown offers a useful theoretical framework for understanding how Wallace's sexual austerities tackle such debt. As part of the epilogue to her study *Undoing the Demos*, her thoughts on austerity are tentative, but they still offer a productive spur to thinking about sacrifice and – in her use of the work of René Girard – scapegoating. For Brown, though neoliberalism diminishes 'venues for active citizenship' (2015: 210), it 'retains and transforms the idea of citizen sacrifice' (210). During a period when 'loyal citizens must "share sacrifice" in accepting austerities' (212), the notion of 'sacrificial citizenship expands to include anything related to the requirements and imperatives of the economy' (211). However, drawing on Moshe Halbertal, Brown suggests that the religious and moral-political nature of sacrifice is 'premised upon a noneconomistic and nonmarketized form of exchange' (215). As such, despite the prevalence of sacrifice in austerity discourse, it remains partly outside its domain: 'as a supplement to neoliberal reason [sacrifice] carries the potential for breaking open or betraying the limitations of that logic' (216). Brown then outlines 'two features of religious sacrifice' (216) that might serve this purpose. First, substitution: if the victims of sacrifices usually function as substitutes for a sacrificer, then this encourages people to ask, 'Who or what might be the object of substitution in neoliberal citizen sacrifice?' (216). Second, restoration: if 'religious sacrifice often aims … to rebalance the force of life and common existence' (218), then accentuating this element within a neoliberal context can potentially spark interrogation of what exactly is said to be out of balance.

Brown's idea that sacrifice offers a position external to neoliberal reason is limited, to some extent, by how it reproduces the ethos of self-interest it attempts to combat. 'A refusal of the encomium to sacrifice' (218) out of the knowledge that one gets nothing in return – in Brown's words, knowing there is no 'guarantee that the benefits of this sacrifice will redound to us' (216) – reiterates, rather than upends, the economization of moral-political questions into cost-benefit analyses. This snag aside, though, Brown's discussion usefully taps into the motivations that *Oblivion* and *The Pale King* display *for* sexual austerity. Restoration and substitution are important to how these texts respectively value sexual indifference as a worthwhile sacrifice, and scapegoat little men who are neurotically oversexed. Following in Brown's footsteps and drawing on Halbertal and Girard's work, moreover, allows one to explore how Wallace's sexual austerities use these ideas. My readings confirm the pertinence of Brown's observations but, contrary to her intent, in ways that are internal to the logic of neoliberal austerity. Through different forms of sacrificing and scapegoating, Wallace's little men bear the burden of solving problems created by 'bigger' ideas of male sexuality, thereby functioning as prime objects for austerity's displacement of responsibility.

'Small *h*-heroes': Sacrificing sexuality

In his Editor's Note to *The Pale King*, Michael Pietsch outlines some of the ways the novel might have been different had Wallace lived to finish it. For one, he suggests that 'the terms "titty-pinching" and "squeezing his shoes" … would probably not be repeated as often as they are' (2012: xi). Wallace uses the former in this novel to designate the meta-fictional aesthetic that its would-be writer 'David Wallace' wishes to avoid (Wallace 2012a: 69), and also, in modified form, to describe Toni Ware's sexual assault as a young girl (65). The latter term, meanwhile, appears regularly in Chris Fogle's account of joining the IRS and refers in particular to the way his father would chide him for his youthful lack of direction (158). Abstracting these terms from their immediate contexts, however, and putting to one side the question of draft imprecision, both concepts are in fact suggestive of *The Pale King*'s interest in sexual austerity. Pinching and squeezing, imagined as reduced consumption in light of economic difficulty, are what this text's little men need to do. The maternal 'titty' is to be rejected for the dependency that it instils, while the preoccupation that Fogle has with a podiatrist's sign of a female foot – the position of which, as a university student, he uses to decide whether he should study or party – compounds the undesirability of such dependence. *Oblivion* displays similar concerns, a testament to how, as Hering explores, this collection to a large extent developed out of Wallace's contemporaneous writing of *The Pale King*.[4] That said, my focus in this section lies with the latter, for it is in *The Pale King* that Wallace most notably suggests that sacrificing sexuality is conducive to balancing a shared spermatic budget.

Sacrifice is a motif throughout Wallace's texts, and as Andrew Warren observes, 'it becomes central to Wallace's mature political and ethical thinking' (2018: 181). However, it is worth considering one of Wallace's earlier and most explicit treatments of sacrifice in relation to male sexuality before outlining how it works in *The Pale King*. In his essay on the tennis player Michael Joyce, Wallace links sexual abstinence with achievement, for Joyce is 'a complete man (though in a grotesquely limited way)' (1997e: 254) because of his 'ascetic focus ... a consent to live in a world that, like a child's world, is very serious and very small' (237). He then suggests that

> athletes are in many ways our culture's holy men: they give themselves over to a pursuit, endure great privation and pain to actualize themselves at it, and enjoy a relationship to perfection that we admire and reward ... and love to watch even though we have no inclination to walk that road ourselves. In other words they do it "for" us, sacrifice themselves for our (we imagine) redemption. (237)

Wallace finds Joyce both inspirational and grotesque for the sacrifices tennis demands of him, and especially in terms of sex. For as he also notes towards the essay's end, Joyce has 'dated some. It's impossible to tell whether he's a virgin. It seems staggering and impossible, but my sense is he might be. Then again, I tended to idealize and distort him' (254).[5] Idealized or distorted, Wallace associates Joyce's probable virginity with his athletic prowess. Having sacrificed sexuality for the good of his game, he allows Wallace to glimpse a 'relationship to perfection' (237) that he is otherwise barred from. Indeed, Joyce may pursue individual glory, 'to have his name known' (254), but his sacrifice, at least in this regard, works for the benefit of another, less disciplined man.

This sacrificing for others takes on explicitly political meanings in *The Pale King*, foregrounding issues such as resource distribution, civic duty and the legacy of America's founding ideals, to name but a few. Central, though, is what Mark McGurl identifies as the novel's 'idealization of debt as the price we should gladly pay for community, national or otherwise' (2014: 54). McGurl aligns *The Pale King* with the primordial debt theories David Graeber elucidates in his *Debt: The First 5,000 Years* (2011). These theories, in McGurl's words, posit a 'metaphysical "existence = debt" equation' (51) that sidesteps the 'global political domination of the indebted' (51) by creditors. It is in the name of gladly paid debt that Wallace has little men in this novel sacrifice sexual desire. Moreover, as many scholars have noted, *The Pale King* marks Wallace's most direct critique of free-market economics, and in part excavates the rise of neoliberalism in the United States more generally. By showing how austerity discourses inform *The Pale King*'s depictions of sexuality, I draw connections to the novel's wider considerations of debt repayment in the context of neoliberalism. However, in doing so, I show how the novel recapitulates austerity's displacement of responsibility for budget deficits onto the vulnerable. It is little men who come to represent the virtues of sacrificing to repay debt, even when they have not themselves accrued it.

Fogle's conversion from being a 'wastoid' (Wallace 2012a: 172) student to being 'one of the low-level True Believers on whom the Service depended' (273) illustrates how sexual austerity is imbricated in *The Pale King*'s broader concerns with budgets, debts and deficits. Fogle, 'bumbling into the wrong building's 311 right before final exams' (218), finds himself in an advanced tax accounting class, where a substitute teacher ends his lesson with an encomium to accounting's 'effacement. Sacrifice. Service. To give oneself to the care of others' money' (233). The speech signals *The Pale King*'s attachment to stereotypical understandings of 1950s rectitude, what Burn describes as the presence in the novel of 'all those old-fashioned hats and odes to fusty values of hardwork and self-control' (2014a: 152). What is most significant for my purposes, though, is Fogle's description of how the class – of which 'nearly everyone ... was male' (Wallace 2012a: 219) – responds to the idea that accounting, in the substitute's words, can be 'an arena for actual heroism' (232): 'It seemed then that a sudden kind of shudder went through the room, or maybe an ecstatic spasm, communicating itself from senior accounting major or graduate business student to senior accounting major or grad business student so rapidly that the whole collective seemed for an instant to heave' (232–3). As Severs notes, Wallace here draws on chapter 94 of *Moby-Dick* (1851), 'A Squeeze of the Hands', 'echoing Melville's homoerotic language' (2017a: 215) to convey an ideal scene of 'communal labor' (215). Robert K. Martin explains how 'A Squeeze of the Hands' depicts a 'scene of fellowship in which work is transformed into sexuality. The subject of the chapter is masturbation, with a play on variations on the whale's "sperm"' (1998: 194). If the shudder Fogle recalls has the ring of an ejaculatory epiphany, it is in the service of recruiting the class into taking 'care of others' money' (Wallace 2012a: 233). The teacher lauds the sobriety of tax accounting as part of his encouragement that the class deny their own self-interest – namely, for avoiding the job's 'sheer drudgery' (229) – and process money envisaged as a communal, spermatic resource. To borrow the title of Michiko Kakutani's 2011 review of *The Pale King*, the point here is 'Maximized Revenue, Minimized Existence': self-denial as a means to strengthen collective budgets. Accordingly, the substitute's speech functions as a corrective to what, up until this point, had been Fogle's 'wastoid' (Wallace 2012a: 172) drift.

Wallace inverts Melville's scene so that, rather than being, in Martin's words, a temporary abandonment of 'the order of work' (1998: 195), the substitute's speech is vocationally inspiring. But much as Melville for Martin 'is too much of a cynic … to let this vision last' (1998: 195), Fogle's reminiscence also slyly undercuts the teacher's speech. For one, he cannot be 'a hundred percent sure this [the 'ecstatic spasm'] was real' (Wallace 2012a: 233). Moreover, Fogle does not know whether the right descriptor for the speech is 'hortation or exhortation' (235). The former, evocative in its first syllable of 'whore', casts the substitute's enthusiasm for self-effacing sperm-handling in a more pejorative light. This ambivalence queries the idea that Fogle's newfound readiness for sacrifice is a straightforward endorsement of austerity. Furthermore, the sexual meanings that I have picked from Fogle's monologue are selective, belying the allusiveness of its ninety-eight pages (the novel's longest chapter). However, that Fogle cannot be sure if the spasm occurred only heightens its status as an ideal to aim for; namely, that of shared sacrifice in the belief that, as the novel's invocatory opening chapter has it, 'we are all of us brothers' (5). His readiness, *qua* Kakutani, to 'minimize' after hearing the substitute is indicative of the sacrifice *The Pale King* values. If male sexuality forms a single (but important) strand in Fogle's conversion to such austerity, though, it plays a central role in the novel's more notable representatives of such. These are Shane Drinion, and the boy who tries to press his lips against every part of his body. The sexual austerity Wallace prescribes for these figures, moreover, defuses interrogation of the toxic male behaviours that have put shared spermatic budgets into debt in the first place.

As Fogle's decision to join the IRS compensates for his former drift, these figures' sacrifices work as restorative measures to this unbalanced budget. Their status as little men is quite often suggestively literal – whether age-wise in how the boy becomes 'newly mature' (399) through his contortionism, or interpersonally in terms of Drinion's social anonymity. Wallace also aligns such littleness with their respective positions outside of sexual desire. In this regard they resemble what David Greven calls the 'inviolate male' (2005: 1). Writing on nineteenth-century American literature, but intimating the figure's presence in late twentieth-century texts, Greven describes the inviolate male as 'sexually and emotionally unavailable … resolutely ungraspable, elusive, a hermetically sealed vessel of chastity and purity' (2005: 1). Drinion and the boy's gnomic peculiarity accords with Greven's description. It is by virtue of their being 'apart from both male collectivity and Woman' (2005: 28) that these characters exemplify a much needed sexual austerity. They represent what Halbertal outlines as '"sacrificing *for.*" … Self-sacrifice for another individual, value, or collective' (2012: 10, italics in original), rather than '"sacrificing to" [which] involves … such questions as ritual, substitution, atonement' (2012: 9). Brown rightly cautions that Halbertal's distinction is unstable (2015: 214), but the notion of sacrificing *for* a collective is useful to understanding how Drinion and the boy function as incitements to reducing sexual spending.

Wallace's contortionist boy is reminiscent of Vito Acconci's 1970 performance art piece *Trademarks*. Sitting naked on the floor, Acconci bit as much of his body as he could reach, before applying printer's ink to the bite marks and stamping various surfaces with his body (Mahon 2005: 273). Rather than bites, though, Wallace describes the boy's pursuit as 'press[ing] his lips' (Wallace 2012a: 396), and once with the word 'kissed'. The appearance of this latter term subtly undercuts its libidinal implications: 'The upper portions of his genitals were simple, and were protrusively kissed and passed over' (399). Added to this, when he reaches his scrotum and anus 'these areas had been touched, tagged on the four-sided chart inside his personal ledger, then washed clean of ink and forgotten' (403). This neutral description of erogenous zones is in one sense attributable to him being 'just a little boy' (403); he indeed begins his self-kissing at six, and is eleven by the account's end. But Wallace juxtaposes the boy's activities with those of his father, 'an entrepreneur who sold motivational tapes' (405), and a man who is '*tortured*' (407, italics in original) by his compulsive need to have extramarital affairs. Connections between the two – for instance, the father maintains his own ledger, albeit to track his social standing (406), and 'almost contort[s] himself' (407) when shaving – reaffirms how they are, in a sense, mirror images. The boy's pointedly non-libidinal pursuit works as a countermeasure to the father's inability to control himself sexually. In this sense, the former's self-kissing is an oblique way of sacrificing desires that the latter cannot.

Significantly, the philandering that results from what the father perceives to be his 'normal male sexual drives' (407) is suggestive of debt. After his first affair, in which the father 'longed to detach from the woman, but he didn't want the woman to be able to detach' (408), the number of women 'with whom he was secretly involved and to whom he had sexual obligations steadily expanded' (408) as he pursues 'the relief and excitement of an attachment freely chosen' (408). Each new sexual debt the father takes on covers his failure to break off the last. He thus continually postpones the hard work of paying off an obligation. Wallace compounds the difference from the son here through how the boy's chiropractor 'liked to say [there] were the two different types of payments for the spine and associated nervosa, which were *Now* and *Later*' (398, italics in original). The father's 'lack of backbone' (407) – a heavy pun, given the context – amounts to a dereliction of responsibility for his situation, enabled through a string of increasingly bad sexual debts. Commenting on the common sense appeal of austerity arguments, Blyth suggests that they can be 'handily summed up in the phrase *you cannot cure debt with more debt*. If you have too much debt, stop spending' (7, italics in original). The boy's non-libidinal self-kissing follows this logic, compensating for this father's sexual debts by being, 'in some childish way, self-contained and –sufficient' (403), even if 'these [goals] were beyond his conscious awareness' (403).

Consequently, this scene displaces responsibility for cutting a sexual deficit the father has created onto the boy. By seeking extramarital sex, the father spends on credit, artificially inflating the amount of spermatic resources available and postponing the time of 'payment' – envisaged as the hard work of ending these affairs, or of submitting to 'marriage's conjugal routines [however] tedious and stifling' (407). By comparison, the boy's 'adult idea of quiet daily discipline and progress toward a long term goal' (398) means that he shows a positive rectitude in keeping with *The Pale King*'s broader interests in self-control. Furthermore, to the extent that Wallace presents the boy's self-kissing as being admirably demonstrative of qualities the father lacks, then he downplays the responsibility that cultural constructions of male sexuality – and behind them an entire heteronormative system that, one can assume, forces the father to be 'wedded at twenty' (407) – have for his 'secret torture' (407). Though the narrator points to this background as the reason for the father's torture, the implication is that, if he had more backbone, he would be able to contain his desires to accumulate within the strictures of marriage. The boy, a literal little man in his commitment to 'adult idea[s]' (398), not only sacrifices sexuality so his father does not have to, but also to transmute a crisis of accumulation with systemic causes (that of male sexuality as heteronormatively constructed) into a question of personally failing to expend correctly. The boy accordingly picks up the tab and, true to austerity's duplicitous emphasis on shared sacrifice, undergoes hardships in the name of balancing a spermatic budget he did not personally upset.

This provides an interesting contrast with the dynamics I explored in Chapter 2. There I showed how Wallace approaches male homosexuality as a risky type of asset or debt which, once securitized in the form of the closet, allows for emotional returns between straight men. In *The Pale King* and *Oblivion*, sexual debts to women seemingly cannot serve the same aim. My second example of little male sacrifice in *The Pale King* furthers the unacceptability of such debt. This is Drinion's conversation with Meredith Rand, a woman so attractive that she 'has been known to produce facial tics even in gay or otherwise asexual men' (449). As the narrator reflects, Rand 'is a cut of pure choice prime, is the consensus, not always unspoken' (449). Rand's 'galvanic' (451) beauty renders men incapable of treating her as anything but an object to 'buy' like a piece of meat. Changing 'as though they were involved in a game whose stakes have suddenly become terribly high' (449), those who do not studiously ignore her respond to Rand by trying to one up one another: 'Some of the male examiners are, by the second round of pitchers, performing for Meredith Rand' (449). She instigates forms of male self-inflation – even her husband, Ed, alters his car engine to make it 'sound more powerful than normal' (458). By spending on credit, the stretching boy's father uses sexual resources he does not truly have; men around Rand artificially inflate their purchasing power, though they, unlike the father, do not succeed in 'buying' her attentions.[6]

Drinion's lack of response to Rand – the fact that he is 'unaffected by the presence of [this] terribly attractive woman' (450) – registers as an admirable indifference compared to these men. His non-reaction indeed fits Greven's description of the inviolate male, but additionally, as a 'nerd and dweeb' (506) whose only interests are tax procedures, and who 'wears an argyle sweater vest … and brown Wallabee knockoffs that might literally be from JC Penney' (457), he is also suggestive of the sexless nerd. McGurl has observed that Wallace's work is invested in 'white nerd identity' (44), but Sherry Turkle's mid-1980s study of hackers and MIT students is more illuminating here. In her interviews with such men Turkle notes the 'insistent antisensuality' (1984: 201) of the culture they are a part of, in which devotion to computers correlates with a sanctioned and celebrated 'denial of the body' (183). Drinion is not a hacker and he lacks the physical ambivalences Turkle identifies in these men. That said, his status as a little man indifferent to sexual desire is indicative of this stereotype. As the stretching boy's non-erotic attempt to kiss himself counterweighs his father's sexual irresponsibility, so Drinion's nerdy inviolateness before the 'wrist-bitingly' (2012a: 449) attractive Rand counters the lechery that she inspires in others. His sacrifice compensates for the sexual deficit created by straight men who, by performing for Rand, promise sexual expenditures that they do not have to begin with.

Building on Mary K. Holland's description of *Infinite Jest*'s Lyle as a 'spokesperson for positive self-forgetting' (Holland, cited in Severs 2017a: 100), Severs argues that Drinion is 'an avatar of the type of extraordinary shared value *The Pale King* urges us to contemplate' (2017a: 234); in fact Drinion 'is one who, by listening, is able to unite many' (237). My reading specifies this idea, as I suggest that the shared value Drinion represents is the possibility of self-denial, by which men can commonly sacrifice sexual desire. Moreover, the same attribute that Severs lauds in fact makes Drinion an exemplar of austerity's ideological displacement. For as with the boy's self-kissing, Drinion's inviolateness draws attention from hideous male behaviours generally and primarily in order to highlight his exceptionality. Second only to the 'Brief Interviews' stories in its exploration of gendered power dynamics, Drinion's conversation with Rand is one of Wallace's most sustained considerations of misogyny, and Rand herself arguably one of only a handful of three-dimensional women to appear in his work. However, this scene's investment in Drinion's non-response does not register as a need to change scenarios in which men vie for Rand as they would for a good piece of meat. Rather, the implication is that men, if they follow in Drinion's footsteps, could better resist the need to figuratively open up bad lines of credit in their attempts to expend on women. Drinion's austerity therefore shifts the focus here from considering male sexual deficits as a systemic problem – and one bound up with sexist male behaviours – towards the need for men to tame their appetites.

The notion that Drinion's lack of sexual interest is a valuable sacrifice other men cannot make, however, points to a telling contradiction. Drinion and the stretching boy may function as ideals of sexual sacrifice, but they are freakish in their inviolateness. Like Joyce, they both 'enjoy a relationship to perfection that we admire and reward … though we have no inclination to walk that road ourselves' (1997e: 237). This singularity distances them from the collectivity their sacrifices aim to interpolate – that is, straight men as the common caretakers of a spermatic budget. If the austerity logics I have outlined shift responsibility for deficit reduction to Drinion and the stretching boy, their exceptionality also dissuades identification with their asceticism. Indeed, this compounds austerity's ideological double movement, whereby statements like 'we're all in this together' legitimate policies that force the poor to compensate for problems created by the rich. As men of impossible emulation – Drinion, for one, also levitates – his and the boy's sacrifices solicit self-denial, but excuse straight men from walking that same road. This contradiction means something more than how Wallace's investment in 'a sacrificial disposition' (2016: 194), as Hayes-Brady sees it, entails a commitment to 'process rather than product' (194). It also exceeds Emily J. Hogg's idea that 'the vagaries of subjective experience' (2014: 60) in *The Pale King* undermine its interests in 'dutiful self-renunciation' (63). It is consistent, rather, with how austerity constitutes what Blyth calls (in relation to post-2008 measures) 'the greatest bait-and-switch operation in modern history' (2013: 73). Namely, although austerity is sold as a form of collective sacrifice, the littlest must bear the heaviest burden.

Austerity in this sense can be said to revamp ideas of the deserving and undeserving poor, albeit in terms of those who are most and least ready to meet its calls to sacrifice. In Allen et al.'s words, this divide in part manifests as 'the thrifty, self-sufficient, hard-working citizen versus the feckless benefits scrounger' (2015: 908). Drinion and the stretching boy are a testament to *The Pale King*'s investment in those on the former side of this binary, their privations working to encourage yet forestall similar thriftiness in others. As lightning conductors for the need to reduce a shared sexual deficit, the sacrifices of these little men ensure that what Wallace presents as a masculine–capitalist drive to accumulate survives. This is despite the fact that in *The Pale King* Wallace continues his preoccupation with what Holland calls 'the bestial male appropriation of the female other' (2017: 7), and not just through how the stretching boy's father, and Rand's would-be seducers, show a dangerous tendency to sexually spend on credit. For instance, Toni Ware's reflections on how her mother would allow men to '*manhandle*' (2012a: 63, italics in original) her, followed by Toni's assault by a man 'manhandling [her] titty with what seemed an absent dispassion' (65), aligns male sexuality with an accumulative objectification of women. This word also appears in the first story of *Oblivion*, 'Mister Squishy', where a marketing company's 'manipulative and abusive' (2004a: 18) questioning of young mothers means that they are 'manhandled, emotionally speaking' (18). *Oblivion* indeed foregrounds a relationship between straight male chauvinism and neoliberal capitalism. As I argue in the following section, Wallace scapegoats little men for their sexual debts in order to illuminate this relationship, thereby pursuing an austerity logic in ways that – perhaps paradoxically – interrogate aspects of neoliberalism.

'Someone at once obtrusive and irrelevant': Sexual scapegoats

The men whom Wallace scapegoats in *Oblivion* fit more easily into traditional ideas of the schlemiel than the stretching boy or Drinion do. Writing on the Yiddish author Sholem Aleichem, Wisse notes that one of 'the characteristic features of the schlemiel' (1971: 51) is that 'the traditional male virtues such as strength, courage, pride, fortitude, are prominent only in their absence' (51). This is certainly the case for my main examples in this section – Schmidt in 'Mister Squishy', Randy in 'Oblivion', and Skip in 'The Suffering Channel'. In contrast to Aleichem's early twentieth-century figure though, *Oblivion*'s schlemiels are indicative of how, as Sanford Pinsker outlines in relation to post-war writers like Saul Bellow, 'the schlemiel-as-victim becomes the victim of himself, the centre turns inward, and the psyche is seen as more important than the situation' (1991: 147). The situations Schmidt or Randy find themselves in are by no means benign, but Wallace dramatizes their sufferings as little men in terms of their feelings of shame, ineptitude and so on. These feelings form the basis of their suitability for scapegoating, as they arise in no small part from how they run up high sexual deficits. Furthermore, Wallace scapegoats these characters in order to reaffirm more virile men who are, themselves, creating dangerous (and sexualized) credit bubbles. He does so to shift responsibility for sexual deficits onto the vulnerable while – paradoxically – noting how 'stronger' men are simultaneously at fault for proliferating debt.

A more detailed theoretical grounding is needed to unpack how scapegoating works in this manner. Brown again proves useful here in her development of the thought of René Girard. She acknowledges that the aspects of Girard's work she draws on to discuss sacrifice are the same that lay the 'groundwork for his renowned notion of "scapegoating"' (2015: 217). Specifically, Brown builds on Girard's suggestion that sacrifice, sharing the same dynamics as scapegoating, is a 'deliberate act of collective substitution performed at the expense of the victim and absorbing all the internal tensions, feuds, and rivalries pent up within the community' (Girard 2013: 8). Such tensions arise as a result of what Girard argues is the mimetic nature of desire. People desire imitatively, so 'we desire what others desire because we imitate their desires' (1987: 122). As Chris Fleming explains, this means that an object is desired not because of its intrinsic value, and not because somebody chooses it – 'it is desired because the subject (consciously or non-consciously) imitates the desire of another (an Other), real or imaginary, who functions as a model for that desire' (2004: 11). Crucially, when this model exists in the same space and time as the subject, they are liable to become a rival for the latter's desired object. For to imitate a model's desire fully would mean that the subject actually *become* that person. As a result of this impasse, conflictual mimesis arises; the subject is compelled to imitate another's desire, yet this other stands in the way of that endeavour.

In Michael Kirwan's pithy summation, 'two hands reach, not quite simultaneously, for the same object. The outcome is bitter rivalry, even outright conflict' (2004: 21). This is not due to the object's scarcity, but a consequence of the incommensurability of imitable desires. If left unabated, this competition for Girard leads to a Hobbesian state of all against all, in which violence begets violence, and even threatens to eradicate the differences between antagonists: they become what he calls 'monstrous double[s]' (2013: 152) of one another. However, when antagonists reach this threshold moment – what Girard dubs a 'sacrificial crisis' (2013: 46) – they redirect their violence at a scapegoat, against whom warring factions can unite in order to restore social order. The scapegoat is accordingly 'a substitute for all the members of the community', and their 'sacrifice serves to protect the entire community from its own violence' (2013: 8). Moreover, from the perpetrators' perspective a scapegoat cannot appear as such, lest it lose its beneficial social effects; it must simply be 'vulnerable and close at hand' (2013: 2). In Wallace's texts, little men like Randy and Schmidt are vulnerable by virtue of their sexual debts compared to other, seemingly autarkic men; indeed, their scapegoating proceeds despite how these latter men also expend sexual credit.

'Mister Squishy', for one, is awash with forms of mimetic desire. Its protagonist, Terry Schmidt, is a market researcher coordinating an all-male focus group on a new snack-cake. Schmidt's superiors have instructed him to divulge selected information to his group about 'the sort of complex system of a large groups' intragroup preferences influencing one another and building exponentially on one another … like a nuclear chain reaction' (2004a: 23). Alongside this explicit focus on how conflictual mimesis can lead to violence, though, Wallace presents the corporate culture that Schmidt is a part of on a similar basis. By the end of the story he shunts Schmidt from the main narrative to focus on his superiors, Scott R. Laleman and Alan Britton, the former of whom is vying for the latter's position. Wallace presents (and parodies) this rivalry in sexual terms, so that the object of mimetic desire is as much an idea of virile masculinity as it is professional advancement. For instance, 'On the rare occasions when he masturbated, Laleman's fantasy involved a view of himself, shirtless and adorned with warpaint, standing with his boot on the chest of various supine men' (64). Accordingly Laleman 'could almost feel the texture of Mr. B's sternum under his heel' (65). Combined with the 'zeppelin-sized cigars' (62) the men smoke, this image ridicules them as participants in a mimetic pursuit of self-sufficient masculinity – a pursuit that, as Laleman's masturbatory war imagery makes clear, contains a barely suppressed violence.

Despite this violent sexual self-sufficiency, though, Wallace suggests that Laleman also inflates himself in ways similar to how the stretching boy's father, or Rand's seducers, spend sexual resources beyond their means. The 'lale' in Laleman is Persian for tulip, which in the context of a story that in part explores the dot.com bubble, is suggestive of the first economic bubble – the 1637 'tulip mania' in Holland. As Alastair Sooke relates, 'Speculators traded the flower's bulbs for extraordinary sums of money, until, without warning, the market for them spectacularly collapsed' (2016). A 'tulip-man', Laleman's masculinity is in this sense based on value he does not possess.[7] The sexual implications of this are evident in the biographical details we receive about him. In college, Laleman accidentally inhales halon gas, and for several days 'he went around campus with a rose clamped in his teeth, and tried to tango with anyone he saw, and insisted everybody all call him *The Magnificent Enriqué*' (Wallace 2004a: 64). Inflated, Laleman becomes a risible Don Juan, at least until 'several of his fraternity brothers finally all ganged up and knocked some sense back into him' (64) – that is, until he is scapegoated for trying to sexually live beyond his means. That 'a lot of people thought he was still never quite the same after the halon thing' (64) implies that, coterminous with the violent self-sufficiency that has him masturbating to the fantasy of men underfoot, Laleman remains prone to dangerous forms of sexual over-valuation.[8]

In terms of the story's attention, though, Laleman pales in comparison with the piece's sexual little man, Schmidt. That Schmidt becomes a scapegoat – indeed, Laleman and Britton are discussing how to replace workers like him with computers – stems in no small part from his sexual indebtedness. As a man 'who did have the customary pocket-protector with three different colored pens in it' (4), he exemplifies the sexless nerd. Unlike Drinion, though, his obsession with a woman – co-worker Darlene – compels him to engage in non-reproductive sexual expenditures. For instance, he forgoes his nightly intention to phone her and instead 'masturbate[s] himself to sleep again' (33).[9] More than this, he has constructed a shrine to Darlene in his bedroom (26) and fantasizes about 'moist slapping intercourse' (16) with her while moaning '*Thank you, oh thank you*' (54, italics in original). His sense of sexual debt is explicit, but Wallace also couches it within more wide-ranging debts to masculine ideals Schmidt cannot fulfil, whether in his failure 'to act as Big Brother for a boy age 11-15 who lacked significant male mentors' (48), or in his fantasies of saving Darlene from bullying (49–50). Schmidt's sense of sexual ineptitude, though, is the presiding index of his lack of self-determination, particularly compared to men like Laleman. Reflecting on his compulsion to thank Darlene in his fantasies, he wonders 'if he even had what convention called a Free Will at all, deep down' (55). In these ways Schmidt – to borrow and invert a description of the banking system responsible for the 2008 crash – is too small to succeed.

'Mister Squishy' points to mimetic rivalry between men like Laleman and Britton as being responsible for Schmidt possibly losing his job, and also as being conducive to creating unsustainable forms of credit. The story sexualizes these dynamics to further align predatory capitalist practices with chauvinistic men. But it is Schmidt, the little man, who suffers the most – Wallace focuses on *his* sexual debts, and particularly his sense of shame for being unable, figuratively, to pay them off. Indeed, adding to his indignities, Schmidt has 'recently refinanced' (9) his condominium. Austerity's ideological displacement is at play here in that a crisis the story acknowledges as being endemic to male–male rivalry becomes, in Schmidt, a crisis of how the littlest overspend. Yet, though scapegoating Schmidt for such overspending, Wallace does leave the door open to considering how Britton and Laleman are culpable, notably through the latter's status as an inflated tulip-man. In this sense the displacement, and the scapegoating, are powerful but not complete. Wallace encourages us to judge Schmidt harshly for his sexual debts, in other words, but he also hints at how Britton and Laleman's cigar-waving rivalry is prone to creating credit-driven crises. This could figure as grounds for critique; exploring the psychic pains of a man who cannot meet his sexual debts could urge questioning of the nature of these debts, and why men deemed more virile do not suffer. But Wallace is intent not only on stressing how Schmidt's debts *do* make him pathetic, but also, through needles and ricin, how Schmidt too displays reprehensibly 'male' attributes.

For Schmidt decides to make a 'dark difference' (32) by poisoning the cakes he is conducting research on. The means by which he does this displays a sexualized self-control that he otherwise lacks, evoking images of penetration and insemination: 'It would take nothing more than one thin-gauge hypodermic and 24 infinitesimal doses of KCN, AS_2O_3, ricin' (30) to do it; the toxin that he settles on is '97% lethal at .00003 g' (58). Schmidt treats this toxic seed with a care missing from his own waste of sexual energies – its lethality in fact derives from its scarcity. He shows a displaced, sexualized threat comparable to that of his superior Robert Awad, who sexually harasses Darlene. Awad performs such harassment at Britton's direction, with 'instructions to behave in such a way as to test for faultlines in Field Team morale' (62). In a context where men's sexual behaviour can be weaponized in the pursuit of nefarious ends, Schmidt's poisonous seed plays a similar role. Tellingly, Darlene's request that Schmidt stop 'com[ing] up behind [her]' unawares occurs 'during the six-month period when SRD Awad really had been *coming* up stealthily behind her' (55, brackets in original, italics mine), linking the two in a common spermatic predation. In these ways, the result of Schmidt's scapegoating is to compel in him the same violently mimetic desires – to be a man big enough to 'make a difference' (30) – evident in his virile superiors.

In this light, 'Mister Squishy' generally (but not completely) displaces attention from what Wallace hints is an endemic crisis of male rivalry to a crisis of individual overspending, only to *then* enlist Schmidt into the same violent male–male rivalries that scapegoat him in the first place. Thus, austerity works: once Schmidt has been sufficiently punished for his sexual debts (if only through his own intense feelings of shame for accruing them), he begins to act in accordance with its imperatives to parsimony and self-control – albeit, by poisoning snack-cakes. Whether or not Schmidt manages, as a result of his product tampering, 'to bring almost an entire industry down on one supplicatory knee' (30) is beside the point. His initial scapegoating and subsequent violence legitimates the broader austerity logic. In other words, displacing the crisis onto the most vulnerable will not only ensure that a masculine–capitalist system can survive, but also that little men like Schmidt – if punished enough – will begin to abide by its dictates. To borrow Hal's description of Hobbes and Rousseau in *Infinite Jest*'s opening scene, Schmidt is Drinion or the stretching boy 'in a dark mirror' (1996: 12). Like those two little men, Wallace forecloses the opportunity to identify with Schmidt, but because of his awfulness rather than this saintliness. Similarly, as with Drinion and the boy, Schmidt acts as a pivot upon which austerity logics re-energize a system in crisis, though by punishing, rather than sanctifying, those unfortunate enough to be at the bottom of the pile.

That these austerity logics occur in a story that skewers advertising, market research, corporate downsizing, managerialism and so on is a notable contradiction. The famous dictum, usually attributed to Fredric Jameson, that 'it is easier to imagine the end of the world than the end of capitalism' is pertinent here. It is easier to imagine how Schmidt's terrorism can destroy, if not the world, then at least his company, than it is to imagine alternatives to a system in which debts must be paid and men's sexual propensity for rivalry and violence must be accommodated. Another reason for why 'Mister Squishy' adheres to austerity's ideological displacements, though, and despite its attempt to interrogate neoliberalism, is the place of women in these dynamics. In the terms Wallace sets up, it is not only that allowing for deficits would validate spending on credit, but also the male violence against women which results from this. Scapegoating little men keeps the masculine–capitalist system that Wallace satirizes running, then, while reiterating the objectionable nature of sexual debts to women on (putatively) feminist grounds. This is particularly evident in *Oblivion*'s title story, in which protagonist Randy Napier juggles his wife Hope's accusations of chronic snoring with suppressing his desires for his stepdaughter, Audrey.

Randy's schlemiel-hood is evident in these psychosexual entanglements with the two main women in his life. References to his haplessness in the face of Audrey's 'prematurely "mature" or voluptuous' (2004c: 193) peers echo *American Beauty*, while nods to David Lynch's *Twin Peaks* (1990–1; 2017) similarly position Randy as a father with incestuous desires. Caught in a 'sad pantomime with pity and disgust' (Wallace 2004c: 194), the story scapegoats him in the service of his father-in-law, Dr Sipe, whom Wallace hints raped Hope and her sister Vivian when they were children, and is possibly grooming Audrey. As 'Mister Squishy' displaces attention onto Schmidt's vulnerability, so too does Randy's crisis take centre stage. To the extent that his desire for Audrey mirrors Sipe's, then, comparable to Schmidt poisoning cakes, Randy also takes part in the same rivalries between virile men that have scapegoated him. Moreover, Wallace undercuts Sipe's virility by stressing his lassitude as a septuagenarian, a form of over-valuation that, like Laleman in 'Mister Squishy', nonetheless takes a backseat to Randy's sexual debts, and namely to notions of masculine purpose he cannot fulfil. At one point, for instance, he even imagines himself storming Audrey's dorm – or 'her machicolated banishment's *donjon*'s fortifications' (231, italics in original) – to express his desire. Wallace reserves the most pronounced example of Randy's indebtedness, however, for the story's conclusion, at which he reveals that Randy's monologue has been Hope's dream all along.

This revelation, to the extent that it reorients Randy's forgoing monologue as occurring in Hope's mind, renders his very existence as being entirely dependent on his wife. That said, the parenthetical interjections that occur throughout the story, and which become particularly violent towards its end (for instance, '("*or hurt you if*")' (236, italics in original)), suggest that Hope's sleeping brain articulates her past sexual abuse through her dreaming of Randy. As Hayes-Brady puts it, Randy's 'vocabulary has infiltrated his wife's mind almost fully, causing the complete collapse of her autonomous identity' (2016: 146). Male sexual debt in this regard is not only objectionable for how it registers as living beyond one's means; it is also to be faulted for how it stimulates non-heteronormative desires which, in their violence, persecute women. Put differently, if men are allowed to indulge in credit spending, inflating their sexual resources beyond what they truly have, they are more liable to carry out the kind of sexual crimes Sipe gets away with and Randy is scapegoated for. Thus, Wallace mobilizes a feminist position (albeit one based on the idea that women, like Avril's diddle-check girls, must be protected from male sexuality) in service of a focus on deficit reduction. The logic of male sexual austerity therefore persists, and despite these stories' critiques of neoliberalism, because of its ostensible efficacy in forestalling – or at least, in broadcasting the nature of – male violence against women.

Nevertheless, this does not mean that *Oblivion* and *The Pale King* forgo an attachment to male violence. In fact, my final example of *Oblivion*'s little male scapegoats – Skip in 'The Suffering Channel' – compounds this attachment as being central to the male sexual austerity at work. That said, as a journalist investigating a man's ability to produce preformed poo sculptures of famous artworks from his anus, Skip is difficult to locate within the operations I have explored. Severs reads him as a liminal figure between *Oblivion* and *The Pale King*, an 'ingenious attempt to resurrect aspects of the ethos of work, especially cognitive labor. … Skip's form of hard-won attention has broad implications for the social world' (2017a: 194–6). Skip does foreshadow *The Pale King*'s focus on the beneficial aspects of little male austerity. For one, like the stretching boy he is inviolate: 'since the end of a serious involvement some years prior, [he was] all but celibate' (2004d: 271). Following Severs, who praises Skip for being a forerunner of the self-denial present in *The Pale King*'s little men, one could connect such celibacy to his professional rectitude – even if it is in the service of a glossy magazine. Skip also shares Drinion's anti-sensual dorkiness, whether in 'the whole awkward issue of his monochrome wardrobe' (298) or 'the fact that he actually carried pictures of his dogs in his wallet' (298). His sexlessness thus correlates with his being 'energetic and competent, a team player' (239), whereby sexual abstinence for Wallace can lead to achievement.

However, alongside those elements that make him a forerunner of *The Pale King*'s little men, Skip also functions as a scapegoat. Like Schmidt and Randy, he is sidelined by the story's end, his project of bringing Brint and his faecal talents to the public's attention commandeered and repurposed by two of *Style*'s interns. Where conflictual mimesis appears in 'The Suffering Channel', it is indeed between the female interns, whom Wallace presents as being in subtle rivalry with each other for job advancement and physical beauty. This is evident in the two women who take over Skip's story – Ellen Bactrian and an unnamed 'executive intern' (316) – who, as they use side-by-side elliptical trainers, discuss how to best exploit Brint's pain so that it involves 'bona fide suffering' (325). Crucially, though, Wallace notes that Bactrian and the executive intern's 'editorial brainstorming sounds like an argument, but it isn't – it's two or more people thinking aloud in a directed way' (317). In fact, the rivalries between women at *Style* lack the intimations of violence that are present in Laleman and Britton's conflict. Similarly, despite the various figures of maternal abuse in this novella, these women do not share Randy or Sipe's hideousness. If the executive intern is 'like a living refutation of everything Marx ever stood for' (293), it is not because she is ruthlessly capitalist, but unthinkingly so – a 'standard of excellence' (293) at *Style* in her managerial acumen. The question arises, then, as to whether or not Bactrian and the executive intern's 'argument' is a bona fide rivalry.

This is an important question as it signals how Wallace's presentation of mimetic rivalry in 'The Suffering Channel' follows an implicit sexism evident in Girard's theory, so that, if *Oblivion*'s stories variously scapegoat little men for their sexual debts, this punishment must take place within and between groups of men in order to be meaningful. As Toril Moi notes, 'Girard himself reveals quite explicitly the fact that his mimetic desire must essentially be taken to mean "masculine" desire' (1982: 25). So, too, must the violence directed at a scapegoat be masculine, for in Moi's words 'among the effects of the sacrificial crisis is the disappearance of sexual difference' (25). If scapegoating restores individuation to groups who are otherwise at risk of becoming undifferentiated through their rivalry, then, as part of this, it also restores the apparent differences between men and women. Wallace's interns are suggestive of the breakdown of difference – for instance, 'no fewer than five of the interns at the working lunch on 2 July were named either Laurel or Tara' (Wallace 2004d: 261). Working in the more obvious monstrous doubling of the World Trade Centres, these interns imply the failure of scapegoating when it is women, rather than men, who are the rivalrous subjects.

The suitably ironically named Mrs Anger, the magazine's executive editor, has 'put *Style* in the black for the first time in its history' (249). Wallace links

Style's balanced budget with its near exclusively female workforce; they achieve a budgetary rectitude that is absent in men like Schmidt and Randy. That 'The Suffering Channel' subtly attacks these women for their blind adherence to neoliberalism, then, compounds how *Oblivion* gears its austerity logics to male sexuality alone. For austerity's scapegoating function to take place in these stories – so that Wallace displaces punishment for debt from 'big' to little men, and in turn affirms the seeming inevitability of the same masculine–capitalist system he satirizes – it must occur between men. Skip's willingness to ignore Brint's pain and deliver him to his superiors is thus something more than a lamentable sign of how, as Olivia Banner suggests, 'the fraternal as well [as the paternal] has slid into a zone of absence' (2009). It is rather a welcome violence to the extent that a 'real' sacrificial crisis can occur, in which male–male antagonism allows for communal affirmation at the expense of a scapegoat. The sexual scapegoats in *Oblivion* may differ in the modality of their ineptness – most notably in how Skip is closer to *The Pale King*'s dutiful workers – but as punishable little men they further legitimate austerity's hold on male sexuality in the collection.

Conclusion

By exploring neoliberal austerity as a phenomenon concerned with cutting budget deficits and high levels of debt, this chapter has inevitably offered a partial reading of the motivations for its implementation. For instance, the fact that cuts in public spending often function as a Trojan horse for reducing the size of the state has not played a part in my analysis. To the extent that *The Pale King* presents a vision of the IRS as an institution best embodied by an array of little men, though, then comparisons can be drawn between the apparent need for a leaner state and Wallace's investment in male diminution. In a similar vein, this chapter has not considered how the impacts of austerity measures are in and of themselves gendered. As Helen Davies and Claire O'Callaghan observe, in the aftermath of 2008, 'a significant strand of the debates surrounding the influence of austerity upon society have been gendered, with concerns expressed that we are in a "man-cession"' (2017: 17). In this respect my readings – particularly of *Oblivion*'s investment in male violence – further an unduly androcentric cultural response to austerity. As I have shown throughout this book, though, Wallace is preoccupied with writing about male sexuality to the detriment of other desiring positions, and austerity conceived as a means of dealing with high debts is central to this in *The Pale King* and *Oblivion*. Similar to my previous readings of how neoliberal ideas of responsibility, risk, contract and property inform sexuality in Wallace texts, this chapter has argued that austerity logics subtend their emphasis on sacrifice and scapegoating.

Chiefly, austerity's displacement of responsibility for creating and reducing budget deficits – from the powerful to the vulnerable – plays out in *Oblivion* and *The Pale King* through how they charge little men with either balancing a shared sexual budget, or taking the blame for said budget's instability. Even when these texts note how systemic forces of male rivalry are at fault for economic crises, they still predominantly focus on little men. Further, the persistence of such ideological displacement in contexts where Wallace's texts critique neoliberalism is suggestive of a reluctance to let go of the systems they satirize – namely, capitalist procedures he aligns with masculinity. Austerity goes all the way down, whether in the sense of forming the imaginative horizons for how *The Pale King* and *Oblivion* depict sexuality, or in the sense of targeting those they present as being the weakest – little men. Wallace not only suggests that male sexual toxicity is immutable, then, but that so too are the capitalist practices he aligns with such toxicity. Drawing on various elements of the two threads that have informed Chapters 1 to 4 – specifically, ideas of non-reproductivity, investment, and waste on the one hand, and violence, blockage and release on the other – this chapter has shown how, to the very last, male sexual toxicity for Wallace cannot change.

Conclusion

'I never signed up for sperm therapy, buster' (Wallace 1987: 332). So says Lenore to her analyst, Dr Jay, who, in accordance with the often slapstick tone of Wallace's first novel, has removed the pull string from his sweatshirt, fixed it to his rear, and begun to emulate the motions of a swimming sperm cell. By making semen a central thread in my investigation of Wallace's texts, I am perhaps in danger of eliciting the same scepticism Lenore shows for her analyst. However, though he is clearly ludicrous in this scene, Jay still proceeds to help Lenore see that she no longer loves her boyfriend, Rick. To some extent my goals have mirrored Jay's, for I too have tried to complicate a prior attachment, namely to Wallace's purported anti-neoliberalism. I have focused on the spermatic imagery in his texts to show how his depictions of male sexuality follow neoliberal logics. In doing so, I have suggested that his work is indebted to neoliberalism, rather than just opposing it. Neoliberal logics regarding responsibility, risk, contract, property and austerity are key to how Wallace positions sexual toxicity as the basis of masculinity. By presenting the notion that men are prone to negativity and violence as a neutral economic fact, these logics dissuade one from thinking about male sexuality differently. Furthermore, Wallace's spermatic imagery, though often not as blatant as Jay's cosplaying, helps to perpetuate the idea that such hideousness is inevitable by appealing to bodily metaphors of investment, waste, blockage and release.

That said, Jay is also badgering Lenore into accepting faux-psychoanalytic theories that Wallace lampoons. Though I hope to have made a strong case for Wallace's hideous neoliberal spermatics, I have avoided arguing that this performative process provides, like Jay's 'membrane-theory' (1987: 330), an analytical master key. My revisionist reading has not tried to replace the idea that Wallace is anti-neoliberal with the idea that he is, in fact, neoliberal. As I have observed throughout this book, there are compelling signs that Wallace tries to critique neoliberalism. However, I have acknowledged these points of anti-neoliberal sentiment not to dilute my argument, but rather to better show how neoliberal logics animate Wallace's texts despite his general hostility to late capitalism. The consistency with which Wallace gravitates to such logics, moreover, is indicative of a tension in his representations of gender. This is the tension that arises from focusing near exclusively on male characters and perspectives in the knowledge that such a focus potentially shores up patriarchal power relations. In other words, by rendering male sexual toxicity an economic issue, neoliberal logics such as responsibilization and privatization situate it as a fact to accommodate, not a contingency to transform. This process allows for the recognition that sexual negativity and violence are objectionable, but it sidesteps the possibility that one can transform them.

Fascinatingly, the same tension I perceive in Wallace's depictions of gender has started to appear in Wallace Studies itself. In a 2018 blog post titled 'Thinking about David Foster Wallace, Misogyny and Scholarship', for instance, Hering reflects upon recent considerations of misogyny in relation to Wallace. 'I'm a man who has read, re-read and written extensively on Wallace', states Hering, 'and these articles have troubled me and caused no small soul searching about my position as a reader and scholar of his work'. Wary of perpetuating the sexism that others have decried in Wallace's texts and their readers, and which he admits has given him 'pause on more than one occasion', Hering suggests that 'when misogyny is present [in Wallace's output], it is to illustrate its toxicity'. To some extent, my readings confirm this notion. Wallace's at times phobic depictions of femininity and of homosexuality are often geared towards adumbrating the toxicity of such depictions. However, in my reading this is not because his texts, in Hering's words, are 'committed to addressing [misogyny] as a major problem of contemporary culture' (2018). Toxicity is not a problem that Wallace wants to solve; on the contrary, he courts it as the immutable fact of male sexuality. Men's sexual hideousness is lamentable, Wallace implies, but it is nevertheless a useful basis upon which to ground masculinity.

Severs has written at length about this desire for ground in Wallace's texts. He suggests that 'to be of interest to Wallace's narrative gaze is often to be sensitive to ground and to alienation from it' (2017a: 9). In contrast to what Brian McHale describes as 'the aspiration to weightlessness' (2015: 139) in postmodern culture during the 1990s, Wallace, in Severs's reading, sought ways of 'getting reacquainted with ground' (2017a: 18). My suggestion that Wallace grounds his depictions of masculinity in ideas of male sexual toxicity chimes with this argument, albeit less literally. Whereas Severs points to specific images of grounding in Wallace's texts (such as feet, mud and shoes), my argument has evoked this notion abstractly. Specifically, my readings cumulatively demonstrate how sexual toxicity is the persistent and – to borrow a term that is central to

Severs's study – axiomatic grounds of Wallace's representations of masculinity. Additionally, whereas Severs generally takes this desire for grounds as being self-evident, I have tried to stress how it is actually a performative process. Hence, although Severs may be right to suggest that a good subtitle for *Infinite Jest* could be 'Philosophical Groundlessness and the Unbalanced Male' (2017a: 95), I have argued that the sexual toxicity in which Wallace grounds his depictions of masculinity is something that he has to actively produce, not a pre-discursive given on which men can find their feet.

I close *David Foster Wallace's Toxic Sexuality*, then, with the pessimistic estimation that Wallace cannot be redeemed as a progressive writer on sexuality and gender. In fact, these issues elicit a knee-jerk conservatism in his work, as when in 'Authority and American Usage' he suggests that a boy wearing a skirt to school is so *outré* as to be almost unthinkable (2005d: 94–6). Nevertheless, there are still interesting questions to ask about Wallace's treatment of sexuality and gender, both despite of and because of this conservatism. For instance, critics could investigate the presence of cross-dressing and transgender identity in his work, and ask why the 'crosswriting' (2012b: 100) he saw himself partaking in with Lenore in *Broom*, or the ambiguous gender identity of Magda in 'Westward', gave way in *Infinite Jest* to his crass depiction of the male to female transgender spy, Helen Steeply. At the same time, there is still much work to be done on Wallace's depictions of masculinity outside the realm of sexuality. Most obviously, sports, addiction and white-collar work offer themselves as worthwhile topics for exploration. Class also begs to be considered in this light as well, especially given how much of *Infinite Jest* focuses on the benighted but heroic lower-class Don Gately. Critics can perhaps consider how the regressive attitudes to gender I have traced in this book inform Wallace's depictions of masculinity in these arguably less libidinal areas. It is fair to say that we are still scratching the surface of Wallace's sexual and gender politics, but also that what lies beneath will probably be ugly.

The question of whether we can or should still turn to Wallace as an anti-neoliberal writer is trickier to answer. His depictions of male sexuality imply a deep sympathy with the neoliberal logics of responsibility, risk, contract, property and austerity for their apparent ability to sidestep political contestation. But to what extent should Wallace's neoliberalism in one area capsize his attempts to write against the same political-economic theory elsewhere? That the neoliberal sympathies that I have traced appear across his corpus, from *Broom* to *The Pale King*, and are as evident in his journalism as in his fiction, suggests that the task is more difficult than simply prioritizing aspects of his oeuvre which are anti-neoliberal over those that are not. There are also biographical details that imply we would we be rash to see him as being automatically adverse to neoliberalism's key figureheads. In addition to voting for Reagan, for instance, he admitted to Lipsky that he had '*sensuous*' (2010: 127, italics in original) dreams about Margaret Thatcher; in the same interview he supportively references Hayek's *The Road to Serfdom* (2010: 158) too. As critics interested in working against the neoliberal logics that Wallace endorses, what are we to do with this information?[1] To answer this question, I want to end by briefly turning to Kadji Amin's book *Disturbing Attachments: Genet, Modern Pederasty, and Queer History* (2017). Amin's concern with Jean Genet, and his importance to queer politics, might seem unrelated to the topics at hand, but his thoughts about the value of engaging with artists who disappoint our political convictions are, in fact, highly productive to thinking about Wallace and neoliberalism.

Amin's book is haunted by one he wanted to write but couldn't – a study of Genet that would further his 'subcultural iconicity' (2017: 1) and 'the impassioned identification he inspires in many of his queer admirers' (1). Genet's non-normativity and his commitment to transgression seems to accord with queer utopian politics, but, in Amin's words, 'as I set about the painstaking labor of research, I grew increasingly disturbed by aspects of Genet's queer relations that would not fit this utopian narrative' (5). Notably, Genet's pederasty, his nostalgia for prison, his racial fetishization of black and brown bodies and his fantasies of terrorism run afoul of the progressive politics Amin thought he might embody. *Disturbing Attachments* meditates on how Genet's more nauseous enthusiasms compromise this politics, and in turn what this might reveal about the current state of Queer Studies. Amin's analysis is complex, and I cannot hope to do it full justice here. However, his suggestions for how we might respond to the unease caused when an artist fails to fulfil the political expectations we bring to them are useful for my purposes. As opposed to 'flaying the object for its failure to be sufficiently transgressive or consistently radical' (9), ignoring unease so we can 'celebrate the object's truly radical aspects' (9), or carrying out work that enhances a critic's 'position of mastery' (9) at the object's expense, Amin encourages us to '*inhabit unease*' (10, italics in original). From this position we can think critically about our attachments to certain political projects and about the possible benefits of being disturbed from them.

I am not suggesting that we should approach Wallace's misogyny or homophobia in the same way Amin approaches Genet's pederasty or racial fetishism. This comparison would work to some extent in that both men present us with images and ideas of sexuality that are contrary to the current literary-critical field's liberal, anti-sexist configuration. Both, in other words, have the power disturb us. But such a comparison would elide the difference between how Genet's transgressions are the rebel-yells of a self-marginalizing queer, whereas Wallace 'transgresses' in the dominant voice of white hetero-patriarchal American culture.[2] When it comes to Wallace's relationship to neoliberalism, though, Amin's thoughts are apt. The readings I have carried out in *David Foster Wallace's Toxic Sexuality* pose a challenge to the idealizing function of much scholarship in this area. I have gone against the grain and cast Wallace as a committed neoliberal – at least, when it comes to male sexuality. To some extent this can be interpreted as the critical flaying that Amin warns against, but I leave it to readers to decide how mean I have been. By unpicking how Wallace follows neoliberal logics of responsibility, risk, contract, property and austerity, though, I hope to have created some unease in the field. If others inhabit this unease, and give credence to how Wallace perpetuates capitalist exploitation, they can hopefully build on my pessimism, conducting further and better readings of his complicity with neoliberal ideas.

To remain attached to Wallace's work is a disturbing enterprise given the dynamics that I have explored in this book. Doing so, though, gives us an opportunity to re-evaluate what we find interesting or enchanting about it in light of what we find unpalatable. This entails more than just acknowledging, in Thompson's words, how 'much of what we admire about Wallace's work is inextricable from those textual moments that we might well want to disavow, or at the very least view as regrettable' (2018: 217). The task, rather, is to consider how his reactionary attitudes towards sexuality and gender, and his support for neoliberalism in these areas, might require us to re-conceptualize or even overhaul some of the field's cornerstones – whether that be his apparent search for sincerity, the desire for reader-author connection, the need to find authentic value in a consumer culture, and so on. This is one way, perhaps, to resist the calcification that canonization can do to a writer, a means to keep not only Wallace's work polymorphous in its meanings and effects, but the criticism on it too. Toxicity offers those of us working in Wallace Studies the chance to reopen foundational ideas and, however uneasy it might make us feel, to think them anew.

Notes

Introduction

1 Catherine Toal (2003), Rachel Haley Himmelheber (2014), Matthew Alexander (2016), and Adam Kelly (2018) can also be added to this list.
2 For Hutcheon the politics of postmodern art (and especially of postmodern literature and photography) can be determined through its degree of critical complicity with the status-quo. As she theorizes, this is 'my own paradoxical postmodernism of complicity and critique, of reflexivity and historicity, that at once inscribes and subverts the conventions and ideologies of the dominant cultural and social forces of the twentieth-century western world' (2002: 11). While Hutcheon understands complicitous critique as being a denaturalizing manoeuvre, in which 'those entities that we unthinkingly experience as "natural" (they might even include capitalism, patriarchy, liberal humanism) are in fact "cultural"' (2), when it comes to male sexuality Wallace moves in the opposite direction. Indeed, his apparent 'critique' of patriarchy in particular works to compound and excuse his complicity.
3 To distinguish between the collection and the short story cycle within it, I will refer to the former as *Brief Interviews* and to the latter as 'Brief Interviews'.
4 In his most recent contribution to the field, *The Wallace Effect: David Foster Wallace and the Contemporary Literary Imagination* (2019), Boswell notes how 'an unmistakable strain of sexual menace' (8) is evident in how Wallace's contemporaries incorporate him into their work through thinly veiled fictional avatars – such as Richard Katz in Jonathan Franzen's *Freedom* (2010), or Leonard Bankhead in Jeffrey Eugenides's *The Marriage Plot* (2011). This adds further credence to my argument that sexual toxicity is an important aspect of Wallace's texts, even though I do not focus on his literary reception in this study.
5 In her article 'Queer Postmodern Practices: Sex and Narrative in *Gravity's Rainbow*', Franco draws on *No Future* to argue that 's/m and queer negativity are in *Gravity's Rainbow* simultaneously symptoms and causes of postmodernist narrative instability' (2017: 147). She develops these ideas further in 'Queer Sex, Queer Text: S/M in *Gravity's Rainbow*', her contribution to the essay collection *Thomas Pynchon, Sex, and Gender* (2018).
6 Bachner notes that 'I identify a wide range of phenomena under the umbrella of "violence"' (2011: 8), and that 'my use of the term violence throughout this book

is not supported by any single consistent theory' (9). Allowing the texts that she examines to guide her analysis of violence, Bachner moves between 'what we might call obvious, commonsense examples of violence, those that entail empirically verifiable injury' (9) and 'structural and symbolic violence' (9). I follow her lead in this regard. Keeping this term flexible allows me to account for how Wallace's invocation of sexual violence, though undergoing modal changes from text to text, still signifies ideas of un-representability and immutability.

7 For a compelling reading of how Wallace's political sympathies accord with Trumpism, see the final chapter of Joffe's unpublished PhD thesis, '"In the Shadows": David Foster Wallace and Multicultural America' (2017).

8 These topics are tackled respectively by Jennifer Backman, 'From Hard Boiled to Over Easy: Reimagining the Noir Detective in *Inherent Vice* and *Bleeding Edge*' (2018), Doug Haynes, '"Allons Enfants!" Pynchon's Pornographies' (2018), and Jeffrey Severs, '"Homer Is My Role Model": Father-Schlemihls, Sentimental Families, and Pynchon's Affinities with *The Simpsons*' (2018).

9 Hungerford treats Wallace's work as a source of *literal* toxicity – a potentially harmful substance that it is best to avoid, unless one wants to run the risk of contamination.

10 Murat Aydemir's *Images of Bliss: Ejaculation, Masculinity, Meaning* (2007) offers a broad study of semen in relation to various cultural and philosophical contexts. Lisa Jean Moore's *Sperm Counts: Overcome by Man's Most Precious Fluid* (2007) is also good on this front.

11 Indeed, I take a different tack to Sloane, who in his blurb to *David Foster Wallace and the Body* describes Wallace's work as belonging to 'the history of literary and philosophical entanglements with the brute fact of embodiment'. This may well be the case, but I set out from the conviction – foundational to the strands of queer and postmodern theory that I draw on in particular – that the 'brute' body should be de-naturalized, rather than taken as a 'fact' in need of clearer understanding. For more on the continued importance of this kind of anti-essentialism in light of recent theoretical rapprochements with materialist thinking, see Jordana Rosenberg's 'The Molecularization of Sexuality: On Some Primitivisms of the Present' (2014), and Min Hyoung Song's 'The New Materialism and Neoliberalism' (2017).

12 For more on the popularity of these ideas in nineteenth-century America, see chapter 2 of Kimmel's *Manhood in America* (2012), 'Born to Run: Self-Control and Fantasies of Escape'.

13 This is not to suggest that it is only with neoliberalism that sexuality began to be treated as an economic concern (or vice versa). In his rigorously researched *The Currency of Desire: Libidinal Economy, Psychoanalysis and Sexual Revolution* (2016), David Bennett draws on a variety of philosophical, sociological, medical, literary and pornographic texts to show how this idea has been present in the West since at

least the Enlightenment. However, although he is right to point out that the human capital approach to sexuality is not as new as it seems, it is still the case that there are logics peculiar to neoliberalism that one cannot simply subsume into the intellectual history he outlines. For instance, when I turn to human capital in Chapter 1, it is in light of the specifically late twentieth-century phenomenon of financialization.

14 Readers will note that I am allowing for some terminological slippage here between sex understood as an activity and sex or sexuality understood as an identity. As Dean himself points out, 'The word "sex" describes both a status and an activity, with the heteronormative assumption being that one determines the other. It is a fallacy of our time … to assume that what you do sexually should give rise to an identity' (2018: 141). I allow for this slippage, though, because it captures the heteronormative assumptions that I detect in Wallace's work. For Wallace, sexually toxic activities *are* an expression of male heterosexual status.

15 I use 'conservatism' here in its simplest, most literal sense – as designating the need to preserve something (masculinity understood as an identity rooted in a propensity for sexual toxicity) from change. For an interesting reading of how Wallace might be seen as a political conservative, see James Santel's 'On David Foster Wallace's Conservatism' (2014).

Chapter 1

1 For a contemporaneous account of Trump's remarks and their fallout on the 2016 campaign trail, see Ben Jacobs et al. '"You can do anything": Trump brags on tape about using fame to get women' (2016). As events would transpire, Trump would win the presidency despite (or because of) his willingness to indulge in misogynistic and racist rhetoric.

2 As others have explored in detail, Wallace at one point considered writing a novel about porn, the raw material for which would find its way into 'Big Red Son', *Brief Interviews with Hideous Men*, and *The Pale King*. For more information on this project, see in particular pages 123 to 128 of Max (2012a), Godden and Szalay (2014), and the last chapter of Hering's *David Foster Wallace: Fiction and Form* (2016).

3 These anxieties also suggest that sex (or, at least, representations of sex) properly belong in the private rather than the public realm. Not only is this distinction incredibly unstable, it has also historically worked to penalize sexual minorities in favour of heteronormative culture and institutions. For more on this topic, see Lauren Berlant and Michael Warner's 1998 essay 'Sex in Public'.

4 There are differences between 'work' understood as any purposeful activity and, in the Marxist sense I evoke here, 'labour' as an alienable commodity in a capitalist

society. I retain this latter term to explore how Wallace depicts male sexuality as human capital. For theories of human capital generalize labour, from employment to all areas of life, as an *economic* idea. Taken to its extreme, human capital renders non-economic 'work' redundant.

5 Given how Wallace figures male sexuality as a resource that needs to be more wisely invested, his suggestion that men look for sexual pleasure in activities other than orgasm amounts to a plea that they diversify their portfolios. As Barclay Palmer explains, this 'is a management strategy that blends different investments in a single portfolio. The idea behind diversification is that a variety of investments will yield a higher return. It also suggests that investors will face lower risk by investing in different vehicles' (2019). Higher emotional return and lower sexual risk are precisely what 'Back in New Fire' encourages in its heterosexual male readers – dynamics that also come into play in Wallace's securitization of homosexuality and AIDS, which I focus on in the next chapter.

6 It is possible to orgasm over the written correspondence of a lover; the same could be said for phone sex. Yet one would be hard pressed to argue that this is what Wallace has in mind. His other examples of preferred sexual activity – holding hands, bodily posture and so on – are strikingly chaste. As I will show in the next section, Wallace's hostility to masturbation forecloses the possibility of positive auto-eroticism.

7 Feher has since developed this idea of working within neoliberalism in order to resist it in his 2018 book *Rated Agency: Investee Politics in a Speculative Age*.

8 Obviously, this is not to say that Halberstam would follow Wallace's enthusiasm for AIDS, a sentiment that places him in the realm of homophobic moralists rather than queer theorists. Indeed, in *How to Have Theory in an Epidemic: Cultural Chronicles of AIDS* (1999), Paula A. Treichler lists some of the many meanings that AIDS has taken on, quite a few of which are directly relevant to 'Back in New Fire': these include 'a condemnation to celibacy or death' (12); 'the result of moral decay' (13); 'the perfect emblem of twentieth-century decadence; of fin de siècle decadence; of postmodern decadence' (13); 'nature's way of cleaning house' (13); 'the price paid for the 1960s' (13).

9 It also sets him apart from some of his more ribald postmodern contemporaries. Consider Mark Leyner's remark that 'as a writer, the notion of being paid to masturbate does not seem odd to me in the least' (1996: 133), or the following reflection by the protagonist of Nicholson Baker's *The Fermata* – 'what else was there in the world beside masturbation? Nothing' (1994: 121).

10 For more on this relationship, see Timothy Aubry (2011), Maria Bustillos (2014), and John Roache (2017).

11 As David P. Rando (2013) shows in his analysis of 'B.I #20', the final story in *Brief Interviews*, the myth of Adam and Eve is a significant backdrop to the collection's

treatment of gender. Wallace uses similar imagery in his review of David Markson's *Wittgenstein's Mistress*, in which he postulates an 'Evian' (2012b: 104) model of misogyny based around guilt as subject as opposed to a 'Hellenic' (104) model of guilt as object. For a close reading of Wallace's interesting but, at times, incoherent review, see Holland (2017).

Chapter 2

1 It is a notable coincidence that the common descriptor for such assets was 'toxic'. In this regard, toxicity is a flexible term of our times – its significations in gender, financial and also environmental contexts deserves further scrutiny. For the latter in relation to *Infinite Jest*, see Hering (2011) and Heather Houser (2014).
2 Martin also draws on securitization as theorized in the field of international relations. In Barry Buzan et al.'s words, this means the 'elevation of specific "threats" to a prepolitical immediacy' (1998: 29), so normal procedures are suspended in order to deal with an immediate danger. My focus is on the financial sense of the term, as I wish to forefront how Wallace presents sexuality in relation to capital. For an interesting analysis of how the risk of AIDS has been understood from an international relations perspective, see Stefan Elbe's essay 'Risking Lives: AIDS, Security and Three Concepts of Risk' (2008).
3 The often dizzying complexity of financial securitization means that my use of the term in relation to images of sexuality necessarily sheds some nuance. I advance, however, in the spirit of Van der Zwan (2014), Martin (2002, 2007), and Haiven's (2014) arguments that financial processes now inform spheres beyond those of hedge fund managers and Wall Street bankers. Indeed, in Haiven's words, securitization 'is not merely the lingua franca of contemporary finance; it is also the biopolitical imperative of financialization. Financialized subjects are to relinquish any hope of actual security and, instead, become savvy virtuosi, counter-levering life's uncertainty into opportunities for self-maximization' (2014: 78).
4 Severs reads Wallace's treatment of risk differently, arguing that he is interested 'in the systematic means by which people build up shared value *against* contingency and risk, such as … governmental insurance' (2017a: 178, italics in original). This may be the case, but it does not preclude Wallace's endorsement of risk taking and risk management when it comes to male sexuality – another example, indeed, of how sexuality is a persistent exception to what is at times his broadly anti-neoliberal vision.
5 Sloane argues that if Wallace 'focuses on the more hideous dimensions of heteronormative sex, he perhaps redeems himself a little in his portrayal of the relationship between Faye Goddard and Julie Smith' (2019: 18), namely in *Girl*'s

opening story 'Little Expressionless Animals'. My focus on male homosexuality excludes a discussion of this story. I would point out, however, that Wallace's sensitive portrayal of this lesbian relationship comes at the expense of any interest in its queerness. As Julie says: 'Lesbianism is simply one kind of response to Otherness. Say the whole point of love is to try to get your fingers through the holes in the lover's mask. To get some kind of hold on the mask, and who cares how you do it' (1989a: 32).

6   That said, I would also join Joffe in expressing reservations about the efficacy of this feminist critique. For a sophisticated reading of Wallace's 'feminism' here, see her essay '"The Last Word": Sex-Changes and Second-Wave Feminism in *The Broom of the System*' (2018).

7   Namely, Wallace's generally scathing review of Updike's *Toward the End of Time*, collected as the second piece in *Consider the Lobster and other Essays* (2005b).

8   For the most impressive reading of the novella in this vein, see Charles B. Harris's essay 'The Anxiety of Influence: The John Barth/David Foster Wallace Connection' (2014).

9   Hearts are an important motif throughout Wallace's work. For more on this, see David P. Rando's (2013) 'David Foster Wallace and Lovelessness', and Richard Godden and Michael Szalay's (2014) 'The Bodies in the Bubble: David Foster Wallace's *The Pale King*'.

10 In this essay Bersani discusses the interrelationship of sex, politics and AIDS, to conclude that sexuality's value lies precisely in its affront to personhood. Indeed, to the extent that he is interested in sex as 'anticommunal, antiegalitarian, antinurturing, [and] antiloving' (1987: 215), then this essay is a key forerunner to Edelman's arguments concerning negativity.

11 An assumption I feel confident in making given that the story's intimations of same-sex desire are associated with secrecy and ignorance. By contrast, these lovers are experiencing the safest of heterosexual prerogatives – waking down the street as a couple.

12 Hal has also inherited this paternal affection – the one-hitters of marijuana he smokes are shaped 'sort of like a long FDR-type cigarette holder' (1996: 49).

13 Many thanks to Bonnie Cuthbert for clarifying my explanation of this process.

14 Of course, one should not miss the irony here. As N. Katherine Hayles notes (albeit, attributing her chosen quote to the wrong character), annular fusion 'is like "treating cancer by giving the cancer cells themselves cancer," Thorp explains (572), a strategy that does not give one hope there will be less cancer in the world' (1999: 688).

15 This is not an exact equivalence, for Kenkle proposes a relationship 'between unwrapping a Christmas present and undressing a *young lady*' (Wallace 1996: 874, italics mine). The change in gender here though does not undermine my point, given that Kenkle clearly does have a (poorly grasped) understanding of Freud's account of the Wolf Man in mind.

16 It might seem strange to class Hal as a heterosexual, given that the narrator explicitly states that he is disinterested in sex: 'Hal is maybe the one male E.T.A. for whom lifetime virginity is a conscious goal' (1996: 634). However, the phrasing here is telling. If abstinence is a 'conscious goal' for Hal, then this suggests existing predilections – or, at the very least, an awareness of such – that he his choosing to disavow. In this regard, he is a forerunner of the sexual ascetics and little men who populate *The Pale King*, which I examine in Chapter 5.

17 For more on the concept of homonationalism, see Jasbir K. Puar's *Terrorist Assemblages: Homonationalism in Queer Times* (2017).

Chapter 3

1 For Beatrice Pire and Pierre-Louise Patoine, 'Wallace seemed to have bridged the gap between the two models that his friend Jonathan Franzen had clearly contrasted in "Mr Difficult," his controversial essay on William Gaddis' (2017: 2). For more on the reception and implications of Franzen's binary, see Smith (2015) and Brooks (2017).

2 That is, for employment contracts, which in their broadest definition necessitates that one party is subservient to another in exchange for a salary, commodities, services, etc. As Chris Fogle reflects in *The Pale King*, 'There's also the social contract' (2012a: 195), where an obligation to others comes into play. These types of contract are not my concern.

3 My references throughout this chapter to 'the reader' beg the question of who this person is. To be clear, I am not trying to account for how actual, specific readers do respond to Wallace's texts. Rather, I use this phrase (as well as 'the spectator') as shorthand for the projected recipient his texts constantly envisage. Essays like 'E Unibus Pluram' address this recipient in broad sociological terms; the passages of *Infinite Jest* that I examine towards the end of this chapter project the more immediate person holding the book.

4 This is slightly different to Amy Hungerford's suggestion that Wallace sets out to 'fuck the reader' (2016: 144). This might be accurate in relation to the early texts Hungerford looks at, but it misses how the agency involved in such 'fucking' pertains as much to the reader as it does to the text (or in her *ad hominem* attacks, to Wallace himself).

5 Severs's 2019 reading of the role of contracts in Pynchon, by contrast, is more compelling. See '"Where all the paperwork's done": Pynchon's Critique of Contracts'.

6 'The Suffering Channel' appears to be a natural fit in relation to my current investigation. However, as I argue in Chapter 5, this story does not figure its desired violence in relation to the gaze, but rather in relation to male–male rivalry.

7 In response to this gazing, 'Gately can see every ashtray on the table shake from the force of Joelle V.'s shudder' (1996: 370). This information furthers the gendered

nature of the gazing taking place and registers Wallace's awareness of objections to it. However, this awareness does not undermine how the following scene solicits the male gaze. As such, this is a good example of how Wallace's texts often acknowledge forms of feminist critique but do not carry them through. My next chapter explores this dynamic in more detail.

8 I am doing a disservice here to the complexity of Lacan's theories of sexuality and feminine *jouissance*. A good critical account of these theories is available in Malcolm Bowie's *Lacan* (1991), while Bruce Fink's *The Lacanian Subject: Between Language and Jouissance* (1995) offers a brilliant explanation of same. For my purposes it is enough to say that, for Lacan, *The Ecstasy of St Theresa* represents an orgasmic pleasure irreducible to a masculine signifying economy; in Bowie's words, 'Theresa and her fellow mystics are borne along on an uncaused, unlocalizable and ineffable pleasure-spasm' (1991: 152–3).

9 Hayes also relates that 'in the same year Irigaray published *Speculum*, 1975, Laura Mulvey published her vastly influential essay on visual pleasure in which she explains how "the male gaze" objectifies and attempts to control those who are looked at' (1999: 353).

Chapter 4

1 In his analysis of the 'Adult World' stories and 'Octet', which along with 'B.I. #20' and 'The Depressed Person' are arguably the most substantial pieces in *Brief Interviews*, Casey Michael Henry makes the case for the importance of orgasm. He argues that the collection's 'moments of affective transcendence' (2019: 138–9) are 'sexual, or orgasmic' (139), an extension of 'the orgasmic-epiphanic mode of structural defamiliarization' (114) that he perceives at work in *Infinite Jest*. Henry is chiefly concerned with how *Brief Interviews* figures moments of empathy in this orgasmic mode. Although different to my own focus, his description of 'sexual desire as a cipher rather than mimetic imprint' (138) in *Brief Interviews* certainly accords with how I understand spermatic imagery functioning in this chapter; as an implicit rupturing, breaking or transcendence of apparently stale feminist discourses of male toxicity.

2 I use 'property' loosely here to suggest both a character trait and an exploitable resource. I do so to draw out the logic by which Wallace presents feminist critique as expropriating a hideousness that, ostensibly, would be best left to men. I complicate these definitions later on in this chapter in relation to the 'Brief Interviews' proper.

3 It is worth remarking here upon the commonalities between this millennial emphasis on depraved masculinities and the ongoing, late 2010s investigation

of sexual crimes committed by male public figures such as Bill Cosby, Harvey Weinstein and Jimmy Savile. It is far beyond the scope of this book to postulate on how the former period relates to the latter, and as I noted in my Introduction, I am more interested in reading Wallace in his own specific historical and cultural context than I am in thinking about how he may have predicted a future he did not live to see. Nevertheless, studies could certainly be carried out on how the era of Chuck Palahniuk's novel *Fight Club* (1996) might inform the era of #MeToo.

4 Franzen is particularly vocal about his attempts to provoke feminist critics in his *Guardian* interview with Emma Brockes, 'There is no way to make myself not male' (2015a).

5 In his marginalia to Foucault's 'What is an Author?', and specifically the essay's argument that an author's name and an ordinary proper name are not isomorphic in their functioning, Wallace has written 'Gobbledegook' (Roache 2017: 2).

6 Wallace groups Foucault with Derrida, de Man, and Barthes, creating a rather broad, and perhaps deliberately strawman image of post-structuralism.

7 These monetary associations may seem arbitrary. However, one can also read the 'check' of diddle-check as a homonym for the American spelling of cheque. Added to the already noted use of 'enclosure', the case for this scene's manipulation of capitalist imagery grows.

8 I am not suggesting that the sexual exploitation of teenage girls is the same as a teenage boy's objectification of a grown woman. Wallace's juxtaposition of the two in this scene, however, presents both as existing on the same continuum of male hideousness.

9 This is slightly different to Rando's suggestion that these processes lead to a 'revelation of lovelessness' (2013: 581). Rando's equation of hideousness with (a supposed) affective deadening elides how these stories forefront men as the bearers of repulsive attitudes and behaviours. Instead of being revelatory, moreover, they confirm and complicate said repulsiveness as a type of pre-set knowledge that feminists ostensibly impute to men.

10 The name 'Dolores Rusk' is also telling. Sharing her forename with Nabokov's nymphet, this Dr's surname is evocative of the famously sexually repressed Victorian man of letters, John Ruskin. The implication is that Nabokov's character has grown up to be a man-hating therapist who works out her frigidity by subjecting male students to psychobabble. That this is in part due to her adherence to a feminism overly broad in its disciplinary application is evident as well – Rusk holds 'doctorates in both Gender and Deviance' (Wallace 1996: 1039).

11 Trump would use this phrase in his inauguration speech, declaring that 'from this moment on, it's going to be America First' (2017). For an intellectual history of the phrase, see Sarah Churchwell's *Behold, America: A History of America First and the American Dream* (2018).

12 Wallace suggests that this vanity arises from the left's ignorance of 'the obvious truth' (2005d: 113) – the 'thoroughgoing *self-interest* that underlies all impulses toward economic equality' (113, italics in original). Such a bald statement of support for economic self-interest strengthens my argument that Wallace follows neoliberal logics.
13 Wallace's description in *Infinite Jest* of Gately's intubation – 'his throat felt somehow raped' (1996: 809) – similarly presents the inability to talk for oneself as sexual violating.
14 Hence, when Kelly asks how Wallace 'might have conceived it [i.e. *Brief Interviews*] as responding and even contributing to the aims of contemporary feminism' (2018: 83), my argument has been that Wallace responded and 'contributed' to feminism by caricaturing it (as being anti-male) and privatizing its critique. Indeed, Kelly argues that Wallace advances a feminist project best understood through 'the so-called French feminists, highly influential in the US academy during the 1980s' (2018: 84). Though compelling on its own terms, to my mind this gives Wallace too much credit. Yes, he may have read the work of Hélène Cixous, Luce Irigaray and Julia Kristeva, but as I have shown throughout, Wallace treats feminist thought as both flawed and worthy of parody. There is little evidence that he was interested in working *with* feminism in pursuit of gender equality – in fact, quite the opposite.
15 This is not to simply equate Bachner's Lacanian invocation of the 'real' with Foucault's description of enunciations that are not 'in the true'. I merely wish to stress how both positions – in their different ways – foreground epistemological limitation.

Chapter 5

1 Another likely source for Wallace's use of the schlemiel is Thomas Pynchon, in whose work this character type appears often. See Severs's essay '"Homer Is My Role Model": Father-Schlemihls, Sentimental Families, and Pynchon's Affinities with *The Simpsons*' (2018). For more on the Pynchon–Wallace connection here, see note 9.
2 Wallace does go on, however, to describe Kafka's humour in terms that are very much reminiscent of the schlemiel's perseverance in the face of hostility. As Wallace's conjoining of Pynchon, Roth, Barth and Allen implies, this essay is not rigorous literary criticism – it is 'the text of a very quick speech' (2005c: 62).
3 The reason why two separate characters share this affliction in *Infinite Jest* – if it is not an instance of authorial oversight – is mysterious. That said, the recurrence of various images, motifs, themes and even phrases throughout this encyclopaedic novel means the doubling of neurotic men with limp penises is not out of place.

4. See the final chapter of Hering's *Fiction and Form* (2016), in which he meticulously traces how *The Pale King* is the confluence of various preceding and overlapping projects.
5. Elsewhere, Wallace notes how 'history's great philosophers never married. … The great mathematicians are nuptially split about 50/50, still way below the civilian range. No cogent explanation on record; feel free to hypothesize' (2003: 200).
6. Notably, Rand suggests that her attractiveness makes her a 'monopsony' (486). As Drinion explains, this is 'the reverse of monopoly. There's a single buyer and multiple sellers' (483). Such a comparison contradicts my reading, as it positions Rand, not the men around her, as buyers of sexual attention. However, it is Ed who teaches her this comparison (483). As such, it is part of his manipulative seduction, which empowers Rand in ways that, cruelly, render her more subject to his control. Similarly, the idea of female sexual empowerment as being an insidious permutation of patriarchal control is consistent with the dynamics I explored in Chapter 4. Indeed, Rand's double bind – wanting to be saved by a man, but being aware of the anti-feminist implications of this same desire – means she exemplifies the kind of postfeminist woman the misogynists E and K hypothesize in 'B.I. #28'.
7. As for the use of Persian here, the tulip is indeed a flower of the East: as Mike Dash notes, 'When exactly cultivation of these wild flowers began is a mystery, but we do know that by about the year 1050, tulips were already venerated in Persia' (1999: 8).
8. Britton, for his part, also has his own 'way of pumping himself up' (2004a: 64).
9. Wallace takes this line from *Gravity's Rainbow*, where it refers to Pynchon's similarly creepy statistician Pointsman: 'Here's an erection stirring, he'll masturbate himself to sleep again tonight. A joyless constant, an institution in his life' (2013: 167).

Conclusion

1. It is not outside the realm of possibility that critics and readers can promote Wallace's work *because* of his neoliberalism. The controversies Hering outlines in his blog post suggest that he can certainly be promoted because of his machismo. The cover image of Penguin's 2018 paperback edition of *The David Foster Wallace Reader* is illustrative in this regard. Dressed in jeans, denim shirt and boots, and with a ragged Star Spangled Banner in the background, Wallace sits on top of a dog cage with his right hand resting near his crotch. The message is crude but clear – opening this book is tantamount to unleashing an animal.
2. This is why Thompson's argument that Wallace's provocative ideas can shock readers out of their complacency is rather misguided (2018). For Thompson downplays the possibility that Wallace means what he says when, for instance, he suggests the

threat of AIDS can have positive effects, or that African American students can only benefit from assimilating into a dominant white supremacist culture. Furthermore, Thompson's argument implies that the 'uncomfortable truths' (2018: 210) Wallace imparts to readers – for instance, that men are sexually toxic – *are* true, rather than statements we can and should challenge.

Bibliography

Aaron, Michele (2007), *Spectatorship: The Power of Looking On*, London: Wallflower Press.
Alderson, David (2016), *Sex, Needs and Queer Culture: From Liberation to the Postgay*, London: Zed Books.
Alexander, Matthew (2016), 'Engaging with David Foster Wallace's *Hideous Men*', *Postgraduate English*, 32: 1–17.
Allen, Kim, Heather Mendick, Laura Harvey and Aisha Ahmad (2015), 'Welfare Queens, Thrifty Housewives and Do-It-All Mums: Celebrity Motherhood and the Cultural Politics of Austerity', *Feminist Media Studies*, 15 (6): 907–25.
American Beauty (1999), [Film] Dir. Sam Mendes, USA: DreamWorks Pictures.
Amin, Kadji (2017), *Disturbing Attachments: Genet, Modern Pederasty, and Queer History*, Durham, NC: Duke University Press.
Arendt, Hannah (1944), 'The Jew as Pariah: A Hidden Tradition', *Jewish Social Studies*, 6 (2): 99–122.
Aspiz, Harold (1984), 'Walt Whitman: The Spermatic Imagination', *American Literature*, 56 (3): 379–95.
Aubry, Timothy (2011), *Reading as Therapy: What Contemporary Fiction Does for Middle-Class Americans*, Iowa: University of Iowa Press.
Aydemir, Murat (2007), *Images of Bliss: Ejaculation, Masculinity, Meaning*, Minneapolis: University of Minnesota Press.
Bachner, Sally (2011), *The Prestige of Violence: American Fiction, 1962-2007*, Athens: University of Georgia Press.
Backman, Jennifer (2018), 'From Hard Boiled to Over Easy: Reimagining the Noir Detective in *Inherent Vice* and *Bleeding Edge*', in Ali Chetwynd, Joanna Freer and Georgios Maragos (eds), *Thomas Pynchon, Sex, and Gender*, 19–35, Athens: University of Georgia Press.
Baker, Nicholson (1994), *The Fermata*, London: Vintage.
Banner, Olivia (2009), '"They're Literally Shit": Masculinity and the Work of Art in an Age of Waste Recycling', *Iowa Journal of Cultural Studies*, 10 (1): 74–90. Available online: https://ir.uiowa.edu/ijcs/vol10/iss1/7/ (accessed 21 August 2019).
Barker-Benfield, G.J. (1976) *The Horrors of the Half-Known Life: Male Attitudes Toward Women and Sexuality in Nineteenth-Century America*, New York: Harper & Row.
Baudrillard, Jean (2009), *The Transparency of Evil: Essays on Extreme Phenomena*, London: Verso.
Becker, Gary S. (1976), *The Economic Approach to Human Behavior*, Chicago: University of Chicago Press.

Benoit, Kenneth (2006), 'Duverger's Law and the Study of Electoral Systems', *French Politics*, 4: 69–83.

Bennett, David (2016), *The Currency of Desire: Libidinal Economy, Psychoanalysis and Sexual Revolution*, London: Lawrence & Wishart.

Benzon, Kiki (2015), 'David Foster Wallace and Millennial America', in Philip Coleman (ed.), *Critical Insights: David Foster Wallace*, 29–45, Ipswich: Salem Press.

Berlant, Lauren (2011a), 'Austerity, Precarity, Awkwardness'. Available online: https://supervalentthought.files.wordpress.com/2011/12/berlant-aaa-2011final.pdf (accessed 21 August 2019).

Berlant, Lauren (2011b), *Cruel Optimism*, Durham, NC: Duke University Press.

Berlant, Lauren and Lee Edelman (2013), *Sex, or the Unbearable*, Durham, NC: Duke University Press.

Berlant, Lauren and Lee Edelman (2015), 'Reading, Sex, and the Unbearable: A Response to Tim Dean', *American Literary History*, 27 (3): 625–29.

Berlant, Lauren and Michael Warner (1998), 'Sex in Public', *Critical Inquiry*, 24 (2): 547–66.

Bersani, Leo (1987), 'Is the Rectum a Grave?', *October*, 43: 197–222.

Biale, David (1997), *Eros and the Jews: From Biblical Israel to Contemporary America*, Berkeley: University of California Press.

Bloom, Allan (1987), *The Closing of the American Mind: How Higher Education Has Failed Democracy and Impoverished the Souls of Today's Students*, New York: Simon & Schuster Inc.

Bloom, Harold (1973), *The Anxiety of Influence: A Theory of Poetry*, Oxford: Oxford University Press.

Blyth, Mark (2013), *Austerity: The History of a Dangerous Idea*, Oxford: Oxford University Press.

Boddy, Kasia (2013), 'A Fiction of Response: *Girl with Curious Hair* in Context', in Marshall Boswell and Stephen J. Burn (eds), *A Companion to David Foster Wallace Studies*, 23–41, Basingstoke: Palgrave Macmillan.

Bollier, David (2003), *Silent Theft: The Private Plunder of Our Common Wealth*, New York: Routledge.

Boswell, Marshall (2009), *Understanding David Foster Wallace*, Columbia, SC: University of South Carolina Press.

Boswell, Marshall (2013), '"The Constant Monologue Inside Your Head": *Oblivion* and the Nightmare of Consciousness', in Marshall Boswell and Stephen J. Burn (eds), *A Companion to David Foster Wallace Studies*, 151–70, Basingstoke: Palgrave Macmillan.

Boswell, Marshall (2014), 'Trickle-Down Citizenship: Taxes and Civic Responsibility in *The Pale King*', in Marshall Boswell (ed.), *David Foster Wallace and "The Long Thing": New Essays on the Novels*, 209–25, London: Bloomsbury Academic.

Boswell, Marshall (2019), *The Wallace Effect: David Foster Wallace and the Contemporary Literary Imagination*, London: Bloomsbury Academic.

Bowie, Malcolm (1991), *Lacan*, London: Fontana Press.
Bramall, Rebecca (2013), *The Cultural Politics of Austerity: Past and Present in Austere Times*, Basingstoke: Palgrave Macmillan.
Brief Interviews with Hideous Men (2009), [Film] Dir. John Krasinski, USA: IFC Films.
Brooks, Ryan M. (2015), 'Conflict Before Compromise: A Response to Rachel Greenwald Smith', *The Account*, 4. Available online: https://theaccountmagazine.com/article/forum-on-compromise-aesthetics (accessed 21 August 2019).
Brooks, Ryan M. (2017), '"The Family Gone Wrong": Post-Postmodernism, Neoliberalism, and the Contemporary Novel's Contract with the Reader', *49th Parallel: An Interdisciplinary Journal of North American Studies*, 39: 22–45. Available online: https://fortyninthparalleljournal.files.wordpress.com/2014/07/ryan-brooks-issue-39.pdf (accessed 23 August 2019).
Brown, Wendy (2015), *Undoing the Demos: Neoliberalism's Stealth Revolution*, New York: Zone Books.
Buchbinder, David (2008), 'Enter the Schlemiel: The Emergence of Inadequate or Incompetent Masculinities in Recent Film and Television', *Canadian Review of American Studies*, 38 (2): 227–45.
Buerkle, C. Wesley (2011), 'Masters of Their Domain: *Seinfeld* and the Discipline of Mediated Men's Sexual Economy', in Elwood Watson and Marc E. Shaw (eds), *Performing American Masculinities: The 21st-Century Man in Popular Culture*, 9–36, Bloomington: Indiana University Press.
Burn, Stephen J. (2012), *David Foster Wallace's Infinite Jest: A Reader's Guide*, 2nd edn, London: Continuum.
Burn, Stephen J. (2014a), '"A Paradigm for the Life of Consciousness": *The Pale King*', in Marshall Boswell (ed.), *David Foster Wallace and "The Long Thing": New Essays on the Novels*, 149–68, London: Bloomsbury Academic.
Burn, Stephen J. (2014b), 'Toward a General Theory of Vision in Wallace's Fiction', *English Studies*, 95 (1): 85–93.
Bustillos, Maria (2014), 'Philosophy, Self-Help, and the Death of David Foster Wallace', in Robert K. Bolger and Scott Korb (eds), *Gesturing Toward Reality: David Foster Wallace and Philosophy*, 121–39, London: Bloomsbury Academic.
Butler, Judith (1990), *Gender Trouble: Feminism and the Subversion of Identity*, New York: Routledge.
Butler, Judith (1993), *Bodies That Matter: On the Discursive Limits of "Sex"*, New York: Routledge.
Buzan, Barry, Ole Waever and Jaap de Wilde (1998), *Security: A New Framework for Analysis*, Boulder: Lynne Rienner Publishers.
Carlin, Gerry and Mark Jones (2010), '"Students Study Hard Porn": Pornography and the Popular Press', in Karen Boyle (ed.), *Everyday Pornography*, 179–89, New York: Routledge.
Carlisle, Greg (2013), *Nature's Nightmare: Analyzing David Foster Wallace's Oblivion*, Los Angeles: Sideshow Media Group Press.

Carroll, Hamilton (2011), *Affirmative Reaction: New Formations of White Masculinity*, Durham, NC: Duke University Press.

Chetwynd, Ali, Joanna Freer and Georgios Maragos (2018), 'Introduction', in Ali Chetwynd, Joanna Freer and Georgios Maragos (eds), *Thomas Pynchon, Sex, and Gender*, ix–xxxii, Athens: University of Georgia Press.

Churchwell, Sarah (2018), *Behold, America: A History of America First and the American Dream*, London: Bloomsbury.

Clare, Ralph (2014), 'The Politics of Boredom and the Boredom of Politics in *The Pale King*', in Marshall Boswell (ed.), *David Foster Wallace and "The Long Thing": New Essays on the Novels*, 187–208, London: Bloomsbury Academic.

Clare, Ralph (2018), 'Introduction: An Exquisite Corpus: Assembling a Wallace Without Organs', in Ralph Clare (ed.), *The Cambridge Companion to David Foster Wallace*, 1–15, Cambridge: Cambridge University Press.

Clarke, John and Janet Newman (2012), 'The Alchemy of Austerity', *Critical Social Policy*, 32 (3): 299–319.

Cook, Simon (2017), '"The Obscenification of Everyday Life": Representing Pornography in Anglo-American Fiction since 1970', PhD, Universiteit Utrecht, Utrecht.

Cooper, Melinda (2017), *Family Values: Between Neoliberalism and the New Social Conservatism*, New York: Zone Books.

Cornwall, Andrea, Frank Karioris and Nancy Lindisfarne, eds (2016), *Masculinities Under Neoliberalism*, London: Zed Books.

Coughlan, David (2015), '"Sappy or No It's True": Affect and Expression in *Brief Interviews with Hideous Men*', in Philip Coleman (ed.), *Critical Insights: David Foster Wallace*, 160–75, Ipswich: Salem Press.

Curtis, Neal (2016), 'Thought Bubble: Neoliberalism and the Politics of Knowledge', in Jeremy Gilbert (ed.), *Neoliberal Culture*, 101–23, London: Lawrence & Wishart.

Dash, Mike (1999), *Tulipomania: The Story of the World's Most Coveted Flower and the Extraordinary Passions It Aroused*, London: Victor Gollancz.

Davies, Helen and Claire O'Callaghan (2017), 'Introduction: Boom and Bust? Gender and Austerity in Popular Culture', in Helen Davies and Claire O'Callaghan (eds), *Gender and Austerity in Popular Culture: Femininity, Masculinity & Recession in Film & Television*, 1–19, New York: I.B. Tauris & Co. Ltd.

Davies, William (2016a), *The Limits of Neoliberalism: Authority, Sovereignty and the Logic of Competition*, Revised Edition, Los Angeles: Sage.

Davies, William (2016b), 'The New Neoliberalism', *New Left Review*, 101: 121–34.

Dean, Tim (2015), 'No Sex Please, We're American', *American Literary History*, 27 (3): 614–24.

Dean, Tim (2018), 'Foucault and Sex', in Lisa Downing (ed.), *After Foucault: Culture, Theory, and Criticism in the 21st Century*, 141–54, Cambridge: Cambridge University Press.

Deleuze, Gilles (1989), *Masochism: Coldness and Cruelty*, New York: Zone Books.

Delfino, Andrew Steven (2008), *Becoming the New Man in Post-Postmodernist Fiction: Portrayals of Masculinities in David Foster Wallace's* Infinite Jest *and Chuck Palahniuk's* Fight Club, Saarbrücken: VDM Verlag Dr. Müeller.

Dines, Gail (2011), *Pornland: How Porn Has Hijacked Our Sexuality*, Boston: Beacon Press.

Dorson, James (2014), 'The Neoliberal Machine in the Bureaucratic Garden: Pastoral States of Mind in David Foster Wallace's *The Pale King*', in Eric Erbacher, Nicole Maruo-Schröder and Florian Sedlmeier (eds), in *Rereading the Machine in the Garden: Nature and Technology in American Culture*, 211–30, Verlag: Frankfurt-on-Main.

Duggan, Lisa (2003), *The Twilight of Equality: Neoliberalism, Cultural Politics, and the Attack on Democracy*, Boston: Beacon Press.

Eagleton-Pierce, Matthew (2016), *Neoliberalism: The Key Concepts*, New York: Routledge.

Easthope, Anthony (1992), *What a Man's Gotta Do: Masculine Myth in Popular Culture*, New York: Routledge.

Edelman, Lee (2004), *No Future: Queer Theory and the Death Drive*, Durham, NC: Duke University Press.

Edelman, Lee (2011), 'Ever After: History, Negativity, and the Social', in Janet Halley and Andrew Parker (eds), *After Sex? On Writing Since Queer Theory*, 110–20, Durham, NC: Duke University Press.

Edelman, Lee, Robert L. Caserio, Judith Halberstam, José Esteban Muñoz and Tim Dean (2006), 'The Antisocial Thesis in Queer Theory', *PMLA*, 121 (3): 819–28.

Elbe, Stefan (2008), 'Risking Lives: AIDS, Security and Three Concepts of Risk', *Security Dialogue*, 39 (2–3): 177–98.

Eugenides, Jeffrey (2011), *The Marriage Plot*, London: 4th Estate.

Evans, Eric J. (2004), *Thatcher and Thatcherism*, 2nd edn, New York: Routledge.

Faludi, Susan (1991), *Backlash: The Undeclared War Against American Women*, London: Vintage.

Feher, Michel (2009), 'Self-Appreciation; Or, The Aspirations of Human Capital', *Public Culture*, 21 (1): 21–41.

Feher, Michel (2018), *Rated Agency: Investee Politics in a Speculative Age*, New York: Zone Books.

Felski, Rita (1996), 'Fin de siècle, Fin de sexe: Transsexuality, Postmodernism, and the Death of History', *New Literary History*, 27 (2): 337–49.

Fink, Bruce (1995), *The Lacanian Subject: Between Language and Jouissance*, Princeton, NJ: Princeton University Press.

Fleming, Chris (2004), *René Girard: Violence and Mimesis*, Cambridge: Polity Press.

Floyd, Kevin (2009), *The Reification of Desire: Toward a Queer Marxism*, Minneapolis: University of Minnesota Press.

Foucault, Michel (1981), 'The Order of Discourse', in Robert Young (ed.) and Ian McLeod (trans.), *Untying the Text: A Post-Structuralist Reader*, 48–78, New York: Routledge.

Foucault, Michel (1988), 'Power and Sex: Discussion with Bernard-Henri Levy', in Lawrence D. Kritzman (ed.) and David J. Parent (trans.), *Michel Foucault: Politics, Philosophy, Culture: Interviews and Other Writings, 1977-1984*, 110–24, London: Routledge.

Foucault, Michel (1998a), *The Will to Knowledge: The History of Sexuality: 1*, trans. Robert Hurley, London: Penguin.

Foucault, Michel (1998b), 'What Is an Author?', in James D. Faubion (ed.) and Josue V. Harari (trans.), *Aesthetics, Method, and Epistemology*, 205–22, New York: The New Press.

Foucault, Michel (2002), *Archaeology of Knowledge*, trans. A. M. Sheridan Smith, New York: Routledge.

Foucault, Michel (2008), *The Birth of Biopolitics: Lectures at the Collége De France 1978-1979*, ed. Michel Senellart and trans. Graham Burchell, Basingstoke: Palgrave Macmillan.

Franco, Marie (2017), 'Queer Postmodern Practices: Sex and Narrative in *Gravity's Rainbow*', *Twentieth-Century Literature*, 63 (2): 141–66.

Franco, Marie (2018), 'Queer Sex, Queer Text: S/M in *Gravity's Rainbow*', in Ali Chetwynd, Joanna Freer and Georgios Maragos (eds), *Thomas Pynchon, Sex, and Gender*, 88–108, Athens, University of Georgia Press.

Franzen, Jonathan (1996), 'Perchance to Dream', *Harper's*, 1 April: 35–54.

Franzen, Jonathan (2002), 'Mr. Difficult: William Gaddis and the Problem of Hard-to-Read-Books', *The New Yorker*, 30 September: 100–11.

Franzen, Jonathan (2012), 'Farther Away', in *Farther Away*, 15–52, London: 4th Estate.

Franzen, Jonathan (2015a), 'There Is No Way to Make Myself Not Male', interviewed by Emma Brockes for *The Guardian*, 21 August. Available online: https://www.theguardian.com/global/2015/aug/21/jonathan-franzen-purity-interview (accessed 21 August 2019).

Franzen, Jonathan (2015b), *Purity*, London: 4th Estate.

Fraser, Nancy (2013), 'How Feminism Became Capitalism's Handmaiden – And How to Reclaim It', *The Guardian*, 14 October. Available online: https://www.theguardian.com/commentisfree/2013/oct/14/feminism-capitalist-handmaiden-neoliberal (accessed 21 August 2019).

Freud, Sigmund (1979a), 'From the History of an Infantile Neurosis (The "Wolf Man")', in James Strachey (ed.), *Case Histories II: The 'Rat Man', Schreber, The 'Wolf Man', A Case of Female Homosexuality*, 227–366, London: Penguin.

Freud, Sigmund (1979b), 'Notes Upon a Case of Obsessional Neurosis (The "Rat Man")', in James Strachey (ed.), *Case Histories II: The 'Rat Man', Schreber, The 'Wolf Man', A Case of Female Homosexuality*, 33–128, London: Penguin.

Freud, Sigmund (2001), 'A Child Is Being Beaten', in James Strachey (ed.), *The Standard Edition of the Complete Psychological Works of Sigmund Freud, Volume XVIII*, 177–204, London: Vintage.

Garner, Bryan A. (2013), *Quack This Way: David Foster Wallace & Bryan A. Garner Talk Language and Writing*, Dallas: RosePen Books.

Gilbert, Jeremy (2016a), 'Introduction', in Jeremy Gilbert (ed.), *Neoliberal Culture*, 7–9, London: Lawrence & Wishart.
Gilbert, Jeremy (2016b), 'What Kind of Thing Is "Neoliberalism"?', in Jeremy Gilbert (ed.), *Neoliberal Culture*, 10–32, London: Lawrence & Wishart.
Giles, Paul (2012), 'All Swallowed Up: David Foster Wallace and American Literature', in Samuel Cohen and Lee Konstantinou (eds), *The Legacy of David Foster Wallace*, 3–22, Iowa City: University of Iowa Press.
Gill, Rosalind (2009), 'Beyond the "Sexualization of Culture" Thesis: An Intersectional Analysis of "Sixpacks," "Midriffs" and "Hot Lesbians" in Advertising', *Sexualities*, 12 (2): 137–60.
Girard, René (1987), 'Generative Scapegoating', in Robert G. Hamerton-Kelly (ed.), *Violent Origins: Walter Burket, René Girard, and Jonathan Z. Smith on Ritual Killing and Cultural Formation*, 73–145, Stanford: Stanford University Press.
Girard, René (2013), *Violence and the Sacred*, trans. Patrick Gregory, London: Bloomsbury Academic.
Godden, Richard and Michael Szalay (2014), 'The Bodies in the Bubble: David Foster Wallace's *The Pale King*', *Textual Practice*, 28 (7): 1273–322.
Graeber, David (2011), *Debt: The First 5000 Years*, Brooklyn, Melville House.
Gray, John (1995), *Liberalism*, 2nd edn, Buckingham: Open University Press.
Greven, David (2005), *Men Beyond Desire: Manhood, Sex, and Violation in American Literature*, Basingstoke: Palgrave Macmillan.
Greven, David (2013), 'American Psycho Family Values: Conservative Cinema and the New Travis Bickles', in Timothy Shary (ed.), *Millennial Masculinity: Men in Contemporary American Cinema*, 143–62, Detroit: Wayne State University Press.
Haddad, Vincent (2017), 'Conjuring David Foster Wallace's Ghost: Prosopopoeia, Whitmanian Intimacy and the Queer Potential of *Infinite Jest* and *The Pale King*', *Orbit: A Journal of American Literature*, 5 (1): 1–28. Available online: https://orbit.o penlibhums.org/article/doi/10.16995/orbit.139/ (accessed 21 August 2019).
Haiven, Max (2014), *Cultures of Financialization: Fictitious Capital in Popular Culture and Everyday Life*, Basingstoke: Palgrave Macmillan.
Halbertal, Moshe (2012), *On Sacrifice*, Princeton: Princeton University Press.
Halperin, David M. (1995), *Saint Foucault: Towards a Gay Hagiography*, Oxford: Oxford University Press.
Hanlon, Gerard (2016), 'Total Bureaucratisation, Neo-liberalism, and Weberian Oligarchy: The Political Economy of Corporate Governance', Review of *The Utopia of Rules: On Technology, Stupidity, and the Secret Joys of Bureaucracy*, by David Graeber, *Ephemera: Theory & Politics in Organisation*, 16 (1): 179–91.
Harris, Charles B. (2014), 'The Anxiety of Influence: The John Barth/David Foster Wallace Connection', *Critique: Studies in Contemporary Fiction*, 55 (2): 103–26.
Harvey, David (2007), *A Brief History of Neoliberalism*, Oxford: Oxford University Press.
Hayek, Friedrich (2001), *The Road to Serfdom*, New York: Routledge.

Hayes, Tom (1999), 'A *Jouissance* Beyond the Phallus: Juno, Saint Teresa, Bernini, Lacan', *American Imago*, 56 (4): 331–55.
Hayes-Brady, Clare (2013), '"…": Language, Gender, and Modes of Power in the Work of David Foster Wallace', in Marshall Boswell and Stephen J. Burn (eds), *A Companion to David Foster Wallace Studies*, 131–50, Basingstoke: Palgrave Macmillan.
Hayes-Brady, Clare (2016), *The Unspeakable Failures of David Foster Wallace: Language, Identity, and Resistance*, London: Bloomsbury Academic.
Hayes-Brady, Clare (2018), 'Reading Your Problematic Fave: David Foster Wallace, Feminism and #metoo', *The Honest Ulsterman*, June. Available online: https://humag.co/features/reading-your-problematic-fave (accessed 22 August 2019).
Hayles, N. Katherine (1999), '"The Illusion of Autonomy and the Fact of Recursivity": Virtual Ecologies, Entertainment, and *Infinite Jest*', *New Literary History*, 30 (3): 675–97.
Haynes, Doug (2018), '"Allons Enfants!" Pynchon's Pornographies', in Ali Chetwynd, Joanna Freer and Georgios Maragos (eds), *Thomas Pynchon, Sex, and Gender*, 69–87, Athens: University of Georgia Press.
Henry, Casey Michael (2015), '"Sudden Awakening to the Fact That the Mischief Is Irretrievably Done": Epiphanic Structure in David Foster Wallace's *Infinite Jest*', *Critique: Studies in Contemporary Fiction*, 56 (5): 480–502.
Henry, Casey Michael (2019), *New Media and the Transformation of Postmodern American Literature: From Cage to Connection*, London: Bloomsbury Academic.
Hering, David (2011), 'Theorising David Foster Wallace's Toxic Postmodern Spaces', *US Studies Online*, 18. Available online: https://www.baas.ac.uk/issue-18-spring-2011-article-2/ (accessed 23 August 2019).
Hering, David (2015), 'Form as Strategy in *Infinite Jest*', in Philip Coleman (ed.), *Critical Insights: David Foster Wallace*, 128–43, Ipswich: Salem Press.
Hering, David (2016), *David Foster Wallace: Fiction and Form*, London: Bloomsbury Academic.
Hering, David (2018), 'Thinking About David Foster Wallace, Misogyny and Scholarship', *Literary Studies: Bloomsbury*, 19 February. Available online: http://blomsburyliterarystudiesblog.com/continuum-literary-studie/2018/02/thinking-david-foster-wallace-misogyny-scholarship.html (accessed 21 August 2019).
Hesse, Carla (1991), 'Enlightenment Epistemology and the Laws of Authorship in Revolutionary France, 1777–793', in Robert Post (ed.), *Law and the Order of Culture*, 109–37, Berkeley: University of California Press.
Hester, Helen (2014), *Beyond Explicit: Pornography and the Displacement of Sex*, New York: State University of New York Press.
Himmelheber, Rachel Haley (2014), '"I Believed She Could Save Me": Rape Culture in David Foster Wallace's "Brief Interviews with Hideous Men #20"', *Critique: Studies in Contemporary Fiction*, 55 (5): 522–35.
Hoberek, Andrew (2018), 'Wallace and American Literature', in Ralph Clare (ed.), *The Cambridge Companion to David Foster Wallace*, 33–48, Cambridge: Cambridge University Press.

Hogg, Emily J. (2014), 'Subjective Politics in *The Pale King*', *English Studies*, 95 (1): 59–69.
Holland, Mary K. (2013), 'Mediated Immediacy in *Brief Interviews with Hideous Men*', in Marshall Boswell and Stephen J. Burn (eds), *A Companion to David Foster Wallace Studies*, 107–30, Basingstoke: Palgrave Macmillan.
Holland, Mary K. (2017), '"By Hirsute Author": Gender and Communication in the Work and Study of David Foster Wallace', *Critique: Studies in Contemporary Fiction*, 58 (1): 64–77.
Houser, Heather (2014), '*Infinite Jest*'s Environmental Case for Disgust', *Ecosickness in Contemporary U.S. Fiction: Environment and Affect*, New York: Columbia.
Huehls, Mitchum and Rachel Greenwald Smith (2017), 'Four Phases of Neoliberalism and Literature: An Introduction', in Mitchum Huehls and Rachel Greenwald Smith (eds), *Neoliberalism and Contemporary Literary Culture*, 1–20, Baltimore: Johns Hopkins Press.
Hungerford, Amy (2016), *Making Literature Now*, Stanford: Stanford University Press.
Hustvedt, Siri (2011), *The Summer Without Men*, London: Spectre.
Hutcheon, Linda (2002), *The Politics of Postmodernism*, 2nd edn, London: Routledge.
Huyssen, Andreas (1986), *After the Great Divide: Modernism, Mass Culture, Postmodernism*, Bloomington: Indiana University Press.
In the Company of Men (1997), [Film] Dir. Neil Labute, USA: Sony Pictures Classics.
Jacobs, Ben, Sabrina Siddiqui and Scott Bixby (2016), '"You Can Do Anything": Trump Brags on Tape About Using Fame to Get Women', *The Guardian*, 8 October. Available online: https://www.theguardian.com/us-news/2016/oct/07/donald-trump-leaked-recording-women (accessed 28 August 2019).
Jackson, Ben (2010), 'At the Origins of Neo-Liberalism: The Free Economy and The Strong State, 1930–1947', *The Historical Journal*, 53 (1): 129–51.
Jackson, Edward and Joel Nicholson-Roberts (2017), 'White Guys: Questioning *Infinite Jest*'s New Sincerity', *Orbit: A Journal of American Literature*, 5 (1): 1–28.
Joffe, Daniela Franca (2017), '"In the Shadows": David Foster Wallace and Multicultural America', PhD, University of Cape Town, Cape Town.
Joffe, Daniela Franca (2018), '"The Last Word": Sex-Changes and Second-Wave Feminism in *The Broom of the System*', *The Journal of David Foster Wallace Studies*, 1 (1): 151–84.
Kakutani, Michiko (2011), 'Maximized Revenue, Minimized Existence', *The New York Times*, 31 March. Available online: http://www.nytimes.com/2011/04/01/books/the-pale-king-by-david-foster-wallace-book-review.html (accessed 21 August 2019).
Kelly, Adam (2010), 'David Foster Wallace and the New Sincerity in American Fiction', in David Hering (ed.), *Consider David Foster Wallace: Critical Essays*, 131–46, Los Angeles: Sideshow Media Group Press.
Kelly, Adam (2014a), 'David Foster Wallace and the Novel of Ideas', in Marshall Boswell (ed.), *David Foster Wallace and "The Long Thing": New Essays on the Novels*, 3–22, London: Bloomsbury Academic.

Kelly, Adam (2014b), 'Dialectic of Sincerity: Lionel Trilling and David Foster Wallace', *Post 45*. Available online: http://post45.research.yale.edu/2014/10/dialectic-of-si ncerity-lionel-trilling-and-david-foster-wallace/ (accessed 21 August 2019).
Kelly, Adam (2017), 'Formally Conventionally Fiction', in Rachel Greenwald Smith (ed.), *American Literature in Transition, 2000-2010*, 46–60, Cambridge: Cambridge University Press.
Kelly, Adam (2018), 'Brief Interviews with Hideous Men', in Ralph Clare (ed.), *The Cambridge Companion to David Foster Wallace*, 82–96, Cambridge: Cambridge University Press.
Kimmel, Michael (2012), *Manhood in America: A Cultural History*, 3rd edn, Oxford: Oxford University Press.
Kimmel, Michael (2013), *Angry White Men: American Masculinity at the End of an Era*, New York: Nation Books.
Kirwan, Michael (2004), *Discovering Girard*, London: Darton, Longman & Todd Ltd.
Kruger, Steven F. (1996), *AIDS Narratives: Gender and Sexuality, Fiction and Science*, New York: Routledge.
Lacan, Jacques (1985), 'God and the *Jouissance* of The Woman: A Love Letter', in Juliet Mitchell and Jacqueline Rose (eds) and Jacqueline Rose (trans.), *Feminine Sexuality: Jacques Lacan and the ecole freudienne*, 137–48, New York: W.W. Norton & Company.
Laqueur, Thomas W. (2004), *Solitary Sex: A Cultural History of Masturbation*, New York: Zone Books.
Leyner, Mark (1996), *Tooth Imprints on a Corn Dog*, New York: Vintage Contemporaries.
Lewis, Holly (2016), *The Politics of Everybody: Feminism, Queer Theory, and Marxism at the Intersection*, London: Zed Books.
Lipsky, David (2010), *Although of Course You End Up Becoming Yourself: A Road Trip with David Foster Wallace*, New York: Broadway Books.
Magnolia (1999), [Film] Dir. Paul Thomas Anderson, USA: New Line Cinema.
Mahon, Alyce (2005), *Eroticism and Art*, Oxford: Oxford University Press.
Malin, Brenton, J. (2005), *American Masculinity Under Clinton: Popular Media and the Nineties "Crisis of Masculinity"*, New York: Peter Lang Publishing.
Markson, David (1988), *Wittgenstein's Mistress*, Champaign, IL: Dalkey Archive Press.
Martin, Randy (2002), *Financialization of Daily Life*, Philadelphia: Temple University Press.
Martin, Randy (2007), *An Empire of Indifference: American War and the Financial Logic of Risk Management*, Durham, NC: Duke University Press.
Martin, Robert K. (1998), 'Melville and Sexuality', in Robert S. Levine (ed.), *The Cambridge Companion to Herman Melville*, 186–201, Cambridge: Cambridge University Press.
Marzullo, Michelle (2011), 'Through a Glass, Darkly: U.S. Marriage Discourse and Neoliberalism', *Journal of Homosexuality*, 58 (6–7): 758–74.

Max, D.T. (2012a), *Every Love Story Is a Ghost Story: A Life of David Foster Wallace*, London: Granta.
Max, D. T. (2012b), 'God, Mary Karr, and Ronald Reagan: D.T. Max on David Foster Wallace', interviewed by John Williams for *The New York Times*, 12 September. Available online: https://artsbeat.blogs.nytimes.com/2012/09/12/god-mary-karr-and-ronald-reagan-d-t-max-on-david-foster-wallace/ (accessed 23 August 2019).
McGurl, Mark (2014), 'The Institution of Nothing: David Foster Wallace in the Program', *Boundary 2*, 41 (3): 27–54.
McHale, Brian (2015), *The Cambridge Introduction to Postmodernism*, Cambridge: Cambridge University Press.
McKinley, Maggie (2015), *Masculinity and the Paradox of Violence in American Fiction, 1950-75*, London: Bloomsbury Academic.
McLaughlin, Robert (2012), 'Post-postmodernism', in Joe Bray, Alison Gibbons, and Brian McHale (eds), *The Routledge Companion to Experimental Literature*, 212–23, New York: Routledge.
Michaels, Walter Benn (2017), 'Fifty Shades of Neoliberal Love', in Mitchum Huehls and Rachel Greenwald Smith (eds), *Neoliberalism and Contemporary Literary Culture*, 21–33, Baltimore: Johns Hopkins University Press.
Moi, Toril (1982), 'The Missing Mother: The Oedipal Rivalries of René Girard', *Diacritics*, 12 (2): 21–31.
Moore, Lisa Jean (2007), *Sperm Counts: Overcome by Man's Most Precious Fluid*, New York: New York University Press.
Motte, Warren F. (2003), *Fables of the Novel: French Fiction Since 1990*, Chicago: Dalkey Archive Press.
Mullen, Patrick (2002), 'Review of *Deficits and Desires: Economics and Sexuality in Twentieth Century Literature*', *Modern Fiction Studies*, 48 (3): 780–82.
Mulvey, Laura (2009), *Visual and Other Pleasures*, 2nd edn, Basingstoke: Palgrave Macmillan.
Nabokov, Vladimir (1995), *Lolita*, London: Penguin.
Nash, Woods (2015), 'Narrative Ethics, Authentic Integrity, and an Intrapersonal Medical Encounter in David Foster Wallace's "Luckily the Account Representative Knew CPR"', *Cambridge Quarterly of Healthcare Ethics*, 24 (1): 96–106.
Nichols, Catherine (2001), 'Dialogizing Postmodern Carnival: David Foster Wallace's *Infinite Jest*', *Critique: Studies in Contemporary Fiction*, 43 (1): 3–16.
Nikunen, Kaarina, Susanna Paasonen and Laura Saarenmaa (2007), 'Pornification and the Education of Desire', in Kaarina Nikunen, Susanna Paasonen, and Laura Saarenmaa (eds), *Pornification: Sex and Sexuality in Media Culture*, 1–22, Oxford: Berg Publishers.
Nixon, Charles Reginald (2013a), 'The Work of David Foster Wallace and Post-Postmodernism', PhD, University of Leeds, Leeds. Available online: http://etheses.whiterose.ac.uk/6873/ (accessed 21 August 2019).

Nixon, Charles Reginald (2013b), 'Variations on Wallace'. Review of *Both Flesh and Not: Essays*, by David Foster Wallace, *The Oxonion Review*, 21 (4). Available online: http://www.oxonianreview.org/wp/variations-on-wallace/ (accessed 21 August 2019).

Office Space (1999), [Film] Dir. Mike Judge, USA: 20th Century Fox.

Oksala, Johanna (2013), 'Feminism and Neoliberal Governmentality', *Foucault Studies*, 16: 32–53.

O'Malley, Pat (1996), 'Risk and Responsibility', in Andrew Barry, Thomas Osborne, and Nikolas Rose (eds), *Foucault and Political Reason: Liberalism, Neo-Liberalism and the Rationalities of Government*, 189–209, New York: Routledge.

O'Toole, Laurence (1998), *Pornocopia: Porn, Sex, Technology and Desire*, London: Serpent's Tail.

Oyler, Lauren (2018), 'When Did Everything Get So "Toxic"?', *The New York Times Magazine*, 2 October. Available online: https://www.nytimes.com/2018/10/02/magazine/when-did-everything-get-so-toxic.html (accessed 22 August 2019).

Palmer, Barclay (2019), '5 Tips for Diversifying Your Portfolio', *Investopedia*, June. Available online: https://www.investopedia.com/articles/03/072303.asp (accessed 23 August 2019).

Paul, Pamela (2006), *Pornified: How Pornography Is Damaging Our Lives, Our Relationships, and Our Families*, New York: Owl Books.

Penney, James (2014), *After Queer Theory: The Limits of Sexual Politics*, London: Pluto Press.

Phillips-Fein, Kim (2017), *Fear City: New York's Fiscal Crisis and the Rise of Austerity Politics*, New York: Metropolitan Books.

Pietsch, Michael (2012), 'Editor's Note', in *The Pale King: An Unfinished Novel*, London: Penguin.

Pinsker, Sanford (1991), *The Schlemiel as Metaphor: Studies in Yiddish and American Jewish Fiction*, Revised and Enlarged Edition, Carbondale: Southern Illinois University Press.

Pire, Beatrice, Pierre-Louis Patoine (2017), 'Introduction', in Beatrice Pire and Pierre-Louis Patoine (eds), *David Foster Wallace: Presences of the Other*, 1–8, Eastbourne: Sussex Academic Press.

Plehwe, Dieter (2009), 'Introduction', in Philip Mirowski and Dieter Plehwe (eds), *The Road from Mont Pelerin: The Making of the Neoliberal Thought Collective*, 1–44, Cambridge: Harvard University Press.

Plummer, Ken (2005), 'Male Sexualities', in Michael S. Kimmel, Jeff Hearn and R.W. Connell (eds), *Handbook of Studies on Men & Masculinities*, 178–95, Thousand Oaks: Sage.

Posner, Richard (1994), *Sex and Reason*, Cambridge: Harvard University Press.

Power, Kevin (2019), 'Hating Jonathan Franzen', *Dublin Review of Books*, 1 February. Available online: https://www.drb.ie/essays/hating-jonathan-franzen (accessed 31 August 2019).

Puar, Jasbir K. (2017), *Terrorist Assemblages: Homonationalism in Queer Times*, 10th anniversary edition, Durham, NC: Duke University Press.
Purdy, Jedediah (2014), 'The Accidental Neoliberal: Against the Old Sincerity', *n+1*, 19. Available online: https://nplusonemag.com/issue-19/politics/the-accidental-neoliberal/ (accessed 21 August 2019).
Pynchon, Thomas (2013), *Gravity's Rainbow*, London: Vintage.
Rando, David P. (2013), 'David Foster Wallace and Lovelessness', *Twentieth-Century Literature*, 59 (4): 575–95.
Roache, John (2017), '"The Realer, more Enduring and Sentimental Part of Him": David Foster Wallace's Personal Library and Marginalia', *Orbit: A Journal of American Literature*, 5 (1): 1–35. Available online: https://orbit.openlibhums.org/article/doi/10.16995/orbit.142/ (accessed 21 August 2019).
Robinson, Marilynne (2012), *When I Was a Child I Read Books*, London: Virago.
Robinson, Sally (2000), *Marked Men: White Masculinity in Crisis*, New York: Columbia University Press.
Roiphe, Katie (2013), 'The Naked and the Conflicted', in *In Praise of Messy Lives*, 63–74, Edinburgh: Canongate Books.
Rosenberg, Jordana (2014), 'The Molecularization of Sexuality: On Some Primitivisms of the Present', *Theory & Event*, 17 (2).
Rottenberg, Catherine (2018), *The Rise of Neoliberal Feminism*, New York: Oxford University Press.
Row, Jess (2019), *White Flights: Race, Fiction, and the American Imagination*, Minneapolis: Graywolf Press.
Rubin, Paul H. and Tilman Klump (2012), 'Property Rights and Capitalism', in Dennis C. Mueller (ed.), *The Oxford Handbook of Capitalism*, 204–19, Oxford: Oxford University Press.
Saint-Aubin, Arthur Flannigan (1994), 'The Male Body and Literary Metaphors for Masculinity', in Harry Brod and Michael Kaufman (eds), *Theorizing Masculinities*, 239–58, Thousand Oaks: Sage.
Santel, James (2014), 'On David Foster Wallace's Conservatism', *Hudson Review*, 66 (4): 625–34.
Sarracino, Carmine and Kevin M. Scott (2010), *The Porning of America: The Rise of Porn Culture, What It Means, and Where We Go from Here*, Boston: Beacon Press.
Saunders, George (2008), 'The Braindead Megaphone', in *The Braindead Megaphone: Essays*, 1–20, London: Bloomsbury.
Sayers, Philip (2014), 'Representing Entertainment in *Infinite Jest*', in Marshall Boswell (ed.), *David Foster Wallace and "The Long Thing": New Essays on the Novels*, 107–26, London: Bloomsbury Academic.
Schatz, Thomas (1981), *Hollywood Genres: Formulas, Filmmaking, and the Studio System*, Boston: McGraw-Hill.
Schrecker, Ted and Clare Bambra (2015), *How Politics Makes Us Sick: Neoliberal Epidemics*, Basingstoke: Palgrave Macmillan.

Schui, Florian, (2014), *Austerity: The Great Failure*, New Haven: Yale University Press.
Sedgwick, Eve Kosofsky (1985), *Between Men: English Literature and Male Homosocial Desire*, New York: Columbia University Press.
Sedgwick, Eve Kosofsky (2008), *Epistemology of the Closet*, Berkeley: University of California Press.
Severs, Jeffrey (2017a), *David Foster Wallace's Balancing Books: Fictions of Value*, New York: Columbia University Press.
Severs, Jeffrey (2017b), 'Spectacles Vehement and Untutored and Rude: Reading David Wallace in the Age of Trump', *Columbia University Press Blog*, 22 February. Available online: https://web.archive.org/web/20180724051518/http://www.cupblog.org/2017/02/22/spectacles-vehement-and-untutored-and-rude-reading-david-foster-wallace-in-the-age-of-trump/ (accessed 21 August 2019).
Severs, Jeffrey (2018), '"Homer Is My Role Model": Father-Schlemihls, Sentimental Families, and Pynchon's Affinities with *The Simpsons*', in Ali Chetwynd, Joanna Freer, Georgios Maragos (eds), *Thomas Pynchon, Sex, and Gender*, 194–208, Athens: University of Georgia.
Severs, Jeffrey (2019), '"Where All the Paperwork's Done": Pynchon's Critique of Contracts', *Textual Practice*, 33 (3): 361–82.
Sex, Lies and Videotape (1989), [Film] Dir. Steven Soderbergh, USA: Miramax Films.
Shapiro, Steven (2014), 'From Capitalist to Communist Abstraction: *The Pale King*'s Cultural Fix', *Textual Practice*, 28 (7): 1249–71.
Simon, William (1996), *Postmodern Sexualities*, New York: Routledge.
Sloane, Peter (2019), *David Foster Wallace and the Body*, New York: Routledge.
Smith, Rachel Greenwald (2014), 'Six Propositions on Compromise Aesthetics', *The Account*, 3. Available online: https://theaccountmagazine.com/issue/fall-2014 (accessed 21 August 2019).
Smith, Rachel Greenwald (2015), *Affect and American Literature in the Age of Neoliberalism*, Cambridge: Cambridge University Press.
Smith, Zadie (2011), 'The Difficult Gifts of David Foster Wallace', in *Changing My Mind: Occasional Essays*, 257–300, London: Penguin.
Sooke, Alastair (2016), 'Tulip Mania: The Flowers That Cost more than Houses', *BBC Culture*, 3 May. Available online: http://www.bbc.com/culture/story/20160419-tulip-mania-the-flowers-that-cost-more-than-houses (accessed 21 August 2019).
Song, Min Hyoung (2017), 'The New Materialism and Neoliberalism', in Mitchum Huehls and Rachel Greenwald Smith (eds), *Neoliberalism and Contemporary Literary Culture*, 52–69, Baltimore: Johns Hopkins University Press.
Springer, Simon, Kean Birch and Julie MacLeavy (2016), 'An Introduction to Neoliberalism', in Simon Springer, Kean Birch and Julie MacLeavy (eds), *The Handbook of Neoliberalism*, 1–14, New York: Routledge.
Starr, Paul (1988), 'The Meaning of Privatization', *Yale Law & Policy Review*, 6 (1): 6–41.
'Statement of Aims' (1947), *The Mont Pelerin Society*. Available online: https://www.montpelerin.org/statement-of-aims/ (accessed 21 August 2019).

Stein, Lorin (2012), 'David Foster Wallace: In the Company of Creeps', in Stephen J. Burn (ed.), *Conversations with David Foster Wallace*, 89–93, Jackson: University Press of Mississippi.

Studlar, Gaylyn (1993), *In the Realm of Pleasure: Von Sternberg, Dietrich, and the Masochistic Aesthetic*, New York: Columbia University Press.

The Hayek Prophecies (2010), [Film] Dir. Arick Salmea, USA: Rising Phoenix Pictures.

Thompson, Lucas (2016), *Global Wallace: David Foster Wallace and World Literature*, London: Bloomsbury Academic.

Thompson, Lucas (2018), 'Wallace and Race', in Ralph Clare (ed.), *The Cambridge Companion to David Foster Wallace*, 204–19, Cambridge: Cambridge University Press.

Toal, Catherine (2003), 'Corrections: Contemporary American Melancholy', *Journal of European Studies*, 33: 305–22.

Tratner, Michael (2001), *Deficits and Desires: Economics and Sexuality in Twentieth-Century Literature*, Stanford: Stanford University Press.

Treichler, Paula A. (1999), *How to Have Theory in an Epidemic: Cultural Chronicles of AIDS*, Durham, NC: Duke University Press.

Trump, Donald J. (2017), 'The Inaugural Address', 20 January. Available online: https://www.whitehouse.gov/briefings-statements/the-inaugural-address/ (accessed 23 August 2019).

Trnka, Susanna and Catherine Trundle (2017), 'Introduction: Competing Responsibilities: Reckoning Personal Responsibility, Care for the Other, and the Social Contract in Contemporary Life', in Susanna Trnka and Catherine Trundle (eds), *Competing Responsibilities: The Ethics and Politics of Contemporary Life*, 1–26, Durham, NC: Duke University Press.

Tuck, Greg (2003), 'Mainstreaming the Money Shot: Reflections on the Representation of Ejaculation in Contemporary American Cinema', *Paragraph*, 26 (1–2): 263–79.

Tuck, Greg (2009), 'The Mainstreaming of Masturbation: Autoeroticism and Consumer Capitalism', in Feona Attwood (eds), *Mainstreaming Sex: The Sexualization of Western Culture*, 77–92, London: I.B. Tauris.

Turkle, Sherry (1984), *The Second Self: Computers and the Human Self*, Cambridge: MIT Press.

Van der Zwan, Natascha (2014), 'Making Sense of Financialization', *Socio-Economic Review*, 12 (1): 99–129.

Wade, Stephen (1999), *Jewish American Literature Since 1945: An Introduction*, Edinburgh: Edinburgh University Press.

Waldby, Catherine (1996), *AIDS and the Body Politic: Biomedicine and Sexual Difference*, New York: Routledge.

Waldron, Jeremy (1991), *The Right to Private Property*, Oxford: Oxford University Press.

Wallace, David Foster (1987), *The Broom of the System*. Reprint, London: Abacus, 2011.

Wallace, David Foster (1989a), 'Little Expressionless Animals', in *Girl with Curious Hair*, 1–42. Reprint, London: Abacus, 2010.

Wallace, David Foster (1989b), 'Luckily the Account Representative Knew CPR', in *Girl with Curious Hair*, 43–52. Reprint, London: Abacus, 2010.

Wallace, David Foster (1989c), 'Lyndon', in *Girl with Curious Hair*, 75–118. Reprint, London: Abacus, 2010.

Wallace, David Foster (1989d), 'Westward the Course of Empire Takes Its Way', in *Girl with Curious Hair*, 231–373. Reprint, London: Abacus, 2010.

Wallace, David Foster (1989e), 'Crash of '69', *Between C & D*, 3–12.

Wallace, David Foster (1992), 'Contributor's Notes', in Katrina Kenison (ed.), *The Best American Short Stories 1992*, 306–15, Boston: Houghton Mifflin.

Wallace, David Foster (1996), *Infinite Jest*. Reprint, London: Abacus, 2014.

Wallace, David Foster (1997a), '#6 E——— on "How and Why I Have Come to Be Totally Devoted to S——— and Have Made Her the Linchpin and Plinth of My Entire Emotional Existence"', *The Paris Review*, 144. Available online: https://www.theparis review.org/fiction/1225/brief-interviews-with-hideous-men-david-foster-wallace (accessed 21 August 2019).

Wallace, David Foster (1997b), 'E Unibus Pluram: Television and U.S. Fiction', in *A Supposedly Fun Thing I'll Never Do Again: Essays and Arguments*, 21–82. Reprint, London: Abacus, 2010.

Wallace, David Foster (1997c), 'Greatly Exaggerated', in *A Supposedly Fun Thing I'll Never Do Again: Essays and Arguments*, 138–45. Reprint, London: Abacus, 2010.

Wallace, David Foster (1997d), 'David Lynch Keeps His Head', in *A Supposedly Fun Thing I'll Never Do Again: Essays and Arguments*, 146–212. Reprint, London: Abacus, 2010.

Wallace, David Foster (1997e), 'Tennis Player Michael Joyce's Professional Artistry as a Paradigm of Certain Stuff About Choice, Freedom, Discipline, Joy, Grotesquerie, and Human Completeness', in *A Supposedly Fun Thing I'll Never Do Again*, 213–55. Reprint, London: Abacus, 2010.

Wallace, David Foster (1999a), 'Death Is Not the End', in *Brief Interviews with Hideous Men*, 1–3. Reprint, London: Abacus, 2011.

Wallace, David Foster (1999b), 'Forever Overhead', in *Brief Interviews with Hideous Men*, 4–13. Reprint, London: Abacus, 2011.

Wallace, David Foster (1999c), 'B.I. #14 08-96', in *Brief Interviews with Hideous Men*, 14–5. Reprint, London: Abacus, 2011.

Wallace, David Foster (1999d), 'B.I. #15 08-96', in *Brief Interviews with Hideous Men*, 15–6. Reprint, London: Abacus, 2011.

Wallace, David Foster (1999e), 'B.I. #3 11-94', in *Brief Interviews with Hideous Men*, 18–22. Reprint, London: Abacus, 2011.

Wallace, David Foster (1999f), 'Think', in *Brief Interviews with Hideous* Men, 61–2. Reprint, London: Abacus, 2011.

Wallace, David Foster (1999g), 'B.I. #40 06-97', in *Brief Interviews with Hideous Men*, 69–72. Reprint, London: Abacus, 2011.

Wallace, David Foster (1999h), 'B.I. #48 08-97', in *Brief Interviews with Hideous Men*, 85–97. Reprint, London: Abacus, 2011.
Wallace, David Foster (1999i), 'B.I. #46 07-97', in *Brief Interviews with Hideous Men*, 98–105. Reprint, London: Abacus, 2011.
Wallace, David Foster (1999j), 'Adult World (I)', in *Brief Interviews with Hideous Men*, 137–55. Reprint, London: Abacus, 2011.
Wallace, David Foster (1999k), 'Adult World (II)', in *Brief Interviews with Hideous Men*, 156–61. Reprint, London: Abacus, 2011.
Wallace, David Foster (1999l), 'B.I. #59 04-98', in *Brief Interviews with Hideous Men*, 181–91. Reprint, London: Abacus, 2011.
Wallace, David Foster (1999m), 'B.I. #28 02-97', in *Brief Interviews with Hideous Men*, 192–200. Reprint, London: Abacus, 2011.
Wallace, David Foster (1999n), 'B.I. #20 12-96', in *Brief Interviews with Hideous Men*, 245–71. Reprint, London: Abacus, 2011.
Wallace, David Foster (2003), *Everything and More: A Compact History of Infinity*, New York: W. W. Norton & Company.
Wallace, David Foster (2004a), 'Mister Squishy', in *Oblivion: Stories*, 3–66. Reprint, London: Abacus, 2009.
Wallace, David Foster (2004b), 'Good Old Neon', in *Oblivion: Stories*, 141–81. Reprint, London: Abacus, 2009.
Wallace, David Foster (2004c), 'Oblivion', in *Oblivion: Stories*, 190–237. Reprint, London: Abacus, 2009.
Wallace, David Foster (2004d), 'The Suffering Channel', in *Oblivion: Stories*, 238–329. Reprint, London: Abacus, 2009.
Wallace, David Foster (2005a), 'Big Red Son', in *Consider the Lobster and Other Essays*, 3–50. Reprint, London: Abacus, 2011.
Wallace, David Foster (2005b), 'Certainly the End of *Something* or Other, One Would Sort of Have to Think', in *Consider the Lobster and Other Essays*, 51–9. Reprint, London: Abacus, 2011.
Wallace, David Foster (2005c), 'Some Remarks on Kafka's Funniness from Which Probably Not Enough Has Been Removed', in *Consider the Lobster and Other Essays*, 60–5. Reprint, London: Abacus, 2011.
Wallace, David Foster (2005d), 'Authority and American Usage', *Consider the Lobster and Other Essays*, 66–127. Reprint, London: Abacus, 2011.
Wallace, David Foster (2005e), 'Up Simba', in *Consider the Lobster and Other Essays*, 156–234. Reprint, London: Abacus, 2011.
Wallace, David Foster (2009), *This Is Water: Some Thoughts, Delivered on a Significant Occasion, About Living a Compassionate Life*, New York: Little, Brown.
Wallace, David Foster (2012a), *The Pale King: An Unfinished Novel*, London: Penguin.
Wallace, David Foster (2012b), 'The Empty Plenum: David Markson's *Wittgenstein's Mistress*', in *Both Flesh and Not: Essays*, 73–120, London: Penguin.

Wallace, David Foster (2012c), 'Back in New Fire', in *Both Flesh and Not: Essays*, 167–72, London: Penguin.

Wallace, David Foster (2012d), 'The (As It Were) Seminal Importance of *Terminator 2*', in *Both Flesh and Not: Essays*, 177–92, London: Penguin.

Wallace, David Foster (2012e), 'The Nature of the Fun', in *Both Flesh and Not: Essays*, 193–202, London: Penguin.

Wallace, David Foster (2012f), 'Just Asking', in *Both Flesh and Not: Essays*, 321–24, London: Penguin.

Wallace, David Foster and Mark Costello (1990), *Signifying Rappers*. Reprint, London: Penguin, 2013.

Warren, Andrew (2018), 'Wallace and Politics', in Ralph Clare (ed.), *The Cambridge Companion to David Foster Wallace*, 173–89, Cambridge: Cambridge University Press.

Weisberg, Jacob (2000), 'Bush, in His Own Words', *The Guardian*, 4 November. Available online: https://www.theguardian.com/world/2000/nov/04/uselections2000.usa5 (accessed 25 February 2020).

Whiteside, Heather (2016), 'Neoliberalism *as* Austerity: The Theory, Practice, and Purpose of Fiscal Restraint Since the 1970s', in Simon Springer, Kean Birch and Julie MacLeavy (eds), *The Handbook of Neoliberalism*, 361–9, New York: Routledge.

Whitman, Walt (1996), 'I Sing the Body Electric', in *Walt Whitman*, 64–71, London: Orion Publishing Group.

Williams, Iain (2015), '(New) Sincerity in David Foster Wallace's "Octet"', *Critique: Studies in Contemporary Fiction*, 56 (3): 299–314.

Wisse, Ruth R. (1971), *The Schlemiel as Modern Hero*, Chicago: University of Chicago Press.

Wolfe, Tom (2012), 'Hooking Up', in *Hooking Up*, 3–13, London: Vintage.

Index

Aaron, Michele   91–2, 94, 98–9, 109
abjection   6, 25, 42, 57, 63, 73, 79, 82, 84, 86–7, 93
abstinence   24, 33, 39, 40, 46, 158, 172, 189 n.16
abuse   11, 109–12, 128–30, 137, 142, 171–2
accounting   159–60
advertising   92, 100, 102, 156, 170
Aitken, Rob   31
Alderson, David   23
Aleichem, Sholem   166
Alexander, Matthew   145, 183 n.1
Allen, Kim   155, 165
Allen, Woody   151–2
   Annie Hall   151
   Everything You Always Wanted to Know About Sex   151
'America First'   139, 191 n.11
Amin, Kadji   180–1
anal sex   7, 57, 60, 65, 68, 76–7, 79–81, 83–5
Anderson, Paul Thomas   119
   Magnolia   119–20, 123
androcentrism   2, 48, 174
Arendt, Hannah   151
Aspiz, Harold   18
Atwood, Margaret   9
Aubry, Timothy   186 n.10
austerity   20, 26–7, 147, 149–75. *See also* little man; sacrifice; scapegoating
   definitions of   153, 174
   history of   150, 153–5
   and responsibility   150, 153–5, 162, 165–6, 175
authorship   126–7, 131, 137, 146. *See also* Foucault; property
Aydemir, Murat   184 n.10

Bachner, Sally   6, 8–10, 90, 108, 115–17, 146, 183 n.6, 192 n.15
Backman, Jennifer   184 n.8
Baker, Nicholson   186 n.9
Baldwin, James   8

Bambra, Clare   90
Banner, Olivia   174
Basinger, Kim   102
Baudrillard, Jean   21–2
Beauvoir, Simone de   8
Becker, Gary S.   15, 30, 36, 50. *See also* human capital
Bellow, Saul   166
Benfield, G. J. Barker   19–20
Bennett, David   184 n.13
Benoit, Kenneth   72
Benzon, Kiki   32
Berlant, Lauren   22–3, 154, 185 n.3
Bernini, Gian Lorenzo   110–11, 113–14, 117
Bersani, Leo   68, 188 n.10
Biale, David   151
biomedicine   25, 75–9, 85
biopower   20–1
Bloom, Allan   70–2, 74
Bloom, Harold   67
Blyth, Mark   153, 162, 165
Boddy, Kasia   68
body   18–20, 22, 38, 161, 184 n.11
Bollier, David   129
Boswell, Marshall   2, 3, 4, 11, 12, 55, 63, 65, 74, 75, 94, 120, 121, 149, 183 n.4
Bourdieu, Pierre   115
Bowie, Malcolm   190 n.8
Bramall, Rebecca   150
Brooks, Ryan M.   13–14, 16, 189 n.1
Brown, Wendy   13, 15, 20, 30, 32, 36, 43, 45, 62, 66, 143, 154, 156–7, 161, 166
Buchanan, Pat   139
Buchbinder, David   151
budgets   26, 150, 153–6, 158–9, 160–1, 163, 165, 174–5
Buerkle, C. Wesley   17, 32
bureaucracy   97, 130
Burn, Stephen J.   93, 114, 116, 159
Bush, George W.   149–50
Bustillos, Maria   186 n.10
Butler, Judith   14, 19

Cameron, David 154
Cameron, James
    Terminator 2: Judgement Day 103, 106–7, 109, 115
Campbell, Joseph 2
capital 12, 14, 15, 24, 96, 99, 108, 112. *See also* human capital
Carlin, Gerry 31
Carlisle, Greg 49
Carroll, Hamilton 123–4
Carter, Jimmy 37
castration 47, 63–4, 80, 91
casual sex 24, 30, 33–5, 40–1, 43, 56, 62, 93
celibacy 172
Chetwynd, Ali 10
choice 14, 37, 45, 101
Churchwell, Sarah 191 n.11
cinema 91–3, 103–8, 112, 124
Clare, Ralph, 2, 12, 16
Clarke, John 154
Clinton, Bill 29
closet 25, 59, 61, 64–74, 79–80, 84, 86, 125, 163
collateralized debt obligations (CDOs) 61
commodification 31–2
competition 14, 21, 129, 153, 167
complicity 3, 9, 24, 91–2, 97–8, 109–11, 113–14, 117, 183 n.2
connection 30, 32–3, 59, 89–90
conservatism 5, 24, 139, 141, 179, 185 n.15
consumerism 17, 31–3, 50–3, 101, 140, 181
contract 14, 25, 89–118, 146
    between reader and text 94, 109
    as constraint 90–1, 93
    employment 90, 95–6, 108, 189 n.2
    masochistic 91–5, 100–1, 103–8, 111–12, 116–17
    neoliberal 90, 112, 116
Cook, Simon 53
Cooper, Melinda 37, 85
Coughlan, David 53, 120–1
Costello, Mark 12
credit 85, 162–9, 171–2
cultural capital 115

Dash, Mike 193 n.7
Davies, Helen 174

Davies, William 13–15
Dean, Tim 22, 185 n.14
death drive 4, 6, 57, 68
debt 21, 150, 156, 159, 161–2, 167–74
deficit 26, 52, 150, 153–4, 156, 164, 166, 174
Delfino, Andrew Steven 19
Deleuze, Gilles 91–2, 94–5, 109. *See also* masochism
DeLillo, Don 9, 55
depoliticisation 13, 85, 143
Dines, Gail 17–18
diversification 186 n.5
Dodson, Betty 51
Dorson, James 2
dot.com bubble 168
Duggan, Lisa 85, 122, 138, 143
Duverger, Maurice 72
Dworkin, Andrea 125

Eagleton-Pierce, Matthew 30, 61, 121–2
Easthope, Anthony 128
economics. *See also* neoliberalism
    and sexuality 1–2, 21–2, 32, 37, 52, 66
The Ecstasy of St Theresa (Bernini) 110, 111, 113, 114, 117, 190 n.8
Edelman, Lee 6, 7, 22, 23, 35, 39, 47, 57, 62, 68, 90, 183 n.5. *See also* negativity
    reproductive futurism 6, 7, 35, 42, 53, 62, 70–1, 76, 87
efficiency 97, 122–3, 137–9, 145
Eggers, Dave 3, 34
ejaculation 1, 4, 18–19, 42–3, 106, 110–11, 119, 133, 136, 139, 147, 160
Ellison, Ralph 8
empathy. *See also* connection
    failure of 49, 53–4
enclosure 129, 132, 191 n.7
entrepreneurialism 14, 30, 43, 62, 99, 161
Eugenides, Jeffrey
    The Marriage Plot 125, 183 n.4
exchange 24, 31, 33, 41–7
existentialism 8–9
expropriation 128, 130–2, 134, 190 n.2

Faludi, Susan 122
fathers 25, 44, 64–7, 70–1, 75–7, 80–1, 161–2

Feher, Michel   15, 36–8, 40, 43, 45, 50, 62, 186 n.7
Felski, Rita   21–2
feminism   171–2, 192 n.14
  as discipline   126, 128, 137–41, 145
  as discourse   125, 133–6, 142, 190 n.1
  caricatures of   125, 138, 145
  feminist critique   26, 56, 63, 91, 113–14, 119–27, 137–9, 143–4, 146–7, 188 n.6, 189 n.7, 190 n.2
  and neoliberalism   24, 51–2
  and pornography   45
  and sexuality   51
finance   18, 31, 52, 55, 61–2
financialization   12, 30–1, 51, 55, 184 n.13
Fink, Bruce   190 n.8
flange   65
Fleming, Chris   167
Floyd, Kevin   23
Ford, Gerald   154
Foucault, Michel   15, 20–1, 43, 192 n.15
  authorship   26, 126–7, 139, 191 n.5
  discipline   126–7, 128, 139–40, 147
  discourse   26, 124–5
  reverse discourse   125, 133–6, 146
Franco, Marie   7, 183 n.5
Franzen, Jonathan   3, 32, 89, 90, 125, 183 n.4, 189 n.1, 191 n.4
  'Contract model'   89
  The Corrections   89
  The End of the End of the Earth: Essays   89
  Freedom   183 n.4
  'Mr Difficult'   89, 189 n.1
  Purity   125
  'Status model'   89
Fraser, Nancy   52
Freer, Joanna   10
Freud, Sigmund   19, 43, 60, 64, 74, 76, 79, 80, 81, 82, 85
  'A Child is Being Beaten'   64
  'From the History of an Infantile Neurosis' (The 'Wolf Man')   79, 80, 81, 82, 83, 188 n.15
  'Notes Upon a Case of Obsessional Neurosis' (The 'Rat Man')   76
  Totem and Taboo   79
Friday, Nancy   51
futurity   62, 67–8, 70–1, 87

Gaddis, William   55, 189 n.1
Garner, Bryan A.   141, 143–4, 150
Genet, Jean   180–1
genre   105–6, 113, 115–16
Gilbert, Jeremy   14, 32, 49
Gilder, George   99–102
Giles, Paul   18
Gill, Rosalind   34
Girard, René   156–7, 166–7, 173
  mimetic desire   167–73
  rivalry   167–75, 189 n.6
  sacrificial crisis   167, 173–4
Godden, Richard   2, 12, 16, 18, 52, 55, 185 n.2, 188 n.9
Graeber, David   159
Gray, John   121–2
Greenspan, Alan   154
Greven, David   124, 161, 163

Haddad, Vincent   18, 32, 59–60
Haiven, Max   15, 61, 67, 187 n.3
Halberstam, Judith   39, 186 n.8
Halbertal, Moshe   156–7, 161
Hall, Stuart   155
Halperin, David M.   134
Hanlon, Gerard   97
Harris, Charles B.   188 n.8
Harvey, David   2, 12, 129
Hayek, Friedrich   90, 121, 129, 180
Hayes, Tom   114, 190 n.9
Hayes-Brady, Clare   2, 3, 11, 12, 32, 117, 135, 137, 142, 165, 172
Hayles, Katherine N.   188 n.14
Haynes, Doug   184 n.8
Henry, Casey Michael   9–10, 32, 82–4, 190 n.1
Hering, David   2, 3, 84, 103, 116–17, 131–2, 137–8, 158, 178, 185 n.2, 187 n.1, 193 n.1, 193 n.4
Hesse, Carla   126
Hester, Helen   102, 106
heteronormativity   53, 70, 156
heterosexuality   2, 35, 37, 61–2, 67, 69–70, 84, 119
hideousness. *See* toxicity
Himmelheber, Rachel Haley   122, 127, 145, 183 n.1
HIV/AIDS   19, 34, 37–8, 40, 59–60, 62, 72–3, 75–9, 82–6, 193 n.2
Hix, H. L.   126
Hoberek, Andrew   9, 90

Hogg, Emily J.   165
Holland, Mary K.   2, 6, 36, 132, 135, 164, 165, 187 n.11
Hollywood   46, 104–7, 124
homonationalism   86, 189 n.17
homonormativity   85
homophobia   25, 59–60, 76, 78, 82–3, 86, 180
homosexuality   7, 15, 25, 34, 38, 57, 59–87, 125. *See also* anal sex; closet; HIV/AIDS
homosociality   65–6
Houser, Heather   187 n.1
Huehls, Mitchum   12, 15
human capital   30, 62, 95, 184 n.13, 185 n.4. *See also* Becker, Gary S.; responsibilization
   definitions of   15, 36, 40, 45
   financialized   15, 24, 30–3, 36, 39, 41, 43, 47, 50–1, 54, 56, 62
   and self-appreciation   24, 30, 36–7, 39, 40–1, 45, 48, 50, 56
Hungerford, Amy   5, 11, 145, 184 n.9, 189 n.4
Hustvedt, Siri   42
Hutcheon, Linda   3, 183 n.2
Huyssen, Andreas   33

individualism   14, 25–6, 30, 32, 38–9, 44–5, 121, 126, 146–7
inflation   37, 154
interiority   25, 60, 64, 68–9, 74–5, 78–9, 81, 83
intimacy   59–62, 64–6, 68–9, 74, 94
investment   30–1, 33, 93
Irigaray, Luce   114, 190 n.9, 192 n.14
irony   6, 100, 102, 104
IRS   2, 158, 161, 174

Jackson, Ben   129
Jameson, Fredric   171
Jenkins, Walter   74
Jewishness   151
Joffe, Daniela Franca   2, 5, 10, 184 n.7, 188 n.6
Jones, Mark   31
jouissance   6, 62, 111, 190 n.8
Judge, Mike
   Office Space   152

Kafka, Franz   152, 192 n.2
Kakutani, Michiko   160
Kelly, Adam   11, 16, 53, 117, 145, 183 n.1, 192 n.14
Kimmel, Michael   10, 184 n.12
Kirwan, Michael   167
Klump, Tilman   133
Krasinksi, John
   Brief Interviews with Hideous Men (film)   124, 127
Kruger, Steven F.   78–9, 83

labour   24, 31, 33–41, 47–8, 112, 185 n.4
Labute, Neil
   In the Company of Men   124
Lacan, Jacques   6, 9, 36, 43, 91, 94, 111, 113–14, 190 n.8, 192 n.15
Laqueur, Thomas W.   42
lesbian   188 n.5
Lévy, Bernard-Henri   125
Lewinsky, Monika   29
Lewis, Holly   23
Leyner, Mark   186 n.9
LGBTQ   86
Lipsky, David   59, 76, 180
little man   26, 149–53, 158–9, 161–4, 174. *See also* schlemiel
loneliness   41, 44
Lynch, David   100, 103–8, 111. *See also* Wallace, David Foster, 'David Lynch Keeps His Head'
   Blue Velvet   104–5, 107–8, 110
   Twin Peaks   171

McGurl, Mark   4, 5, 159, 163
McHale, Brian   178
McKinley, Maggie   8–9
McLaughlin, Robert   9
McSweeney's   34
Mailer, Norman   3, 8
male gaze   25, 91–3, 97, 100, 102–17, 190 n.9
Malin, Brenton J.   151
Maragos, Georgios   10
market   1, 15, 21, 32, 42–3, 50, 85, 89, 121, 129, 143, 159
Markson, David   6, 36, 187 n.11
Martin, Randy   15, 31, 61–2, 67, 187 n.2, 187 n.3

Martin, Robert K.   160
Marxism   12–13, 15, 23, 173, 185 n.4
Marzullo, Michelle   38
masculinity. *See also* negativity; non-reproduction; toxicity; violence
   and emotional repression   69
   phallic and testicular   19
   white male backlash   10, 123–4
masochism   25, 91–2, 95–6, 98, 109–11, 115
masturbation   160, 168, 186 n.6, 186 n.9
   addiction to   50, 52–3, 119
   and exchange   41–7
   female masturbation   41, 50–1, 54
   loneliness of   41, 169
   and negativity   41, 43, 46, 53–4, 93
   as waste   7, 17, 19, 24, 42, 52
Max, D. T.   13, 109, 120–1, 150, 185 n.2
   Every Love Story is a Ghost Story   13
#Me Too   191 n.3
Méliès, George   112
Melville, Herman
   Moby-Dick   160
Mendel, Gregor   140
Mendes, Sam
   American Beauty   152, 171
meta-fiction   68, 76–7, 85, 92, 97, 157
meta-watching   98–9, 104, 106, 113
Michaels, Walter Benn   14, 25, 90, 95–7, 108
Might   34
Mises, Ludwig von   90
misogyny   11, 48, 63, 134, 138, 140–1, 145, 156, 164, 178, 180, 186 n.11, 193 n.6
Moi, Toril   173
money   2, 19, 37, 44–5, 66, 159
money shot   17–18, 42
Mont Pelerin Society   129
Moore, Lisa Jean   62, 184 n.10
Motte, Warren F.   152
Mullen, Patrick   21
Mulvey, Laura   91, 113, 190 n.9

Nabokov, Vladimir   65, 128, 191 n.10
Nash, Woods   67, 69
negativity   6–7, 10, 23, 34, 39–41, 43, 46–7, 53–4, 56–7, 62, 90, 93, 188 n.10

neoliberalism. *See also* austerity; contract; property; responsibility; risk
   as common sense   15–16
   as constructionist project   14
   definitions of   2, 11–12
   extension to all aspects of life   21–2
   logics of   12, 14–15, 23
   relation to liberalism   14, 36, 41, 108, 121, 153
Newman, Janet   154
Nichols, Catherine   43
Nicholson-Roberts, Joel   5
1990s   15, 29, 34
1997 Asian financial crisis   52
Nixon, Charles   34, 46–8
Nixon, Richard   52
non-reproduction   25–6, 33, 39–40, 49, 53–4, 71, 156, 169

O'Callaghan, Claire   174
Oksala, Johanna   52
O'Malley, Pat   74
Onania (Anonymous)   42
orgasm   33, 37, 40, 45–6, 49, 96, 106, 109–10, 113, 115, 134, 186 n.6, 190 n.1. *See also* ejaculation
Oyler, Lauren   5

Palahniuk, Chuck
   Fight Club   190 n.3
Palmer, Barclay   186 n.5
Patoine, Pierre-Louise   189 n.1
patriarchy   3, 24, 35, 49, 51, 68, 70–1, 74, 87, 91, 117, 146, 178, 183 n.2, 193 n.6
Pelosi, Nancy   154
Penney, James   23, 60
performativity   14, 18, 93, 177, 179
Perot, Ross   13
Phillips-Fein, Kim   154
Pietsch, Michael   157
pinkwashing   86
Pinsker, Sanford   166
Pire, Beatrice   189 n.1
pleasure   32, 38, 54, 111, 190 n.8
Plehwe, Dieter   129
Plummer, Ken   134
political correctness   141–3, 145

pornification   24, 29, 31–8, 40–1, 44–5, 47–9, 51, 53–6, 101–2, 107
pornography   11, 44–8, 101–2, 185 n.2. *See also* pornification
  addiction to   45, 50
  hardcore   17, 29, 102, 106
portfolio   15, 50, 52, 186 n.5
Posner, Richard   15
postmodernism   3, 16, 22, 92
post-postmodernism   9
post-structuralism   66, 126–7, 131, 191 n.6
Power, Kevin   89
primal scene   79–82, 85
privatization   26, 122–3, 137–46, 178
property   4, 26, 119–47. *See also* expropriation; privatization
  definitions of   133
  private property   26, 121–3, 126–33, 136–7, 140, 146
  rights to   121, 127, 129
psychoanalysis   63–4, 76, 79, 81–2, 86, 91, 177
Puar, Jasbir K.   189 n.17
Purdy, Jedediah   16
Pynchon, Thomas   7, 9–11, 152, 183 n.5, 184 n.8, 189 n.5, 192 n.1, 193 n.9
  Gravity's Rainbow   7, 193 n.9

queer theory   6, 7, 22–3, 39, 60, 86, 180, 183 n.5, 184 n.11, 186 n.8, 189 n.17

racism   4, 8, 34, 180
Rando, David P.   2, 6, 135, 142, 186 n.11, 188 n.9, 191 n.9
rape   104–5, 109–10, 119, 142–5, 171, 192 n.13
Reagan, Ronald   13, 138, 180
rectum   68, 76, 86
regulation   97
responsibility   24, 29–57. *See also* austerity; human capital
  neoliberal ideas of   39, 55
  responsibilization   24, 30, 33, 37, 39–40, 46–7, 49, 51, 52, 53, 54, 56
  and self-investment   37–8, 43
risk   15, 24–5, 31, 38, 59–87, 187 n.4. *See also* HIV/AIDS; securitization
  financial   31, 61–2

  and homosexuality   60–1, 68, 70, 72–7, 85–7
  neoliberal attitudes to   74
Roache, John   126, 186 n.10, 191 n.5
Robinson, Marilynne   155
Robinson, Sally   93, 123–4
Roiphe, Katie   3
Rosenberg, Jordana   184 n.11
Roth, Philip   3, 8, 152, 192 n.2
Rottenberg, Catherine   52
Row, Jess   5
Rubin, Paul H.   133
Rumsfeld, Donald   154
Ruskin, John   191 n.10

Sacher-Masoch, Leopold von   94–5
sacrifice   26, 150, 153, 155, 156, 157–66, 175
sadism   25, 91–113, 116
Saint-Aubin, Arthur Flannigan   19
Santel, James   185 n.15
Sartre, Jean-Paul   8
Saunders, George   29
Sayers, Philip   93, 103
scapegoating   26, 150, 155, 156, 166–74, 175
scarcity   1, 18, 167, 170
Schatz, Thomas   105–6
schlemiels   26, 149, 150, 151, 152, 166
Schrecker, Ted   90
Schui, Florian   153
secrecy   50, 53–4, 60, 71, 87, 128, 162. *See also* closet
securitization   7, 15, 25, 38, 57, 61–85, 187 n.3
Sedgwick, Eve Kosofsky   59, 60, 65, 70–2, 75
  Epistemology of the Closet   60
self-care   30, 170
self-denial   26, 164, 172
self-help   45, 149
self-interest   192 n.12
semen. *See* spermatics
Severs, Jeffrey   1, 12, 13, 16, 30, 35, 52, 54, 55, 89, 90, 96–7, 160, 164, 172, 178, 179, 184 n.8, 187 n.4, 189 n.5, 192 n.1
sex. *See also* pornification; pornography
  disenchantment of   29, 32, 34–5, 37–8, 44

and emotional connection 32–5, 38, 39
in queer theory 22–3
sex aids 31, 33, 50–1, 53
sexism 24, 33, 48, 49. *See also* misogyny
Shapiro, Steven 12
Simon, William 22
Sloane, Peter 2, 7, 8, 19, 184 n.11, 187 n.5
Smith, Rachel Greenwald 12, 13, 15, 99, 189 n.1
Smith, Zadie 1, 4
Soderbergh, Steven 119, 121, 136
Sex, Lies, and Videotape 119, 123, 136
Solondz, Todd
Happiness 42
Song, Min Hyoung 184 n.11
Sooke, Alastair 168
spectatorship 91–2, 98–101, 103–5, 189 n.3
spermatics
blockage and release 19, 25–6, 93, 123, 147, 177
investment 25, 30, 54, 56, 177
metaphors 4, 18–19, 23, 25, 30, 93–4, 106, 147, 177
spermatic economy 17, 19–20, 42
waste 24–5, 37, 56, 93, 170
Springer, Simon 21
stagflation 154
Starr, Paul 138
state 30, 73–4, 86, 121–2, 129, 138–9, 144, 153–5, 174
Stein, Lorin 124
Studlar, Gaylyn 91
suicide 71, 86, 90, 112–14, 153
suspense 105–15
Szalay, Michael 2, 12, 16, 18, 52, 55, 185 n.2, 188 n.9

Tarantino, Quentin 92, 104, 105
television 92, 98–103
tennis 158
Thatcher, Margaret 11, 138, 180
Thompson, Lucas 2, 4, 12, 41–2, 70, 151, 181, 193 n.2
Toal, Catherine 183 n.1
torture 90, 92, 95, 107, 108, 109, 114, 116

toxicity. *See also* negativity; non-reproduction; violence
definition of 5–11, 187 n.1
immutably male 2, 4, 40, 54, 56, 60, 93, 146, 178
'toxic masculinity' 5
transgender 179
Tratner, Michael 21, 155
Treichler, Paula A. 186 n.8
Trnka, Susanna 39
Trump, Donald J. 10, 16, 29, 184 n.7, 185 n.1, 191 n.11
Trundle, Catherine 39
Tuck, Greg 42–3, 51
tulip-mania 168
Turkle, Sherry 163–4
2007–9 subprime mortgage crisis 61, 150, 153, 169
2010 Eurozone debt crisis 153

Updike, John 3, 65, 141, 188 n.7

value 30, 33, 36–40, 43, 46, 54–5, 62
Van der Zwan, Natascha 30–1, 62, 187 n.3
violence 4, 6, 92, 107
definitions of 8–10, 183 n.6
male sexual 104, 108–16, 142–4
prestige of 8–9, 90, 108, 115–17
unrepresentable 8–10, 25–6, 90–3, 108–9, 111–13, 117, 146, 183 n.6
virginity 35, 155, 158, 189 n.16
voyeurism 91, 98, 102, 107

Wade, Stephen 151
Waldby, Catherine 72, 78
Waldron, Jeremy 133
Wallace, David Foster
'Adult World (I)' 24, 33, 50–7, 66
'Adult World (II)' 24, 33, 41, 50–7, 66
'The (As It Were) Seminal Importance of *Terminator 2*' 106–7
'Authority and American Usage' 16, 141–5, 179, 192 n.12
'Back in New Fire' 24–5, 29, 33–41, 43–50, 56, 60, 62, 66, 154, 186 n.5
'B.I. #3' 144
'B.I. #14' 119, 133–4, 136, 139, 147
'B.I. #15' 122
'B.I. #20' 43, 135, 141–2, 186 n.11

'B.I. #28'   140, 193 n.6
'B.I. #40'   133, 135–6
'B.I. #46'   142–4
'B.I. #48'   94–9, 105, 116
'B.I. #59'   126, 132–3
'Big Red Son'   24–5, 29, 33, 39, 44–8, 50, 56, 101, 106, 141
Both Flesh and Not   34
Brief Interviews with Hideous Men   1, 5, 29, 32, 39, 47, 120, 132, 141
The Broom of the System   6, 15, 25, 60, 63–6, 86, 90, 150, 179
'Certainly the End of *Something* or Other, One Would Sort of Have to Think'   141, 188 n.7
Consider the Lobster   141, 188 n.7
'Crash of '69'   55
'David Lynch Keeps His Head'   25, 92, 103–8, 116
'Death is Not the End'   132–3
'The Empty Plenum'   6, 36, 186 n.11
'E Unibus Pluram: Television and U.S. Fiction'   13–14, 25, 92, 98–100, 102–5, 116, 189 n.3
Everything and More: A Compact History of Infinity   193 n.5
'Forever Overhead'   1, 2, 5
Girl with Curious Hair   60, 63, 79, 84
'Good Old Neon'   86, 123, 135
'Greatly Exaggerated'   126–7
Infinite Jest   19, 25, 41–3, 55, 60, 63, 75, 76–85, 86, 90, 92–3, 96, 100, 103, 107–17, 122–23, 125, 128, 145, 155, 164, 170, 179, 189 n.3, 192 n.13
'Just Asking'   150
'Little Expressionless Animals'   187 n.5
'Luckily the Account Representative Knew CPR'   67–70, 72, 74, 75, 77
'Lyndon'   59, 71–5, 77, 83, 86
'Mister Squishy'   149, 156, 165–7, 169–71
'The Nature of the Fun'   41, 44
'Oblivion'   171–2
Oblivion   4, 26, 86, 100, 147, 149, 150–8, 165, 175

The Pale King   2, 12, 15–16, 18, 26, 37, 55, 59, 116, 149–51, 153–65, 172, 175, 185 n.2, 193 n.4, 193 n.6
Signifying Rappers   12
'Some Remarks on Kafka's Funniness from Which Probably Not Enough Has Been Removed'   152
'The Suffering Channel'   100–2, 106, 149, 156, 166, 172–4, 189 n.6
'Tennis Player Michael Joyce's Professional Artistry as a Paradigm of Certain Stuff About Choice, Freedom, Discipline, Joy, Grotesquerie, and Human Completeness'   158–9
'Think'   24, 48–50, 54, 56–7
This is Water: Some Thoughts, Delivered on a Significant Occasion, about Living a Compassionate Life   149
'Up, Simba'   142, 150
'Westward the Course of Empire Takes Its Way'   67, 123, 179
Warner, Michael   185 n.3
Warren, Andrew   79, 158
waste   17, 19, 24, 37, 137–8, 143, 170
Weinstein, Harvey   190 n.3
Welch, Raquel   109–10
welfare   74, 121
white male backlash   10, 122
whiteness   10, 123, 151
Whiteside, Heather   153–5
Whitman, Walt   17–19
Williams, Iain   38
Wisse, Ruth R.   151, 166
Wittgenstein, Ludwig   66
Wolfe, Tom   29–30
women. *See also* misogyny; sexism
  and consumerism   33, 49–50, 101, 140
  as objects   113–14, 163, 165
  as Other   36, 111, 114
  sexual agency   33, 35, 43, 47, 48, 50
work   35–6, 185 n.4

Yiddish   151, 166

www.ingramcontent.com/pod-product-compliance
Lightning Source LLC
Chambersburg PA
CBHW072232290426
44111CB00012B/2068